MOONLIGHTING

An Oral History

MOONLIGHTING

An Oral History
Scott Ryan

Cover design by Scott Ryan
Photo courtesy of ABC Promotions
Inside photos courtesy of ABC Circle Films & ABC Publicity Photos,
IMDb, Debra Frank, Jay Daniel, and Don Giller
Edited by David Bushman
Book designed by Scott Ryan

Published in the USA by Fayetteville Mafia Press
Columbus, Ohio

Contact Information
Email: fayettevillemafiapress@gmail.com
Website: fayettevillemafiapress.com
Twitter: @FMPBooks

ISBN: 9781949024265
eBook ISBN: 9781949024272

"Isn't it nice to know a lot? And a little bit *not*."
—Stephen Sondheim
"I Know Things Now" *Into the Woods*

Dedicated to Joyce Ryan. She forced me to watch the pilot of *Moonlighting* in 1985 and, in doing so, sent me on the path to becoming a writer. Thanks, Mom.

CONTENTS

The Anselmo Case Suspects
(In order of appearance)

Glenn Gordon Caron	Creator, Executive Producer, Writer
Jay Daniel	Executive Producer, Director
Roger Director	Writer, Producer, Season 4 Showrunner
Cybill Shepherd	Cast Member "Maddie Hayes"
Allan Arkush	Director
Bob Butler	Pilot Director
Curtis Armstrong	Cast Member "Herbert Viola"
Allyce Beasley	Cast Member "Ms. Agnes Dipesto"
Suzanne Gangursky	Production Coordinator
Ron Osborn	Writer, Producer
Reuben Cannon	Casting Agent
Jeff Reno	Writer, Producer
Debra Frank	Writer
Melissa Gelineau	Assistant
Chic Eglee	Writer, Producer, Season 5 Showrunner
Peter Werner	Director
Sheryl Main	Postproduction
Karen Hall	Writer
Neil Mandelberg	Editor
Will Mackenzie	Director
Dennis Dugan	Cast Member "Walter Bishop," Director
Chris Leitch	Director
Mel Harris	Actress
Dana Delany	Guest Star
David Patrick Kelly	Guest Star
Sandahl Bergman	Dancer
Bill Landrum	Choreographer
Margie Arnett	Maddie's Stand-in/Photo Double
Ray Wise	Guest Star

Introduction

Television in 1985 was *very* serious. It was serious about money on *Dallas* and *Dynasty*. It was serious about crime on *Murder, She Wrote* and *Spenser: For Hire*. Tom Selleck may have flashed a smile in his shorty shorts and Hawaiian shirt on *Magnum, p.i.*, but he always took his investigations very seriously. Television was even serious on its sitcoms. *Family Ties* was getting serious about alcoholism with guest star Tom Hanks. When Natalie wouldn't date Tootie's cousin on *The Facts of Life*, it turned into an intense lesson about racism. Television had no space for shenanigans of any kind. In the middle of a decade known for collecting the most toys, the viewing population had no appetite for silly—but that was about to change. Enter writer Glenn Gordon Caron and his creation of the television show *Moonlighting* (1985-1989). Suddenly it was pie fights, rhyming secretaries, and chase scenes. Television was about to get a much needed "Boink."

Moonlighting was a detective series (sure it was) starring real-life movie star and model Cybill Shepherd as Maddie Hayes. Maddie was a model turned detective. (Wait, what?) There sure is *nothing* serious about that idea. She was saddled with unknown real-life bartender Bruce Willis as David Addison. David was a wisecracking "detective" who may or may not have ever solved a case. Somehow ABC heard this pitch and gave the keys to a network television series, along with a blank checkbook, to Glenn Gordon Caron, whose main credits up to that point were as a supervising producer/writer on *Remington Steele* and the TV adaptation of *Breaking Away*. He decided to do a detective series in which the cases *wouldn't* be front and center. Instead, it would be an old-fashioned 1940s screwball-comedy love story between the two main characters. Everything old became new again.

The series premiered on March 3, 1985. It was a midseason replacement, so the first season contained only six episodes. These first episodes were normal detective stories in the sense that there was a mystery and they *mostly* solved them, but it was the dialogue and chemistry between Maddie and David that sparked viewers' interest.

The first-season finale included an average scene for a detective series at that time, but ended up being anything but typical. The detectives went undercover to try to stop an assassination. When David approached the security guard for entry into the party, he said, "We're looking for a man with a mole on his nose." The guard asked, "What kind of clothes do I suppose would be worn by a man with a mole on his nose, who knows?" David immediately responded, "Did I happen to mention, did I bother to disclose, this man that we are seeking with a mole on his nose, I'm not sure of his clothes, or anything else, except he's Chinese—a big clue by itself." How'd he do that? Maddie and viewers wondered. "Gotta read a lot of Dr. Seuss," Addison quipped.[1] That was the kind of banter that Season 1 brought to the small screen. This was revolutionary. Trust me, Jessica Fletcher didn't rhyme.

In Season 2, the series became a bona fide hit. It continued with the traditional case format, but started to up the antics in the chase scenes, a staple of detective series in the eighties. On *Moonlighting*, the criminals and detectives slid across hallways in soapsuds and had a car chase in a hearse, and characters rode around the luggage carousel at an airport. This season contained the "Black and White" episode, which was introduced by legendary film director Orson Welles. The main characters also started talking to the camera and acknowledging the plot right in the middle of scenes. David and Maddie—not Bruce Willis and Cybill

---

1   *Moonlighting*. "Murders in the Mail." Directed by Peter Werner. Written by Kasica, Scheff, Caron. ABC, April 2, 1985.

Shepherd—introduced an episode by reading letters from viewers. They danced with the Temptations in another and apologized for a 3D episode gone awry, all before the opening credits. In 1985, prime-time series were not doing cold opens. They didn't include scenes during the end credits. Television shows existed only between the credits. There were rules that prime time followed. Well, someone forgot to tell that to the *Moonlighting* writers. In their Christmas episode, snow started falling *inside* Maddie and Dave's office, and Maddie and Dave just walked off the set to be met by the entire production staff and their families singing Christmas carols. This season contained the most scripts the series ever produced in a single season: eighteen. This was back when twenty-two to twenty-four episodes were the norm.

In Season 3, the series went from hit to pop culture icon. There was nothing in 1986-1987 as hot as *Moonlighting*. Also, nothing as hard to find. As production problems increased, new episodes became scarcer than sightings of Cybill and Bruce eating together in the 20th Century Fox commissary. Yes, tabloid stories started to spill out from the set that there was trouble behind the scenes. But even while the rumors splashed across the cover of the *National Enquirer*, the series continued to churn out creative and radically different episodes from week to week. One episode contained a seven-minute dance sequence set to the Billy Joel song "Big Man on Mulberry Street." The dance number was directed by *Singin' in the Rain* director Stanley Donen. You don't complete an undertaking like that and stay on an eight-day shooting schedule. So reruns piled up, and so did the bills. As tensions and pressure rose, the series started to focus more on secretary Ms. Agnes Dipesto[2] (Allyce Beasley) and introduced her love interest, Herbert Viola (Curtis Armstrong). Someone had to fill those fifty minutes with fast-talking dialogue.

The series even started to make fun of itself. One episode began with Hollywood reporter Rona Barrett declaring, "No new episode, AGAIN!" It became a mantra for fans who waited patiently from week to week for a fresh episode. Sometimes viewers didn't find out if the episode was a rerun or an original until they turned on their television set at nine o'clock

---

2   Spelling confirmed by Allyce Beasley.

on Tuesday nights. But that didn't take any of the shine off the series. ABC, which also owned the series, didn't contest the missed deadlines or the rising budgets, because the series had such huge ratings that today they would be considered Super Bowl-size ratings. The episode "It's a Wonderful Job" had a 26.1 rating and thirty-nine share.[3] The biggest price tag came from an episode called "Atomic Shakespeare," which was written in iambic pentameter and featured Maddie and David in the Renaissance in an homage to the Shakespeare play *The Taming of the Shrew*. The episode was an Emmy magnet—director Will Mackenzie and writers Ron Osborn and Jeff Reno were all nominated, and Mackenzie won—so ABC was still all in. Later in the season, Mark Harmon guest starred to stand in between David and Maddie. His four-part arc ended in an episode entitled "I Am Curious . . . Maddie," in which Maddie and Dave finally had sex. It became the show's highest-rated episode (over sixty million viewers)[4] and had the entire country talking in rhyme . . . for a moment.

What happened next? Well, that is the question this book asks. How did a show that was hotter than the Rubik's Cube or "Baby on Board" signs get canceled less than two years and twenty-eight episodes after airing its most-watched episode? The media dubbed it the "*Moonlighting* Curse." The conventional wisdom became that if two main characters from a series got together, the show died. It happened on *Moonlighting*, so therefore it will happen on *The X-Files* or *Felicity*. This is why *Castle*, *Bones*, *Friends*, *Downton Abbey*, and every show since 1987 delayed, at all logical costs, their main characters getting together. But was this really the cause of the cancellation? I wanted to solve this mystery more than knowing who was the real killer in the Flamingo Cove murder.

In 1987, I was a huge *Moonlighting* fan, just like half of America. (It's true that close to half of all television sets were tuned in to watch "I Am Curious . . . Maddie.").[5] The difference was that I stayed a fan in 1988 and 1989, and still am today. I never believed that it was the

---

3   Carter, "2 Disappointments for ABC, Low Ratings and an Ending," *New York Times*, May 9, 1989.

4   Klauss, "Maddie and Dave Do It," davidandmaddie.com/doit.htm, 2003-2004.

5   Ryan, Interview with Glenn Gordon Caron. May 2020.

consummation that consumed my beloved series. Some of my favorite episodes of the series, "Cool Hand Dave," "Here's Living with You, Kid," and "A Womb with a View," all aired after this moment and during the final two seasons. Something happened, but what? In the fourth season, the two leads appeared together in the season premiere in September 1987, but didn't share the screen again until February 1988. Why did the writers choose to do this? Who thought America wanted to watch a romantic comedy without its two leads? Who made this decision, and what factors caused it?

The only way to get to the bottom of this mystery was to tackle it like it was the Anselmo case (the unsolved case that the Blue Moon detective agency worked on over the final three years of the series). I needed to do a Herbert Viola type of investigation to get to the bottom of this mystery. I just couldn't stand the idea of reading another article blaming *Moonlighting* for a television couple not getting together. I wanted to talk to everyone who had worked in front of and behind the camera and get them to tell me *exactly* what happened thirty years ago. Easy as picking a locked door while doing the Hokey Pokey.

First step was to see if anyone had already written that book. A quick search showed that no one in over thirty-five years had ever written a book about *Moonlighting*. A series this popular and there were NO books on it? That's strange. Curtis Armstrong, who gleefully played Herbert Viola on the series, wrote the following sentence about this *Moonlighting* fact in his memoir, *Revenge of the Nerd*: "The low points were so low that it may explain why now, after decades, no one has written the real history of the show."[6] Well that's not daunting at all.

I began my investigation with the creator himself. Not God, but Glenn Gordon Caron. I had interviewed him in 2015, for *The Red Room Podcast*, and hoped he would be open to the idea. He gave me his blessing and an updated interview. Then I approached executive producer Jay Daniel. We spoke weekly for a few months over the summer of 2019. We went through the detailed notes he had kept during the filming of the series. Information and answers that had sat unread for years. I

---

6   Armstrong, Curtis. *Revenge of the Nerd Or . . . The Singular Adventures of the Man Who Would Be Booger.* (Thomas Dunne Books/St. Martin's Press, 2017.) 262.

proceeded to talk to directors, writers, cast members, postproduction artists, dancers, editors, and everyone and anyone I could find who had worked on the series. I was lucky enough to get to speak with Allyce Beasley (no, she doesn't just speak in rhymes). She shared so much of her heart, pain, and love for the series. The writers and I went through their scripts. The directors talked about directing an experienced actress and a future action hero. Curtis Armstrong was so thoughtful and had such respect for the series. He was extremely gracious even if this book would cause his memoir to be forever incorrect. (Curtis, you are still the *capo di tutti capi*[7] to me.) Cybill Shepherd was more than excited to help me in any way she could. She decided to rewatch the series and called me after watching an episode. Nothing can give your day a boost like looking at your phone and seeing that Cybill Shepherd is calling you. She was a delight, kind, helpful, and a wonderful asset to the book.

This book pieces together those interviews into one combined memory to create the story of *Moonlighting*. We all know that memory is a tricky thing. People will contradict one another, and I allow it. Memory is better than fact anyway, because it's created by feelings. One of my favorite quotes from Maya Angelou is "They may forget what you said—but they will never forget how you made them feel." This book contains what people *felt* about creating *Moonlighting*. What is the danger in that? Well, you could start with the fact that the quote *isn't* from Maya Angelou; it's actually from Carl W. Buehner,[8] but everyone attributes it incorrectly to Angelou because it *feels* right. So I have dutifully tried to balance memories with facts, all in the context of the era in which the series aired.

Moonlighting originated in the latter half of the 1980s. It would be an understatement to say times have changed since then. In 2021, the "times" have changed since I started to write this very sentence. The focus of the interviews was to find out what it was like to make groundbreaking television in the 1980s. There was something going on back then that was unwisely called the Battle of the Sexes. This isn't a history book about

---

7   *Moonlighting*. "Cool Hand Dave: Part 2." Directed by Allan Arkush. Written by Director & Eglee. ABC, December 1, 1987.

8   Evans. *Richard Evans' Quote Book*, (Publishers Press, 1971).

that war, but I think we can all agree both sides were losing badly in the eighties. I have no intention of looking at the plots, characters, and behaviors through the lens of 2021. This is not a critical analysis of the series, but a look at the creative process. Everyone would have behaved differently today, because things *are* different today, and we are all working to be more inclusive and more sensitive. But if we revise history while we cover it, then we can't learn from it. So all "bad" behavior from the past should stay there. Everyone had the best of intentions, and no one set out to hurt anyone or make any sweeping statements about the opposite sex. It was, in the end, a comedy show. David Addison wouldn't get past even the most lax HR representative today. In the eighties he was revolutionary; today he would be the poster child for the cancel-culture revolution. Some walk by day, some fly by night.[9]

Moonlighting: An Oral History is a look at the series through the words of the people who created it, how the series was shaped and cared for and how it finally slipped away from the hearts and minds of the same American audiences who once had catapulted it to the top. I also had no interest in covering gossip or tawdry tales, so readers will have to look elsewhere for those stories. My interest was to find out how a massively successful series could have so many production problems that, as Bill Carter of *The New York Times* reported, it "used more reruns during its four years on the air than any other series."[10] Why? Can the Anselmo case finally be solved? Find out on tonight's all new episode of *Moonlighting*.

So gather the kids, the dog, Grandma, and lock them in another room and sit back and enjoy[11] *Moonlighting: An Oral History*.

9   Jarreau, "Moonlighting," 1985.

10   Carter, "2 Disappointments for ABC, Low Ratings and an Ending," *New York Times*, May 9, 1989.

11   *Moonlighting*. "The Dream Sequence Always Rings Twice." Directed by Peter Werner. Written by Caron, Frank, & Sautter. ABC, October 15, 1985.

Chapter 1
His Girl Maddie

If birds do bird and bees do, in fact, bee, there is a good chance the reason they do it is for Maddie Hayes. Maddie, a former cover-girl model, was what the world in the midst of Ronald Reagan's America feared most—a beautiful woman with remarkable intelligence. As a spokeswoman for Blue Moon shampoo, Maddie Hayes racked up wealth that would have made Gordon Gekko from *Wall Street* jealous. She was set to retire from her modeling career when she paid a hefty price for trusting her business manager with access to all of her money. He walked away with everything, and she was left with nothing. Well, *almost* nothing. She was left with a detective agency that was created for her to lose money, as a tax write-off. (If you ask me, she should have known her business manager was shady when he came up with that idea, but it was the decade of greed.) This is the moment where *Moonlighting* viewers met Maddie Hayes—broke and at the end of her rope. When she walked into the (then named) City of Angels detective agency, she planned to fire the staff and liquidate the assets, but she didn't quite expect to run into the likes of David Addison—who ever does?

Maddie Hayes was not what television was used to when it came to female characters. She was extremely complex. She was flawed, emotional, a businesswoman, funny, stunningly beautiful, and the boss. These were the traits that writer Glenn Gordon Caron gave Maddie Hayes. But it was movie star Cybill Shepherd (*Taxi Driver*, *The Last Picture Show*) who brought her to life.

In 2020, Bob Dylan released a song called "I Contain Multitudes." I submit he wouldn't have had the inclination to write this song in the sixties, or the eighties, when *Moonlighting* aired, because the idea that people were more than one thing wasn't news. Today, one narrative is all it seems this culture can handle. "You're either with us or against us." Simple. In the midst of the current one-adjective era, Dylan wanted to remind us that people are complex. That we need to hold more than one thought in our minds at the same time—especially when you are viewing human beings. Bob Dylan wasn't thinking of Maddie Hayes or Cybill Shepherd when he wrote the following lyric, but it does apply: "I fuss with my hair and I fight blood feuds. I contain multitudes."[1] Maddie Hayes was a multitude of complexities.

Glenn Gordon Caron (Creator): I was writing the pilot. I think I was half done with it. And it occurred to me that Maddie Hayes was Cybill Shepherd, but I didn't really think I could get Cybill Shepherd. Very much to my amazement, my agent read it and felt the same way and somehow knew how to make that connection. Jay Daniel and I had lunch with her.

Jay Daniel (Executive Producer): We met with Cybill Shepherd at a restaurant called La Serre in Studio City in July of 1984. Cybill was late, which was a very Cybill thing to be. She walked in, all dressed in white, and came over to the table. Of course, we stood. She asked us a question. Glenn's answer was, "Hummina, hummina." He could not get any words out.

Glenn Gordon Caron: To me, Cybill Shepherd was very much a movie star. So the idea of putting food in my mouth while I was in her presence, there just was something wrong about that.

---

1   Dylan, "I Contain Multitudes," *Rough and Rowdy Ways*, 2020.

Jay Daniel: He was so enamored. And so was I. She was very delightful at that lunch, and we were sold. It didn't take a whole lot of convincing for the network to say yes. So we had Cybill long before we found David.

Glenn Gordon Caron: Cybill looked at me and said, "It's a Hawksian comedy, isn't it?" I had no idea what a Hawksian comedy was. I had no idea that she was referring to director Howard Hawks.

Roger Director (Writer): Cybill had a longtime relationship and friendship with Peter Bogdanovich [the director of *The Last Picture Show* and *What's Up, Doc?*], so she knew so much about film and knew so much about romantic comedy. So when she walked in to do that part, she was just absolutely perfect for it.

Cybill Shepherd (Maddie Hayes): Glenn had fifty pages done. I immediately thought of Howard Hawks comedies. I got to meet Howard Hawks, but never worked with him. Peter was interviewing him for something. We went out to his house in Palm Springs.

Glenn Gordon Caron: She lived for an extended period of time with Peter Bogdanovich, and he would show her classic American films to teach her the history. So she was much more conversant with this stuff than I was. A lot of what I was doing, I was doing out of instinct, not out of any sense of "Oh, there's an old movie style here." She seemed to understand what it was in ways that even I didn't.

Roger Director: Cybill has been in some of the greatest movies. And when you look at some of the films that she has been in, no one else could have done *The Last Picture Show* or *Heartbreak Kid*.

Allan Arkush (Director): I spent a lot of time talking with Cybill about old movies. We had a long discussion about silent Ernst Lubitsch comedies. She admitted to me in those discussions that she was playing Cary Grant. She said, "Cary Grant is the greatest reactive actor in the history of movies. There is never one second on the screen where he's not thinking or reacting." That's what she tried to do with Maddie, because

Maddie doesn't have the joke lines.

Bob Butler (Director): I remember believing that Cybill was certainly the straight man. It wasn't up to her to be funny. It was up to Bruce to be funny. That was the design. That's always the situation with the comedy couple, one is straight and one is not.

Glenn Gordon Caron: She had read half the script and said, "If the second half is as good as the first half, I'd be interested in doing this." That was a huge thing. I was very excited.

Cybill Shepherd: It was very fast-paced. There weren't any pauses for laughs like in a sitcom. It just moved like wildfire. It reminded me of *His Girl Friday* and *Bringing Up Baby*.

Allan Arkush: In a way, *Moonlighting* is as much reflective of the eighties and a certain kind of feminism as, say, *His Girl Friday* or *The Philadelphia Story* are emblematic of the early forties. You kind of synthesize those relationships and these people live in a little fantasy world, as the *Moonlighting* characters do.

Curtis Armstrong (Herbert Viola): Glenn was playing with Cybill's persona and bringing as much baggage as he could to it. Because if you were of a certain age, Cybill had instant recognition, going back to— really the late sixties, right?—the modeling days. She seemed to be the perfect person to present Maddie Hayes's character, because everybody at that time had an instinctual knowledge of who she was.

Allyce Beasley (Ms. Dipesto): Maddie was an ex-model who had seen more successful times financially and better times in the limelight. When she takes over the Blue Moon detective agency, she needs that business to survive. Also, she needs that business as her raison d'être, to have something that she could do, to be committed to in the world.

Suzanne Gangursky (Production Coordinator): Maddie definitely had more of the golden ride through life. She became a top model. But when push comes to shove, she's not going to take crap from anybody. Beneath that beautiful exterior is not an airhead. There's somebody in there that is sharp and smart and is *also* nobody's fool.

Ron Osborn (Writer): Maddie was a generally good person with a very type A personality. As worldly as she was, she needed more of the world exposed to her. It isn't that she was uneducated or unworldly in any way, shape, or form. She was set in her opinions and probably needed some of those opinions broken down. In the David-versus-Maddie opinion, which was the basis for all the show, it isn't to say that David was always the right one.

Reuben Cannon (Casting Agent): You have Maddie, who lived by the rules, who played by the rules, who has realized how limited her life has been, because of perhaps self-imposed guidelines she put on herself.

Jeff Reno (Writer): Her veneer was colder, kind of "keep her distance, stay at arm's length from people." She's also a romantic inside. When the show started she had been horribly wronged by her accountant stealing her money and leaving her this detective agency. She had a lot of adapting to do. She had to find some strength, and she probably had to exercise that strength by being a lot harder and colder.

Debra Frank (Writer): Maddie Hayes is someone who is more caught up with image and how she's perceived by the public, by the world. When she loses everything, she's really destroyed by that. That almost becomes her identity in a way, which is why she is uptight. I don't think it was because of that; I think that was inherently her personality. But this exacerbated everything, because when she fails, she fails in front of the world. She's famous, and her reputation was very important to her. Which is really what led to some of their great arguments.

Melissa Gelineau (Production): I think Maddie Hayes certainly cared about how people thought of her. And as the seasons went on, she got slightly looser.

Chic Eglee (Writer): She's at an age where, especially back then, the culture wasn't too kind to postglamour figures. There's a real kind of vulnerability in her. On the one hand, she's really drawn to the bad boy, that bruises, but on the other hand, she is completely offended by everything about it.

Peter Werner (Director): Well, she's a shiksa goddess. The idealized Christian blonde, beautiful model. She is smart, funny, and vulnerable. In today's television, you put lots of faults into characters. But at that time, just having people with real flaws and imperfections took them out of being *Charlie's Angels* and cartoons. Yet they weren't soap operas, self-pitying or anything like that. In a way, she was Glenn's version of the ideal woman.

Roger Director: She was a person who had a lot of hot air thrown at her. She had to deal with a lot of phony people, so she was a person who was strong-willed but had some inner turmoil that left her doubting herself.

Maddie Hayes lost it all in the pilot and spent the series rebuilding her fortune and her life.

Sheryl Main (Postproduction): Maddie was a very strong female. She owned her own agency. She was also smart. She was a really great character for that time on television. But when she opened up, and just let it go, there was some fun there.

Chic Eglee: She's an ice queen. And beneath the ice facade is a really caring, vulnerable, romantic woman, and she dare not show that in a world where women were now having to compete head-to-head with men.

Allan Arkush: Maddie Hayes was the feminist character who came along at the right time. She's an old-fashioned female icon of a sexist society. She takes all that and says, "Screw that. I'm gonna make my own life." She was in control of her life. So that was an important characterization at that point in the eighties. That's one of the reasons the show was successful, because of the male and female of it. Maddie symbolized that in a glamorized way.

Jeff Reno: We didn't have a credible romance unless she was as strong as David was. That notion was responsible for the success of the show, combined with the way it was executed. Those two were such appealing people, and the writing was different from anything that was on at the time—played by two characters that could hold their own against each other. I think the equality of the characters was a huge strength of the show.

Glenn Gordon Caron: I think she represents something slightly more conventional. At first blush, you look at David and you go, "OK, that's anarchy." And you look at Maddie and you go, "OK, that's reason. That's convention." But then that is sort of subsumed by the fact that she's so beautiful, and he's so masculine, that you immediately jump to "What's the possibility that they're going to get together?" Even though they seem so opposite to each other.

Chapter 2
Bringing up David

In the history of leading men on television there is "before" David Addison and there is "after." Men on television were MEN, until David Addison watched a bucket fall on Ms. Dipesto's head and told her she was looking "a little pail today." Leading actors didn't smash up their cars when they got angry. They didn't stand on office desks and sing "Limbo Rock." David Addison changed everything. It was easy for him to do, because he was everything. David Addison was the collection of everything that came before—alive and swimming all around inside of him at once. David was the most fun person in every room, but could pout and be as moody as a teenager. He was a sexist male chauvinist pig, but gladly worked for a woman and always took care of Ms. Dipesto. He had no visible ties to his family, but then lost all control when his dad was about to remarry. He had no past, but then out of nowhere had an ex-wife. He was a blue-collar East Coaster but could fit in at any LA bar. He could reference a rock 'n' roll song and follow it up with a classical-music joke. David Addison was everything all at once.

Because a character like that had never been created on television before, finding him became casting legend. The search finally landed on Bruce Willis, an unknown bartender. Bruce Willis wouldn't be satisfied with just changing television. In a few short years, he would tear down, for good, the barrier that kept actors from going back and forth between movies and television. He would rewrite what an action hero looked and sounded like. He was a man of his time, and that time has long since passed. Without doubt, a character like David couldn't exist in our world today. His comments would be scrutinized on Twitter, and his internalized self-doubt would be overlooked. David Addison was everything good and bad about men in the eighties; he reflected it all.

Glenn Gordon Caron (Creator): David Addison was my reaction to the men that I saw in movies and television, none of whom I recognized or felt any kinship with in my own life. I was always amazed when I flipped on the television, because the men had these manners. I grew up on Long Island and in sort of a working-class neighborhood. And just none of it felt familiar to me. So I think David was a reaction to that.

Melissa Gelineau (Assistant): I think David Addison was a combination of Glenn Caron and Cary Grant. I can't speak for Glenn, but I think everyone has that character that they want to be, and that's what David Addison was. I think that character was a labor of love from Glenn.

Roger Director (Writer): David's one-third Bruce Willis, one-third Glenn Caron, and one-third television. He was a living, breathing person who lived on the planet television, and he was always aware of it. He knew he was on a TV show, but he was thoroughly human. And Bruce could do all those things. I think almost no one else could have done it. And no one other than Glenn could have breathed life into that character.

Karen Hall (Writer): When you're not the showrunner, what you're doing is basically trying to read the showrunner's mind and write what they would have written if they had the time. So David Addison was part Glenn Caron and part Bruce Willis and me trying to figure out what they were doing.

Jay Daniel (Executive Producer): David Addison comes from, and I hardly ever use this word, the genius of Glenn Caron, and from Glenn's own inner self. I really do believe that nobody else could have written that role. You'd never seen this David Addison type on TV before.

Peter Werner (Director): It's funny how I always think of him as Bruce. He's a combination of two people. He's Bruce Willis and a young, idealized Glenn Caron. That was in some ways the genius of Glenn's writing, as he was able to identify, stylize, and idealize himself as this character. The combination produced a performance and a show that is often imitated, never duplicated. I don't know that Glenn has ever quite entered the soul of one of his characters as much as he did David.

Glenn Gordon Caron: David came from my sense of rebellion in boredom, and probably a bunch of egomania thrown in there. The problem was, sort of like being a songwriter, you write these things and then you hope someone can sing them. Interesting complications came up when we went looking for David, and we didn't find him for an awfully long time.

Allyce Beasley (Ms. Dipesto): Oh, well, he's Bruce Willis. I mean, he just is. Everything that Bruce is is what David is. Glenn looked through how many thousands of people? When he found Bruce, he knew Bruce was David. And every aspect of the person who Bruce is or was in that time—fast-talking, wisecracking, womanizing, smirking—that's who David was and who Bruce was.

Allan Arkush (Director): It's Bruce. It's whatever Bruce found in himself. That was David Addison.

Jeff Reno (Writer): He is Bruce with some great writing. He's cool. He enjoys life. He's a smart-ass. He's a romantic at heart, which people don't really remember about him. He adds a lot of very hip cool to that persona.

Curtis Armstrong (Herbert Viola): I guess David Addison is Bruce Willis. I mean, I never saw much difference between the two of them except on very surface levels.

Allan Arkush (Director): The success of the show was that Bruce was an ex-bartender, as a person. What could be more male, in an urban setting, than a blue-collar worker? He was someone who dealt with men and women all the time—that bartender's personality. He just took that personality and put it in that character. Bruce is just so much like that character. Especially when the show was climbing and it was a giant hit, I didn't see a line between them. He was having such a good time in life and on stage.

Debra Frank (Writer): David was this kind of free-spirited guy who enjoyed life, who had a good time. I don't think he really had any aspirations as far as success. The detective agency was set up to lose money. So here's a guy who is not interested in being successful. He's just into enjoying life. I think that became the magic of the character. He was just so playful and so off-the-wall—and all his thoughts, which were not what you expected from anybody that was on television at the time.

Sheryl Main (Postproduction): We had *Miami Vice*, *Cosby*, and *The Golden Girls*. When you look at what was happening, there was nothing like *Moonlighting*. There weren't any characters being written the way Dave and Maddie were written. David was a smart-ass, but he was a charmer, and was loopy, and goofy, but he was smart. That's what those other TV shows were trying to do, but they were kind of white bread. *Moonlighting* had pimples and freckles. With Bruce, you could put him in a suit or a motorcycle jacket, dress him up, or have him running around—put him in a black-and-white episode, dancing, a Shakespeare episode. I don't know that you had that range before in a contemporary, youthful actor.

Allan Arkush: I asked Bruce, "How did you learn to do that?" He said, "It's easy. No matter where I am, I'm David Addison. I'm David Addison in the Middle Ages. I'm David Addison in the 1940s. I'm David Addison in jail. I don't have to spend a lot of time on the script. I am the same guy, who everything keeps changing up on." I thought that was as pure an explanation of how someone deals with a TV character. There is some evolution in a television character, but it tends to be glacial.

Bob Butler (Director): In David Addison's case, that character didn't learn anything. That famous old dramatic chestnut where the character must evolve, change, mature, and learn wasn't true with that character. He was a good-time know-it-all, period.

Neil Mandelberg (Editor): David Addison is the coolest cat I have seen in my life. Everything he did had a class to it. No matter how we handled Bruce's character, he always came out shiny. And that's a testament to Glenn and Bruce. David Addison is your wise guy, smart aleck, who grows on people.

Jeff Reno: He very much goes by emotion and says the first thing that comes to his mind. It just happens to be very carefully worked out by a writers' room. But it feels like the first thing that comes to his mind. David wears his heart on his sleeve. It's very interesting because of what Bruce's career became, it is exactly not the strong, silent type. That is probably a great big difference between earlier and later leading men, including the leading man he became in his action movies.

Reuben Cannon (Casting Agent): David Addison is a likable, charming, super hip guy with exceptional people skills. If you talk about emotional IQs, David Addison's is off the charts, because he can read a situation and calibrate a response so fast. There's a scene where he was talking to Maddie. He says, "Oh, you want to talk about Vietnam? Let's talk about Vietnam." And she says, "You were in Vietnam?" He says, "I could have been!"

Jeff Reno: It was his sense of humor that made him stand apart. He was a leading man that bantered with a very rough edge. I don't believe there was much of that around back then. I don't believe very many leading men had that kind of fast-paced sense of humor.

Debra Frank: He was a cad—but he wasn't a cad, because he really had a heart. He had depth that you got to see a little later on. He did care; he was loving. There were so many things to be able to play with, because he was not one-dimensional.

Chic Eglee (Writer): David is a blue-collar guy: kind of cocky, a show-off with a good deal of Bruce in him. This is the conception of the show that Glenn got so right. The idea that on some level he looks at somebody like Maddie Hayes, who's just so out of his league. She's famous and she's got that, it's not so much in the culture now, but there was a certain sort of genteel quality about her that is very kind of Waspy. David Addison was a kid from New Jersey, like Bruce was, and the idea that here's this ice queen who represents something kind of unattainable—on some level, it's a challenge. But on another level it's a component of unworthiness.

Ron Osborn (Writer): David Addison is clearly a man of history. We always wanted to keep it that way, because this allowed us to give him various talents. He probably had a lot of con artist in him. He probably fell into this job.

Suzanne Gangursky (Production Coordinator): Well, first of all, I grew up on the East Coast. So he is kind of a typical fast-talking Jersey boy—charismatic, with a real edge and street sense to him. That being said, if he's your friend, he's loyal to you. But he's a survivor. He's going to do what it takes to survive in the world.

Reuben Cannon: Maddie's a pretty smart gal. So for her to fall for David, David had to have something in him that's redeemable.

Sheryl Main (Postproduction): David Addison was a guy you wanted to be friends with, but I don't think you ever want to be in a relationship with him. He had a very sharp wit, but he had a big heart. He was kind of an intellectual fuckup.

Chic Eglee: For all of David's swagger and bravado, he really cared. The tension in that show was that nobody wanted to expose enough vulnerability to tell the other person that they had feelings. We just opened them up in a way that they just don't want to be vulnerable. Whatever the heartache was in Maddie's life, whatever heartache was in David's life, they're both kind of playing a role. It's a classic screwball comedy. There's more depth to them, and they are more real. Whether it was pride, vulnerability, or fear, they couldn't say "I love you."

Jeff Reno: He was actually sad when Maddie wouldn't respond to him. He was heartbroken at times. Things bothered him in a lot of ways. Leading men were most often above all that.

Glenn Gordon Caron: Just before I sat down to write *Moonlighting* I saw *Ghostbusters*, and the amazing performance that Bill Murray gave. It was just a style of comedy going on with young actors like Tom Hanks. It was an irreverence, but that irreverence wasn't reflected in prime-time television at all. If it was anywhere, I suppose, it was in that first David Letterman daytime show, but nobody saw that. I thought that I'd love for there to be that sort of music, that sort of sound, on a television show. I, like everybody else my age at that time, wanted to make movies, but you kind of can only go where they'll have you. At that moment in time, the place that would have me was in television. So I thought, "Well, I'm going to do television as if it was a movie." And that was a lot of where David came from.

PHOTO COURTESY OF DON GILLER AND WORLDWIDE PANTS

Bruce Willis was an unknown in 1984 when he auditioned for David Addison. By December 1985, he was David Letterman's guest.

Chic Eglee: My dad was a "greatest generation" type. A real kind of straight-ahead Republican guy. When I moved from *St. Elsewhere* to *Moonlighting*, my dad watched the show. My parents were actually a Nielsen family, with a Nielsen box in their house. Do you think that my parents on Cape Cod would have done a solid for their son and help bump the ratings up by watching *Moonlighting*? No. My dad gets on the phone and says, "Well, son, I watched that new show you're on. I can tell you one thing: I think you've taken a step down in your career." *Moonlighting* was just the hottest thing ever! I felt incredibly lucky to get on that show. And my dad says, "This David Addison character—I don't care for him one bit. He needs a good shave. And he's a wiseass." David just offended everything about my father's sensibility.

Allan Arkush: We were doing a two-shot with the car. And there's a certain point when we had to change the film. So we stopped and Cybill and Bruce said, "Can you let us out?" Which they normally didn't ask for. So they're standing outside the car, and a bunch of boys jog by. They see Bruce and Cybill. All the guys are yelling, "Bruce, Bruce, Bruce. I bet you're gonna score on her"—like Cybill wasn't even there. And she got kind of pissed. David Addison is the adolescent in all of us. He's the part of us that is never going to grow up. And that's what made the energy work, because she had grown up. She was the adult in the room. But if it wasn't for him, she would never learn anything in life.

Jeff Reno: David was kind of a smart-ass sixteen-year-old boy. That's probably not a bad description of him.

Chapter 3
Glenn's Rib

Maddie Hayes and David Addison have since etched themselves into the history of television, but they came to life in the pilot episode of *Moonlighting*. It aired on March 3, 1985. But before America could meet the two detectives, the script had to be written, the cast had to be cast, and the rhymes had to be . . . well, you know.

Glenn Gordon Caron (Writer of the pilot): I was a big snob. And I say that kind of proudly. I didn't feel like most TV was particularly good at that particular moment, but I didn't understand why it couldn't be. I know how snooty that sounds, but it's actually true, and I was very young.

Jay Daniel (Producer of the pilot): Glenn, Bob Butler, and I had done two pilots together, *Concrete Beat* and *Long Time Gone,* that didn't get picked up.

Reuben Cannon (Casting Agent): I would say out of all the scripts Glenn wrote, *Moonlighting* was by far my favorite. I was his kind of go-to guy for casting. I had cast two other pilots for Glenn that didn't go to series, and the third time was the charm.

Glenn Gordon Caron: I started writing pilots and Bob directed them. We did three two-hour pilots together. *Moonlighting* was the last one. I learned at his knee, and he was very generous.

Bob Butler (Director of the pilot): The three of us knew each other very well. We knew each other's foibles very well. We just allowed for them and never fought, never quit.

Glenn Gordon Caron: Bob Butler's friendship was something that I sought out when I first came to Hollywood. He directed the pilots for *Hill Street Blues, Batman, Hogan's Heroes, Star Trek*, and *Remington Steele*. I thought, "If I ever get lucky enough to write pilots, I want that guy to direct them. I want to learn from him." And that's what I did.

Will Mackenzie (Director): Bob Butler is the dearest man in the world. He was honored at the Directors Guild—all of us directors adore that man. *Moonlighting* is one of the best damn pilots I've ever seen. That was another reason I wanted to do the series.

Jay Daniel: Bob Butler is one of the finest directors that I've ever worked with. He knows how to talk to actors better than anybody that I've seen. What's the subtext of this scene? He has a sort-of-shorthand version of that on set. So he brings out the actor in a way that not everybody can do. He's not one of those "move the camera at all costs" directors. So when the camera moves, it's with a purpose.

Glenn Gordon Caron: Bob was in a much more vaulted place. He was a guy who did pilots, and he was paid very handsomely to do those pilots. He got a royalty every time one of his pilots that he directed became a television series.

Jay Daniel: Glenn called and said, "I've got an idea for a project. I'm going to be pitching it at the network. Would you do it if it gets picked up?" I said, "Yeah, of course." It was *Moonlighting*. I was thrilled, because I thought Glenn was the best writer I'd ever worked with.

Roger Director (Writer): Glenn has immense talent, and is a creative genius, as seen with his enduring, incredible career producing and making television. He had worked previously on *Remington Steele*. So I think he hadn't fully developed a sense of the character of the "TV detective." He took it one step beyond, to a TV detective who knew he was a TV detective.

Jay Daniel: I was hired by Glenn in the offices of *Remington Steele*. That's where I met him.

Glenn Gordon Caron: I was on *Remington Steele* for, like, ten episodes, and then ABC called. They said, "We're going to do your pilot." So I left *Remington* to concentrate on this pilot. I had no idea how television really worked. I didn't know that the network can give you notes. I didn't know that the studio comes down and says you can't keep shooting. I didn't know any of that. And I didn't care. I was very young, very arrogant, although I think I tried to wrap it up in a pleasant demeanor. Nonetheless, it was a lot of youthful arrogance.

Jay Daniel: *Moonlighting* was a total departure from either of the other two pilots. They were both very dramatic and serious with a little touch of humor. *Moonlighting* is absolutely a different animal.

Melissa Gelineau (Production Assistant): I was Glenn's assistant. So I literally typed the pilot on a Selectric IBM typewriter. It was a two-hour pilot. If I remember, that script was probably 120 pages. Because it was a typewriter and not a computer, I had to start over a lot. Glenn didn't like cutting and pasting. I can't tell you how many times I retyped that, and he was constantly improving it.

Glenn Gordon Caron: I remember seeing *Adam's Rib* and thinking, "This is interesting." It's clear that these people have an extraordinary amount of affection for each other, and in that affection they find a freedom to get to an honest place with each other where they are capable of saying things that no one else could say to someone. That's informed by the fact that there's some sort of a carnal thing going on that you can't put your finger on.

Melissa Gelineau: I remember Glenn watching a ton of screwball comedies while he was developing it for the rhythms and the fast pace. I just knew Glenn's rhythm, and he was all about the dialogue.

Bob Butler: I remember believing that *Moonlighting* was a little "off the ground." It was a little "Let's pretend. Let's have a good time." Glenn is very masterful in that area.

CASTING

Jay Daniel: We read a lot of actresses for Ms. Dipesto.

Reuben Cannon (Casting Agent): Allyce Beasley was living with another character actor, Vincent Schiavelli. Vince and I had an audition, and either he said or her agent said, "Reuben, you should meet Vincent's girlfriend."

Allyce Beasley (Ms. Dipesto): I do remember first reading the pilot and having to go up two times. The first time was with Reuben Cannon. I went up to meet Glenn, Jay, and Bob Butler. And then I had to do the whole thing again in front of the network to get network approval. I had never done anything like that. I had only been in LA for about a year. I wasn't frightened of anything, because I'd never been through it before.

Glenn Gordon Caron: Allyce went to the same high school that I went to. When she came in to audition, it was just like a gift.

Allyce Beasley: When I got up there, there were still two other women besides myself who were reading for the role. I met them, and they are actually both still working today. We were totally different people. The three of us went out to get a bite to eat afterwards. I'm a New York-trained actor, and I love other actors. You're not really ever competing

against anybody else but yourself. I think I got a call later that day that they had cast me.

Jay Daniel: Allyce was just amazingly special. I think once we found her, Glenn was able to write to her, who she really is. She's a lovely, lovely woman, and a lot of fun. I don't even remember if we had anybody that we thought was right until she walked in.

Reuben Cannon: What she ended up playing is not necessarily what Glenn wrote, because what was great about Glenn was that he would be open to changing a character when he saw a piece of talent. So once he saw how unusual and special she was, she became Ms. Dipesto.

Allyce Beasley: At the second audition, Glenn said to me that they had seen me on *Cheers* and *Taxi* and they couldn't believe I was available to do this.

Reuben Cannon: Cybill Shepherd was always on the list, a very short list. Maybe the only one we talked about. David Shapira was her agent. I had met with Cybill—she was living in Tennessee or somewhere—when I was on a nationwide search for *The Winds of War*. So I knew her.

Melissa Gelineau: Glenn had envisioned Cybill. He wrote Maddie with her in mind. He just could not find a David.

Cybill Shepherd: I had top billing. I didn't get top billing very often. It was rare for any women to get top billing on a project, especially back then.

Reuben Cannon: Glenn gave a prototype: "If this was a feature, we'd be doing Bill Murray and Jessica Lange." That would be the energy—this kind of freestyle rogue of a guy and this blond, uptight lady.

Jay Daniel: I'm not sure of the accuracy of this, but we saw approximately three hundred actors for the part of David Addison. That's obviously a rounded-off figure. We had a whole trip to New York to look for people.

Reuben Cannon: This was like the search for Jimmy Hoffa, in terms of casting directors around the country—if not around the world, with Canadian casting directors. I must have had maybe five to six casting directors along with the ABC network casting department. So the search for David was extensive.

Glenn Gordon Caron: I think we looked at eleven hundred men. Reuben really did look all over the continent.

Jay Daniel: It was a search that I've neither before nor since been through. We saw so many people. The first person that the network mentioned that they would like us to take a look at was Rick Dees, who was a radio personality in Los Angeles. That was the first casting meeting that we took.

Reuben Cannon: What I've always done is expand the possibility. David Alan Grier almost set the standard in terms of what the reading could be. Now, in that era they weren't ready for interracial partners, let alone a blonde white woman and a brother. But David Alan Grier, and his brilliant acting, gave a preview of how good it could be because he was just so electrifying.

Glenn Gordon Caron: Other people would come in who could do it, but you couldn't cast them. They weren't the right type of person. Bill Maher came in and gave a really interesting audition, but he was not a romantic figure. Dennis Dugan came in and just nailed it.

Dennis Dugan (Actor): I think it was the best audition I ever gave. I was just loose. I was ad-libbing. They were encouraging me to riff. I was in the Tim Matheson-John Ritter zone of actors of that time. We were perfect network people because we were Midwestern, funny, unthreatening guys. Glenn wanted a guy with an edge, and Bruce had it. There wasn't anybody else that could have played that part.

Jay Daniel: I remember the day very clearly when Bruce Willis came in. I think on that same day we had just seen Desi Arnaz, Jr. We'd yet to really zero in on anybody. We had a couple of candidates, but nothing that we were really saying, "That's the guy." And then Bruce came in.

Reuben Cannon: Most actors, if they were a leading man they were playing leading men. And if they were character actors they were playing characters. They were afraid to step outside those boxes. I don't think Bruce ever categorized himself. He was just an actor. In fact, he was more of a jazz musician than he was a classical musician in terms of his acting style.

Glenn Gordon Caron: When Bruce came in, he could sing the song, and he made the song better. We weren't wildly dissimilar as young men. We were virtually the same age. He came from Delaware. I came from Long Island. Neither one of us could quite believe that we were in Hollywood, much less that they'd actually let us make a television show.

Reuben Cannon: I get a call from Jenny Delaney, an agent at William Morris: "We have a client who's understudying Ed Harris in a Sam

David Addison could only be played by a certain type of actor.
That type: Bruce Willis.

Shepard play. Will you meet with him?" I said, "Sure. Have him come see me around noon." So Bruce came to my office. I think he was in LA on vacation.

Jay Daniel: Bruce came out from New York to read for a feature Oliver Stone was directing.

Glenn Gordon Caron: Bruce was in town for a *Desperately Seeking Susan* audition, and it was just sort of a last-minute decision to bring him in for this.

Reuben Cannon: I remember he was wearing khakis or something—a khaki shirt, khaki slacks.

Jay Daniel: He came in wearing camouflage and had actually pretty much shaved his head. He for some reason—don't ask me why—decided he would read from on top of the table that we were sitting at. So he got on the table with his legs crossed, and that's how he read for the part.

Reuben Cannon: He immediately hopped up on the file cabinet, sat there, and performed the scene. It was like hearing it for the first time, even though we'd heard it hundreds of times. We all agreed something special had happened.

Glenn Gordon Caron: He may well have jumped up on a table. I just don't remember anymore. But I remember when he was done thinking, "Eureka! That's the guy." I started talking to everybody about it and it became clear to me in about thirty seconds that they thought I was talking about the person that was in before Bruce.

Bob Butler: My first memory is not being impressed with Bruce.

Jay Daniel: We were really just sort of flabbergasted that he was so cocky. He was a bartender from New York. He'd done a few little things, but hardly anything at all. He really kind of created the role for us in how he read the scene. Glenn had something like him in mind all along, but it wasn't something you could really describe, even as glib as Glenn was.

Glenn Gordon Caron: I ran outside to try and stop him because I wanted him to come back another day. He was wearing earrings and he was very pimped out. I had a sense that would be a tough pill for ABC to swallow. I remember thinking, "Oh my God, there's someone that can do it."

Dennis Dugan: Bruce Willis comes in, and he's got a New York accent, loose, funny, and he's crazy. He can sing and can dance and he was just everything that none of the rest of us were.

Jay Daniel: We said, "Let's clean him up. Get him in a suit, and out of his camouflage outfit, and let him read for the network."

Dennis Dugan: Glenn even called me after my audition. He said, "You gave a great audition, but I just wanted to call you personally and tell you that I am not taking you to the network because the guy I want is this actor named Bruce Willis. I don't want you to be any competition for him when we go to the network." I said, "Thanks for being honest with me." And he was right. I wouldn't have been anywhere near as good as Bruce Willis.

Reuben Cannon: I called Jenny Delaney and said, "I want to make a two-week holding deal for Bruce." Something like $35,000 for the pilot and $12,000 per episode for the first season. She said, "Really?" I said, "Yeah, two weeks exclusive. We have first position."

Jay Daniel: We took Bruce to the network with a couple of other actors that we didn't really want. They didn't like Bruce. They didn't care for the other guys either.

Melissa Gelineau: They did bring Bruce to the network. At the time, I think, his hair was really short. He had an earring. They looked at the surface, and they thought that was not David Addison.

Chic Eglee (Writer): The president of the ABC Broadcast Group at the time was Tony Thomopoulos, and he didn't want Bruce Willis at all. I've had this happen many times in my career. I almost got fired trying to cast a character on *Dark Angel*. The network wanted somebody who was hot and I said, "How about we just hire the best actor?" And they were like, "Can you believe what Chic just said? Hire the best actor? It's sweeps!"

Bob Butler: I remember one of the executives not liking Bruce's profile and advising me that I'd have to fix that. I don't know what the hell he meant, which is often the case with network executives. They speak a different language.

Reuben Cannon: I believe it was Lew Erlicht, president of the network at the time, who said, "Reuben, obviously you don't know what a leading man is. I'd like for you to step off the project. Let me bring in Lynn Stalmaster," who was a top independent casting director. I was in essence fired for bringing Bruce Willis in three times—really the only time in my entire career I was replaced.

Chic Eglee: This was just another in the long history of network executives always wanting to cast the wrong guy. Glenn was so committed to Bruce, I think Glenn actually paid his own money to shoot a screen test, if I recall. Tony Thomopoulos was saying, "I don't want to hear about this Bruce Willis guy; he's dead to me."

Curtis Armstrong: The fact that Glenn had to fight so hard for Bruce with the network—Glenn was looking at it as somebody who personified the character and read the lines the way Glenn heard them in his head. He was trying hard to get somebody who brought no baggage with him, which certainly Bruce didn't. That's the reason that Glenn fought so hard. This was David Addison, not somebody who could *play* David Addison.

Glenn Gordon Caron: To me, Bruce instantly was a romantic figure, even though ABC didn't see that when I first showed him to them. That was the point of contention, that he's not a leading man. "You can't put him next to Cybill Shepherd. No one will believe it."

It took two screen tests to convince ABC that Bruce Willis was sexy enough to stand next to Cybill Shepherd.

Melissa Gelineau: They said, "Let's do a screen test." The first screen test they did, from my recollection, was not with Cybill. It was with another actress. They filmed it, and still the network said, "Not the guy."

Cybill Shepherd: I don't think I met with any other actor. I remember the minute Bruce Willis walked into the room that my temperature went up ten degrees. This was in an office somewhere.

Jay Daniel: So we finally said, "We've looked, and this is the guy for us. How do we prove that to you? Can we do an actual screen test, with Cybill and Bruce?" This was for ABC network and their production company, ABC Circle Films, making the commitment to pay for *another* screen test. So they did it. We shot the screen test. Bruce and Cybill met the first day at the rehearsal for that screen test. It all went very well. I don't think they'd met prior to that.

Reuben Cannon: Cybill, in the meanwhile, had agreed to do the screen test with Bruce—which she was reluctant to do.

Cybill Shepherd: I was afraid if I did the screen test that they would decide I wasn't right for the part. [Laughs.]

Reuben Cannon: This is where relationships and friendships come into play. Because of my relationship with David Shapira, I asked to have her do it. It would be done in private. She agreed.

Jay Daniel: I think the network had in mind that we would do something very simple, just get the two of them together, but I decided to make it look like it would go on TV. So we got a stage at Warner Bros. They made it a very romantic setting, with little twinkle lights and black curtains behind them. We filmed the scene where they dance together, chat, and are basically falling in love. It ended up costing about $50,000.

Reuben Cannon: We showed that test to Lew Erlicht and Tony Thomopoulos. Someone in the room said, "Do a test of the test." An audience test was done, and the question to the people they had provided to participate was: "Would you watch this man on TV every week?" It was a resounding "yes." The chemistry was there; the writing was there.

Cybill Shepherd: The one thing I learned very early on about chemistry between actors is if you have chemistry with an actor, the last thing you want to do is act on it, because familiarity can breed contempt. I don't believe that chemistry between two actors can be acted. Bruce and I were so turned on by each other. We were living in the Valley in a townhome. He came over to see me with a bottle of Jack Daniels or something. I opened the door and let him in. It got very hot. I had a La-Z-Boy chair in my living room. We were making out, and you know how La-Z-Boys keep going back and your feet go up? We were going back in the La-Z-Boy and it was hot between us and we were making out and Bruce suddenly pulls back and says, "You know what, we may be working together for a long time." I said, "You're right." We said, "Let's not do this." But we came close in that La-Z-Boy. It was key that we didn't, to keep the chemistry on screen.

Melissa Gelineau: Bruce actually came there and walked through, and all the women were like, "He is so sexy."

Chic Eglee: They're watching the screen test at ABC and this woman executive named Ann Daniel said, "I don't know. There is something about that guy. He just looks like a dangerous fuck."

Jay Daniel: We showed the network that on September 28, 1984. And then on October 1, 1984, they gave us the green light. We had six days for rehearsal, and then we started shooting.

Allyce Beasley: Glenn wrote it and cast it, if I do say so myself, excellently. He knew what he wanted, and he held out until he had exactly that.

Melissa Gelineau: Bruce credits Glenn with giving him his career. I mean, his daughter Rumer's middle name is Glenn.

FILMING

Glenn Gordon Caron: Before we made the pilot, we watched *His Girl Friday*.

Bob Butler: I used *His Girl Friday* on the *Remington Steele* pilot to show that forceful, quick delivery and a lot of pace.

Jay Daniel: *Moonlighting* was the rapid-fire overlapping dialogue shown in *His Girl Friday*. Bob, Glenn, and I talked about how the pace of this thing worked, allowing the characters to overlap each other. It gave energy to the scenes, and we did our very best to make that the rhythm of the show.

Bob Butler: That movie is famous for me because it somehow retains its reality, such as it was, and is lots of fun and still drives "a show" into our souls rather than complete true life. It's a great example of farce and reality meeting.

Allyce Beasley: When I had my first costume fitting, Glenn said to [costume designer] Robert Turturice, "What was she wearing in the audition?" I was wearing a little T-shirt dress. It was the eighties, so we wore big, oversized men's jackets over that. So I *didn't* end up wearing sexy little T-shirt dresses as Ms. Dipesto, unfortunately. It could have been good for my career. It turned out to be a very useful concept later on when I was pregnant during the series, because my character wasn't pregnant.

Bob Butler: There are no costume mistakes anywhere on *Moonlighting*. That job of costuming by Robert Turturice was *really* good.

Melissa Gelineau: Robert Turturice was extremely creative, a brilliant costumer, and was able to hide flaws. His wardrobe was very structured, and I think he knew how to design for Cybill in the most flattering way. All of Cybill's wardrobe was custom-made.

Cybill Shepherd: Robert was a genius. I didn't have a say in my wardrobe. I just trusted him. I tend to trust the people I am working with. My feet are very wide, so if I had to wear pumps I would only wear them in the shots where you see my feet. So I would wear them in that shot at the elevator where you see my feet as I am walking out. That was the only time I actually had the heels on.

Allyce Beasley: I remember the first table read being so nervous and out of my mind. I had no idea who Bruce was, but Cybill Shepherd was *the* cover girl when I was growing up, and I was just bowled over to be in the same room with her.

Jay Daniel: Glenn has a very unique, unexpected sense of humor. When ABC greenlit *Moonlighting*, one of the first meetings that we had with Bob was up at Bob's house. We're sitting around—Glenn, Bob, and I—

talking about the script. There's a scene where we meet David Addison. He calls Ms. Dipesto into his office, she opens the door, and a bucket falls on her head. David says, "Ms. Dipesto, you're looking pail today." Bob and I are going, "Is this OK?" Glenn said, "Yeah, that's David." We had no reason to doubt him, but that was so unconventional. I think it's one of the best introductions to a character I've ever seen.

Bob Butler: I have discovered in teaching that Dave and Maddie's meeting scene—all the way till they end up at the elevator—that half the time I believe it's a little off the ground and half the time I believe it's moderately close to screen reality.

Glenn Gordon Caron: I didn't know anything. I was trying to amuse myself, honestly. I just feel like if something amuses me, or catches my attention in some way, then maybe it will to somebody else. I remember going to Bob Butler's house. I remember going through the script. But I remember that moment playing out on set as we were rehearsing it.

Allyce Beasley: Of course I remember shooting the pilot, because of how many times the basketball and wastepaper basket fell on my head. That took a lot of time.

Glenn Gordon Caron: Bob saw that bucket drop on Allyce Beasley's head. He just looked at me and said, "Really? We are doing this?"

Bob Butler: Is it physically possible for that basket to fall on her head? Not really. You have to do a lot of engineering in life to find the right kind of door with the right kind of lever on it to make that work. That's number one. It's not very real, statistically. At the end of the day, it's a blatant joke. Now it's very good-natured and very lighthearted, which takes the cursor away from it. Allyce, who played that part, was delightful.

Allyce Beasley: They didn't film it by physics, let me put it that way. It was just something that Glenn wanted, and I was willing. I don't know if I would still be that person that would be willing to have that happen over and over again until we got it right. A couple of times it kind of hit

It's Maddie's first meeting with David, but Ms. Dipesto gets the laugh.

me upside of my head. A couple of times it just kind of hit my shoulder and fell off. I mean, it wasn't twenty times, but it could have been a good seven to ten.

Bob Butler: There were more things for it than against it, but it was a rather mechanically fake exaggeration of the truth. That's pretty damning. When you get one of those, you have to be very careful to make it believable. It's admittedly biased, certainly from the director's perspective.

Glenn Gordon Caron: I was always saying, "Let's do it again, only faster." I felt that the clip of it was very important. It gave it a kind of a irreverence. Bob was very concerned and said, "I think people are speaking so quickly that the audience won't be able to comprehend it." We did a couple of tests. We literally would do a scene, then we'd do it faster, and then we do it faster still. Then we go back to dailies at lunch, and without fail, the fastest take was easily the best.

Bob Butler: Bruce was kind of rock-solid. All I did was tweak the edges of his work. He knew how to use his hands or eyes and just included it in the pattern. He knew that things had to go a thousand miles an hour. And he was very comfortable doing that.

Jay Daniel: Bruce was really a willing participant in that he took Bob's direction; he lapped it up like a sponge. Cybill also responded well to it, because Bob treated her with respect. He talked to the cameraman about "Can we get the light a little softer on her?" She needed to hear all of that. She needed to know that she was being taken care of.

Cybill Shepherd: In the pilot my hair looks very different than it does in the series, because everybody thought it was taking too long to have my hair done. So we decided I had to get my hair done, so it was stuck that way for the rest of the day. "No more time on her hair!" In the pilot it is very simple and classic, and then the rest of the show it's kind of bushy and some kind of crazy-looking perm.

Bob Butler: Cybill was very savvy. She is just a great dame. It was Maddie's place to be insulted. I didn't say that at the time, because that would be directing the result rather than discussing the character. But that was the truth of the matter as I saw it.

Jay Daniel: There were elements of Cybill that fit Maddie like a glove, and a lot of the other stuff was acting. Bruce totally got it. His little smirks, you can't write that. But boy, did those words fit into that mouth.

Glenn Gordon Caron: He immediately saw the melody in it, the music in it. He's musical and would hear the meter—so much so that later on in the series he would call me from the stage and say, "You better get down here. They are messing with your stuff." They didn't hear the meter. Everybody's got to hit their note or it won't work.

Jay Daniel: Even on the pilot, getting Cybill out of her trailer was not the easiest thing in the world, because she wanted to look perfect, and rightfully so. Makeup people come in between takes whether she needed a touch-up or not, so that she knew that she was being taken care of. But Bob knew she needed to be taken care of. He spent a lot of time one-on-one, not talking in front of the crew—going and talking directly to her.

Bob Butler: I do remember telling Cybill in the scene where she is tied up with Bruce to cross down screen. I qualified that because she couldn't, since she was tied to a chair. But I said, "That's the classic comedy move at this point, for you to advance and get closer to Bruce." I said, "I think it'll be entertaining if you try to make that move and do it awkwardly."

Cybill Shepherd: Bruce gets untied and waits to untie me. I don't like being tied up. It's not my thing. I was doing exactly what I would have done as a woman if a man got untied, and then delayed in untying me. I would be furious, and I would jump on that chair next to him and then I would punch him and knock him out! Nobody was ever gonna mess with me.

Jay Daniel: Cybill did some wonderful work on the show. I go back to the pilot, and one of the scenes that stands out to me is the scene where

Cybill Shepherd shows off her comic skills in this scene from the pilot.

43

they're tied up together back-to-back. They're sort of arguing and he calls her a ball of fluff. And the way she reads, "BALL of *fluff.*" That was so hilarious to me. I was on the set, and I had to cover my mouth and turn and walk away. It just broke me up.

Cybill Shepherd: I remember that fondly. It was easy to play. When you have a brilliant writer, a creator like Glenn Gordon Caron, it's a gift from heaven.

Bob Butler: Bruce was trying to be real or significant when he gets totally hateful of the villain, rather than smirky or joyful. I tried to talk him out of it. He didn't really respond at all. So the moment is still in there. And I say wrong in a way. He's tied up and the villain is warming up a hot dog or something on the grill to torture him. Instead of being amused, as he should have been, he was beginning to plot revenge.

Jay Daniel: There wasn't money in the budget on the pilot to build much of anything. Everything in the pilot was shot practical. That means we went to an empty office building and brought in some elements to change how it looked. The detective agency was in an office building in Century City. Maddie's house was a real house in Beverly Hills, but I don't remember exactly where that was. The interior was built on stage when we got picked up for the series, to match what the interior of that house looked like.

Bob Butler: In downtown LA there is a huge four-sided clock. One side is straight down to the street and the other three sides are to the roof. Well, that gave us a perfect chance to shoot those few daring shots straight down to show Bruce in depth and build a platform.

Jay Daniel: We thought maybe we'd shoot on the top of the Capitol building downtown in Hollywood. It looks like a stack of records. You couldn't have possibly shot it on top of that building, no way. Then we found the Eastern Columbia Building in downtown Los Angeles.

Neil Mandelberg (Editor): I edited that scene at the clock with Jay, and it turned out to be wonderful. I was just the most excited person in the world. It was the greatest.

Jay Daniel: So when you see the front of the building and you see David and Maddie climbing up the clock and he says, "Yes, I am looking up your dress," all of that is shot on the side clock with the roof. The clock that we actually shot most of the close-ups on with Maddie hanging on the clock has a big roof under it. But the clock that you see on screen goes straight down to the street. The clock scene took six days to shoot, plus a day of second unit. That's how complex it was.

Neil Mandelberg: There were a few cuts where you take a little gasp. That's the greatest because that was in the days when they didn't really have visual effects, and it felt real.

Jay Daniel: Bruce was out there, wired up. The ladder was extremely solid and completely anchored. But he was willing to go out there. There were wires that we got rid of in post that were attached to him.

Cybill Shepherd: The person climbing up the clock is a stunt person. That clock is fourteen feet above the platform. The hairdresser wouldn't come up to that top floor. They built a scaffolding under that clock. If I had fallen, it would have been a two-story fall. I get up there and I am so terrified because I have to get off the scaffolding and get on the clock. They have seven cameras on me. One is hanging out over where I would fall if I fell off the scaffold. It was like doing a stunt. They were smart to get it with seven cameras. If I had fallen, I would have survived, but it would not have been fun. I grabbed Jerry Finnerman's [director of photography] jacket and he had headphones on to talk to the camera operators. I screamed, " I CAN'T DO THIS!" He takes off his headphones and says, "Did you say something?" I said, "No." That is what you call a trooper. It was easy to pretend I was terrified.

Bob Butler: I remember Jay trying to get a particular shot at the clock. He thought it should be framed a certain way, and I just wasn't interested. He persisted, but because that was technically my turf, it didn't get ugly.

Jay is a strong guy, very knowledgeable and very smart. So he didn't dismiss it all. He tried to get that shot. His director didn't agree with him and didn't do it. But barring that, we just really sailed through.

Jay Daniel: We shot a wide shot of them hanging from the clock. I wanted a shot from above them hanging off the clock. It got too complicated to do. So I gave up on it. When I saw the scene cut together, we didn't need that shot. Once again the director wins out. It was all in good fun.

Neil Mandelberg: The pilot was shot beautifully. Jerry Finnerman shot the shit out of the show. He was given the time. The height was felt.

Bob Butler: If the director wants the camera down the lion's throat, it's the DP's job to get it there. That was Jerry's approach. He was very much of that school. He was more experienced than I was.

Jay Daniel: We finished shooting on November 5, 1984. It took twenty-seven days, total. They tested the pilot, and it did quite well.

THE RESULT

Will Mackenzie: When I saw the pilot, I thought, "This is phenomenal." Cybill, being how gorgeous she was, was able to clip along, and Bruce had that—I always equate it to a young Jack Nicholson.

Allyce Beasley: On the way to the screening of the pilot, my manager at the time said, "I just can't wait to see this. I mean, everybody's talking about how Bruce Willis is going to be the next Jack Nicholson." I was like, "What?" I didn't really see that. Not that I had a chance to see it. I mean, I just basically had a few scenes with him.

Jay Daniel: We edited over Thanksgiving. It was long hours in the editing room. We had worked on the clock scene ad nauseum.

Neil Mandelberg: Glenn called and said, "We got this pilot called *Moonlighting*. Do you want to cut it?" My brother Artie cut it and I assisted. Jay and Glenn were there all the time.

Melissa Gelineau: I remember that when I saw that pilot it was the most unique TV show I could remember seeing. It was fun.

Debra Frank (Writer): I was invited, along with several other writers, to go to Fox and view the pilot before it was ever on TV. It was absolutely amazing. Afterwards, I'm in the restroom, and Kerry Ehrin and her writing partner, Ali Marie Matheson, were there. We're at the sink, washing our hands. We're talking about how great and exciting we thought the pilot was.

Jeff Reno (Writer): A lot of people say, "*Remington Steele* or *Hart to Hart* or *Castle* are similar." They are completely unlike *Moonlighting*. I don't mean to be immodest, but it was an elevated kind of dialogue. It moved faster and was a different kind of thing than TV had done at that point.

Bob Butler: It was just a good, solid job. When the material is good and the actors are beginning to show prowess in those first two days of dailies, why, people really leave you alone because they don't want to be responsible for any crises.

Jay Daniel: We delivered a cut of the pilot to them on November 30. We were picked up as a midseason replacement on December 4, 1984.

Reuben Cannon: Series themes are important. Mike Post had a monopoly, but Glenn went outside the box and chose Al Jarreau.

Glenn Gordon Caron: When I was writing the pilot, Al Jarreau's "After All" was the song stuck in my head. When we edited the pilot and submitted the rough edit to ABC, I used "After All" even though I didn't have the rights. We went to get the rights from Jarreau's management, and they said no. They thought that song was going to be a hit and didn't want to give it away. But they asked, "Would you consider doing an original song by Al?" I had no idea what that involved. Lee Holdrige had agreed to score the pilot and was mostly famous for being an orchestrator. He had worked with Streisand [*Songbird, Butterfly*]. I asked him to collaborate with Al Jarreau. They set a studio date, and Al showed up. My daughter was born the night before. I had never been in a recording studio and I was so excited, but at the same time, I felt enormous guilt that I wasn't with my wife, who was home with our newborn. Al and Lee got together on the melody, and Al had some lyrics. I asked for a few changes on some of the lyrics, but once I heard them sung with the tune, it didn't really matter. It just had the feeling of *Moonlighting*. ABC was knocked out by the song. We had a long version and a short version. We used the song in the end credits of the pilot. I loved Al Jarreau. I don't think I realized how different it was from what other shows were using at the time. It ended up being a hit song.

Reuben Cannon: Glenn sent me first the instrumental version. I remember it was a cassette. I played it in my car on the way home. Then came the Al Jarreau version. I remember being on the soundstage when it was being recorded, and Al was there in a booth.

Glenn Gordon Caron: I kind of did what I wanted. I had a willing compatriot in Bruce and in Jay Daniel, and in Bob Butler during the pilot. And sometimes I got scolded. ABC said, "You can't do that." But then they would screen it and all the secretaries would come in, and the executives would hear all these good, working people laughing and they'd go, "OK, don't touch it." A lot of *Moonlighting* was done like that.

Chic Eglee: ABC was not allowed to produce, air, and distribute their own material because that would be in violation of the consent decree. *Moonlighting* was produced by ABC Circle Films. It was on ABC, and it was distributed by ABC, and that happened in the Reagan era, under the Reagan administration. Republicans never met a monopoly that they didn't love. ABC was able to own, produce, air, and distribute that show because Reagan wasn't going to enforce any of that. It was kind of the beginning of what was to come in the way television was made and distributed. But it was also purely a function of the Reagan years.

Chapter 4
What's Up, Blue Moon?

With the pilot completed, Glenn Gordon Caron and Jay Daniel now had to produce a series. Bob Butler left to direct other pilots. Jay handled the line producing, which included running the set, editing, casting, scheduling, and hiring directors. He also had a hand in the creative side of producing. Glenn handled the writing and concentrated on making sure the show didn't fall into the hands of "average television." Glenn was determined to write something different every week. In fact, he was so sure that what he was doing was outside of the norm that he wrote this actual disclaimer on the cover of the script for "Gunfight at the So-So Corral," which was the first hourlong episode of *Moonlighting*. Thanks to Suzanne Gangursky for saving her copy from 1985.

Attached is the first script for our new series "Moonlighting." No doubt the first thing you will do is flip to the back page and gasp. Yes, this is longer and heavier than most one hour episodic scripts. No need for panic, however. Let me remind one and all that our two-hour pilot script was 156 pages and our first assembly off of that script was five minutes short. Our people talk very fast, fast-talking producer, fast-talking people. An average "Moonlighting" script is about 80 pages long, accept no substitutes! Seriously. We look forward to your comments, thoughts and impressions. Thanks for your patience. *Glenn*

Neil Mandelberg (Editor): We were shooting easily seventy-five to eighty pages per episode. When they got into rhythm, I would be checking dialogue and turning pages a lot. On normal shows, the average is a minute per page. Our show was under thirty seconds per page—always. So you can imagine how many pages Glenn has to write for a fifty-two-minute show. The episodes weren't forty-two minutes, like they are now.

Jay Daniel: It was pretty hectic to go that quickly from pilot to series. The normal thing is that you know well in advance that you've got a series to do, and you put your staff together. We were cutting the pilot while all of that was being put together. The episodes had to be ready to go so quickly. We had to shoot exteriors while the sets were being finished on Stage 20 at 20th Century Fox. We also had to move offices. We were at ABC Circle's building for the pilot. We now had to move to Fox for the series. We had two stages. Stage 20 was the main stage, with the detective office permanently built there. Stage 11 was Maddie's house. We had to have all that ready in time for Episode 1. We started shooting that first episode on January 21, 1985.

Sheryl Main (Production): I moved out to LA from New York, and I heard about an actor needing an assistant. So I went to the meeting and it was Bruce Willis, who I knew from New York as Bruno the bartender at Cafe Central. I wasn't right to be his assistant, but he asked Glenn to put me on the show, and I became the writers' assistant. This would have been after the pilot was shot. I had no idea what the hell I was doing. I was using typewriters to type scenes.

Melissa Gelineau: It was one of those "being in the right place at the right time" in terms of becoming Glenn's assistant. He had a deal at ABC Circle Films, and I was working there. I went to film school, and I was his receptionist, but I made it much more. So I was Glenn's assistant, and then I also inherited Jay.

Suzanne Gangursky: I was the production coordinator, and everything ran through our office. I worked closely with the production managers when a script would come out—I didn't say how often a script would come out. [Laughs.] We were responsible for getting all the pages out to the set. Many times we were flying by the seat of our pants.

Sheryl Main: I was always typing. I got to be a part of the creative process that I hadn't really been exposed to. These guys were high-level writers. They're writing stuff that breaks the fourth wall. I was on the inside of that and that was very exciting for me. Sometimes they would drop pages off at my house at ten at night that we would be shooting in the morning. *Moonlighting*, if nothing else, was a creative endeavor. And the creative process was a process! [Laughs.]

Melissa Gelineau: I was on call every single weekend. I was in my early twenties, and my overtime checks were three times my paychecks.

Suzanne Gangursky: I think in the beginning I worked seven days a week for like a month straight. I mean, it was crazy. We had multiple crews going at any given time. Many times three crews shooting at once.

Jay Daniel: In that first season, everything went through Glenn's typewriter. It's why everything is so consistent in terms of how the characters talk. The writers were good, but they understood that their work was going to be rewritten, and sometimes greatly rewritten, by Glenn because the series was his voice. That's a very unique voice for a writer to capture, so it's no reflection on them. It's just having seen the first drafts, and then Glenn's first pass, that was what had to happen for the show to be the show.

Peter Werner (Director of "Gunfight"): Even in the first episode of the first season, we did not have a finished script. And there were days where we would be waiting on the stage for the pages to come down. We'd get our copies and read the first part of a scene and you'd be laughing, and then it would stop halfway through the scene. So we were behind.

Jay Daniel: Peter Werner came in and was very congenial in terms of getting along with Bruce and Cybill. He took their thoughts seriously. The one thing I had to do was to make certain that from the staging standpoint at least, that we adhered to the template that Bob set up in the pilot.

Peter Werner: I remember literally having to walk Bruce out of his trailer when we were shooting the first scene downtown. It was actually in an alley. It was the scene where Maddie wants to go into this bar. Bruce is basically saying, "You'll stick out like a sore thumb." Then he kneels down, tears her dress, and ruffles her hair. He wasn't like, "I'm not coming out." But he was nervous. I walked him to the alley, and we did the first take and he just threw himself into it to a point where I am certain there's a shot in the cut where he's ripping her dress and she's just beginning to crack up. I think Bruce from that moment on was like, "I got this."

Debra Frank: When I was writing on the series, Bruce and Cybill got along great because it was at the beginning, I can remember watching dailies just before the scene would start, and Bruce would say to Cybill, "Do you think the show's gonna take off?" I thought that was absolutely adorable. It was just these sweet little conversations between two actors.

Peter Werner: We were shooting the scene in the parking garage where David distracts the bad guy. I knew it was expensive to rent a Century City garage, which we had to have complete control over. So in blocking this scene, I had Bruce come out from behind the pillar, where the bad guy was standing, and sing in front of him, which was not the most artful solution. Jay came up to me and said, "I don't mean to tell you how to direct, but don't you think it would be better if he came out down there?" I said, "But it'll take us an extra hour to light it, and we're already in the twelfth or thirteenth hour." He said, "But which do you like better?" I said, "I like walking from the pillar to pillar." He said, "OK, well let's just shut down and come back tomorrow." A producer saying that to a director is unheard of.

Cybill Shepherd: We shot in that parking garage a lot. I had a bus that was a dressing room and my daughter Clementine was sitting in it one time, and some guy off the street just walked in and said something to her. It was scary, but luckily he just walked out. After that I tried to get a little more security.

Suzanne Gangursky: I loved the excellence that it was striving for. It wasn't just about "Let's crank this out and make our money." It was "Let's make some really great television and do things that people have never done before. Let's show that TV can aspire to be excellent like movies."

Glenn Gordon Caron: I wouldn't put out pages just so we would have something to shoot. If it wasn't right, I wouldn't put them out, and we'd have nothing to shoot. Which for somebody in Jay's position could be very frustrating. And he probably got yelled at a lot for it. I would go to him and apologize and say, "This is not right yet." He'd say, "We can't schedule creativity to come." Can you imagine? I mean, I was a kid, and to have somebody support you in that way was quite something.

Peter Werner: Once they did the pilot, I believe that Glenn really began to realize how he could go way out writing for Bruce and Bruce would be able to pull that off. I directed the first, third, and fifth episodes of the first season. Glenn has often said it wasn't really until the third episode, which was my episode, "The Next Murder You Hear," that it all came together—the style, the characters, the writing, the cinematography. I think that's often the case in television: you don't always get it in the pilot.

Glenn Gordon Caron: I was exhilarated, but at the same time I was always scared that I wouldn't be able to top myself, because it was a sort of a high-wire act. Every week viewers tune in, and I felt we had some obligation to startle them and entertain them—really entertain. Not the sort of benign entertainment that a lot of television was back then. But get them talking and get them excited.

Peter Werner: The scene I remember shooting most of all was in "The Next Murder You Hear" because it was so emotional. Cybill is chasing after a guy who is supposed to have been murdered. She chases him in the rain. I think it was the last shot of the night; afterward Cybill broke down. She's a very strong person, but she is also very vulnerable. She just wept afterward. When I say break down, it was a mixture of exhaustion, rain, and doing it a few times. If there's a point to it, it's just the level of commitment that was on the part of everybody on the crew as well as the actors to make these scenes as dramatic and funny and actually physical. We did it a few times. It was virtually a hundred-yard dolly shot. To me, this is what you live for as a director. It rains, it's night, you yell "Action," you are pushing the dolly with the actor running along, and then you call "Wrap." And then she just fell into my arms sobbing, and it was like I was in some kind of a director's movie.

SEASON 1 FINALE

THE FINALE OF Season 1 was called "The Murder's in the Mail." This was the episode that contained the "man with a mole on his nose" banter mentioned in the introduction. Filming this episode was the first pressure-packed moment of the series. Because all of the first-season episodes were taking longer to shoot than episodes of other series at the time, the production team was pushing against the deadline to get this episode filmed before it had to air. This was the season finale, and it had to be completed and aired in order for ABC to look at the numbers and decide if the series would be picked up for Season 2. The episode, besides having tongue-twisting dialogue, ends in a massive food fight filmed on location at a hotel in downtown LA. One of the main causes of the delay was that there wasn't a finished script while they were shooting.

Jay Daniel: We *started* shooting on March 18, 1985, and the air date was April 2. Right there you can see the problem. We shot with two units on two of the days during that shoot. We also had to come in on a Saturday. My notes that day say: "Glenn is writing this afternoon's work this morning." So we shot in the morning and we got the script for that afternoon sometime *in* that afternoon. We were waiting at the hotel shooting the scene we didn't have yet. [Laughs.]

Peter Werner: We had a deadline on "The Murder's in the Mail." We'd gotten so far behind that by the time we were doing that episode, it was days before it was supposed to be on the air.

Jay Daniel: We shot on Saturday, which is expensive to do. My note for that day: "Glenn is still writing <u>today's</u> work. Cybill doesn't want to work on Sunday." Glenn finally finished writing the script on Sunday the twenty-fourth.

Peter Werner: Cybill and Bruce were total professionals when it came to shooting. They may not have liked each other, and it may have taken them a while to get out of their trailers, but you'd never know that in some of the dialogue scenes between them. They just threw themselves into that. They knew they had great material.

Cybill Shepherd: I would lie down on the couch, and I would close my eyes and kind of rest for about ten minutes. Then I would wake up and my brain would be refreshed and I could remember the lines better. It doesn't really matter how long you relax; you just don't want to think about it.

Filming this scene became the first time crunch on the series.

Jay Daniel: We filmed the food fight on March 25. We shot that unbelievably fast for what it was. My notes say: "Written yesterday. This is nuts! Filmed all night long till 6 AM."

Cybill Shepherd: I think we did one day that was like twenty-five hours. I had gone to Glenn and said, "At the end of this, I think we should be hit in the face with pies." Glenn said, "Who is gonna throw the pie at Bruce?" [Laughs.] It worked out pretty cool. I liked that scene a lot.

Peter Werner: That last day we actually shot for thirty-six hours. We had to bring in another crew because it was so expensive to shoot with the same crew in overtime that it became less expensive to bring in different people. We were shooting at the Biltmore Hotel. There was a big scene that ends with pie fights and stuff like that. It was the scene that begins with the guy doing the Dr. Seuss rhyme, and he could not get it. I don't know whether he was nervous or it was the dialogue. I think we probably spent two or three hours just shooting, trying to get him to do that correctly. But it was so late. We'd been working for probably twenty-four hours by that point. Everybody was giddy. It was both frustrating and hilarious.

Jay Daniel: I have a memory of myself walking down this big hallway, and off of that is the room where we filmed the food fight. I walked out of that hallway and went outside through a side door to go to my car, and the sun was up. [Laughs.] We had worked all night. Then we scrambled that day on the twenty-sixth because there was supposed to be rain the following day. We had to get our exteriors that day, so we had to swap out what we shot. We finished shooting on March 27. There was so much pressure on us to get that episode out. The network wanted those numbers to know about next season. After the network saw the rough cut of the previous episode ["Next Stop Murder"], they ordered seven scripts for next season. The reason they said seven scripts is because once they say you are picked up, you can start work. Then you have the scripts to work from. But the turnaround between the end of Season 1 and getting into Season 2, with our seven-script order, which became more than that when we did get picked up, was a short turnaround. So we were always behind on scripts.

Peter Werner: That first season, both of them were rather hoping the show would not get picked up. Bruce had a feature possibility and Cybill was back. I never saw two people that were less happy when their show was picked up for another season.

Jay Daniel: On the twenty-eighth, we edited all day and worked till 1:00 a.m. We only had five days till we got the episode on air. We polished the cut on the twenty-ninth and worked till 2:00 a.m. Then we did some looping on Saturday the thirtieth. Mixed the score and did the postproduction on the thirty-first and worked until 8:00 p.m. that night. Glenn, Artie Mandelberg, and I went to the Brown Derby to celebrate that we were finished on the thirty-first. It aired on Tuesday. It was one of those! I wrote on Tuesday, April 2: "COMPLETE COLLAPSE!!!" 'cause that was a bitch.

Peter Werner: At the end of the first season, we had a wrap party. We went up to the bar and we ordered drinks. I turned to walk away and Bruce reached in his pocket and put a $20 bill down. I was like, "You know it's free?" He said, "Yeah, I know. But I was a bartender, and these people don't get paid very well." Ever since that day, I leave a tip at every cash bar that I go to just because of Bruce.

Jay Daniel: On Wednesday, we had the wrap party for the season. It was also Glenn's birthday. I finally got a day off on April 4. I think I was comatose. Everybody was happy with the work. The series was doing well as far as the network was concerned. They aired reruns over the summer, and those episodes really started to draw audiences. The reruns were like number nine, number twelve, and continued to win their night. So everyone was obviously pleased by that. There were a few little things that sort of foreshadowed what might be coming later, but overall, we came away feeling pretty good about everything.

Glenn Gordon Caron: I remember when we were done with the first season, they were already growing apart, and I had taken them into a trailer and sort of given them a talking-to. By the way, Bruce and I are virtually the same age, and Cybill's maybe two years older, so I'm a child at this point and I'm talking to this huge star and scolding her and saying, "You've got to behave," and turning to him and saying, "And *you've* got to behave." But I always remember she was leaving to do a miniseries, *The Long Hot Summer*, with Don Johnson. She turned to me and said, "Now I'm going to go do some real work." I thought, "What?" For whatever reason, she wasn't participating in it. I wasn't sure anybody was going to watch, but I knew we were doing something we'd be proud of for a long time.

THE START OF SEASON 2

Roger Director: I remember I had been hired to write for *Moonlighting* and I was sitting in Glenn's office in the summertime. I guess it was 1985. ABC still hadn't cemented a schedule. I was sitting in his office and he said to me that he wasn't sure the show was gonna go because at that point Aaron Spelling sort of ruled the airwaves at ABC. They were uncertain about whether or not there was a spot for *Moonlighting*. I remember thinking, "Oh, goodness, I've come to this show and we don't even know if it's going to go." Thankfully it did. I distinctly remember sitting in his office and Glenn wrote "Brother, Can You Spare a Blonde?" I'd been working at *Hill Street Blues*, where we sat in a room and beat out every story beat. We had a tight outline, we knew what every scene was going to be about, and Glenn just rolled a piece of paper in a typewriter and wrote: "Fade In." It completely blew my mind, because I was not used to writing that way.

Jay Daniel: We started shooting Season 2 on June 17, 1985. We finished "Brother, Can You Spare a Blonde?" a half day over. We finished "The Lady in the Iron Mask" on July 12. It took nine and a half days to shoot that one. We shot "Money Talks - - Maddie Walks" on the fifteenth of July and finished it on the twenty-fourth. Then we shut down for eight days because of a lack of scripts.

THE SECOND EPISODE of Season 2, "The Lady in the Iron Mask," contains one of the most classic chase scenes of the series. A female client, wearing a black veil, hires Blue Moon to find the man who disfigured her face years earlier. The episode ends with everyone wearing a black dress and a face covering as they run through a hotel and slide down a hallway into a bunch of soapsuds, all set to the *William Tell* overture. Unfortunately, in the DVD version of this episode, the original music is replaced with a new score. It's a shame, because this scene was edited perfectly to the music and was certainly the first classic chase scene, which became a staple of the series.

Chris Leitch (Director of "The Lady in the Iron Mask"): Glenn was wielding a lot of executive-producer vision, and he was hands-on. He was a perfectionist. It was supposed to be a nine-day shoot. It ended up being a thirteen-day shoot, which was not uncommon for *Moonlighting*. It puts a lot of strain on the budget, which gets thrown out when you're way over. My job is to get the shot, get the performances, and get the story. But it's tough for a lot of people.

Roger Director (Writer of "The Lady in the Iron Mask"): I was hesitant to pitch the overall idea about a person who had been so jealous that they disfigured a lover by throwing acid in their face along with a zany chase. I didn't know if a one-hour show could encompass something so horrible and include something so crazy. But I think it sort of did, thanks to Glenn.

Chris Leitch: For this particular episode, Glenn was very clear that there was a Hitchcockian element to it, sort of mixed with a screwball comedy. I went to film school at NYU; my film-history knowledge was pretty strong. So I knew exactly what he was talking about when he was talking about the suspense and the Hitchcockian elements.

Roger Director: I had this idea that we would end the show with this bizarre chase, where everyone had a black dress and a black veil on—which was cuckoo. But Glenn said, "OK, do that." That was the wonderful thing about working for Glenn. He would entertain the wildest notions. You had such extraordinary freedom to just think of what would be different. He always wanted you to go for things that no one had seen before. That was rule number one. If you haven't seen it before, do it. And so we did this bizarre chase.

Chris Leitch: There was a lot of drama behind the camera. And because of that, how can I put this delicately? But maybe I shouldn't put it delicately. There were a lot of cooks in the kitchen. Glenn was very demanding. He was very nice and really sweet. But if it wasn't exactly what he wanted, you would have to reshoot it. Glenn had this process where the script that you were given was never the script that you actually shot. The story would remain the same, but Glenn was constantly rewriting during the shoot. Oftentimes I'd get a call late at night during the shoot and Glenn would say, "You're going to get new pages tomorrow; don't worry about it. We'll try and get it there at call, and then I'll come down, and we can talk about the scenes." That happened two or three times. From my standpoint, I'm just sort of the director. It's my job to fulfill Glenn's vision and to make it work. The problem is that it created chaos for the actors.

The famous ending of "The Lady in the Iron Mask" was a soapy affair.

Jay Daniel: Cybill and Bruce were up for the soapsuds chase scene. They were game for it. We had done big food fights and stuff like that. I don't recall anybody worrying about their clothes or what they were going to look like after. They probably had as much fun doing it as we did watching. Some of the things weren't that much fun to shoot, but I never heard any real bitching about it. They just wanted to make sure you had enough cameras rolling so you didn't have to do it three, four times.

Cybill Shepherd: I don't know why I don't remember filming that chase scene in this episode. I guess there wasn't time to remember anything because we were constantly doing another episode. It was like helter-skelter in the best sense. I was always game for a chase scene. I feel enormously grateful to be a part of this.

Chris Leitch: There was a fountain in the lobby and the initial thought was "Everybody will end up in the lobby, the police show up, and everybody falls in the fountain." Then, I forget whose idea it was, either [stunt coordinator] Chris Howe or I said, "What about a slip and slide?" We had a guy who is supposed to be cleaning the floor and we had all these bubbles, which is obviously ridiculous, but it covered the slip and slide that we put down. All the slip-and-slide work was done by stunt doubles, and then the real actors came out of the bubbles.

Cybill Shepherd: Chris Howe was incredible. I did some stunts on *Moonlighting* that I would never have even tried on other shows. You have to have complete trust in your stunt coordinator if you are going to put your life at risk. We were shooting in an indoor mall, and there were escalators. David is coming up the upside and I am going down the other. In between the escalator there was a space I had to jump on and slide down. During rehearsal, the escalator wasn't moving. So the rubber handles weren't moving, and I could control my descent. But once we were shooting the scene, I could no longer control my speed. I can't hold on because they were moving in opposite directions. I had such speed that I flew off the escalator, and I went a long way, and there was Chris to catch my head so I didn't get hurt. Chris Howe was the greatest.

Jay Daniel: You had to be prepared, wardrobewise, to do it three times. That's really the rule of thumb that you follow. You hope that you don't have to, but sometimes it's just filmmaking. The actors could be perfect, and something happens to the camera on that particular shot.

Chris Leitch: The chase scene was the centerpiece for the episode. The way that we conceived it as a team was "screwball comedy meets the Three Stooges" while trying to maintain some semblance of Hitchcock— although by the time you get there, it's totally screwball. One of the things that inspired Bruce, as an actor, was the Three Stooges. Because everyone is in dresses and masks, the whole thing was "Who's who? Who's where?" We had pretty open access to the Ambassador Hotel.

Cybill Shepherd: It was such a great location, because it wasn't open as a hotel. We shot there all the time. I think that location was key to that scene. People sliding into the bubbles at the hotel.

Chris Leitch: We just took over a bunch of hallways, rooms, staircases, and elevators. We had a whole stunt team of doubles. There must have been at least a dozen people in dresses and masks. [Laughs.] First of all, when you put those pumps on it's hard to run. Certainly Bruce was pretty athletic, but we don't want to ask the guest stars to do it. You can get hurt pretty quickly. Since nobody's talking and there's no other action in the frame, we shot a lot of it at eighteen or nineteen frames per second to give it that silent-movie quality. It just looks like they are running much faster.

Neil Mandelberg: If I remember right, we cut it to the *William Tell* overture. Glenn was great with the music choices. We would include the final music as we made future passes in the editing. Once we got the threads of the scene together, we would then put the music in and make our adjustments to the music. This chase scene was cut with that in mind.

Chris Leitch: I directed early on in the show, so there wasn't sort of this off-screen conflict that evolved. When I was working with Cybill and Bruce, they were delightful. They were incredible and very excited. Bruce was really excited to be doing the series. They were professionals, and it came together pretty quickly. They would do anything. After just rewatching this episode, I'm just kind of amazed at how good the two of them are together—really good acting, amazing interpretations, staying within the characters and the emotions.

WITH THE FIRST nine scripts completed and the formula for the series in place, production came to a halt because the show was out of scripts. Most shows never shut down during the filming of a season, due to the cost and because multiple writers are usually on staff, but Glenn Gordon Caron was writing the final version on every script and just couldn't keep up with this pace. The reasons were complex and would only grow more so as the series continued. Simple answers were never a part of *Moonlighting*. The show was never that black and white.

Except for that one time . . .

Chapter 5

Gentlemen Prefer Black & White

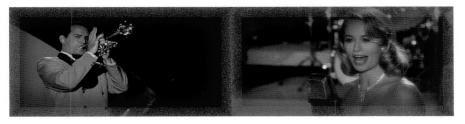

"Good evening, I'm Orson Welles. Tonight broadcasting takes a giant leap backward. In this age of living color and stereophonic sound, the television show *Moonlighting* is daring to be different and share with you a monochromatic, monophonic hour of entertainment."[1]

—Orson Welles

And what an hour of entertainment "The Dream Sequence Always Rings Twice" provided. Written by Debra Frank and Carl Sautter and directed by Peter Werner, it was only the *tenth* episode of *Moonlighting* ever. Why wait to break the mold? It was introduced by Orson Welles, the legendary director of *Citizen Kane*, a film that invariably sits atop the list of the greatest American films ever made. You want to talk about laying down the gauntlet at the top of an episode?

The episode began in typical fashion. Dave and Maddie deliver pictures to a client for a case they are working on. They meet the client at the Flamingo Cove, an old, rundown club. They learn that there was a famous unsolved murder committed at the club. The suspects were a man and a woman who were having an affair. The victim was the woman's

---

1 *Moonlighting*. "The Dream Sequence Always Rings Twice." Directed by Peter Werner. Written by Caron, Frank, & Sautter. ABC, October 15, 1985.

husband. Both suspects went to the electric chair claiming it was the other one who actually did it. David thinks the woman must have done it. Maddie is certain the man did it. Twelve minutes into the episode, the screen turns to black and white and we see Maddie's version of the Flamingo Cove murder. When she awakens from her dream, she calls David, says "I told you he did it," and hangs up on him. Then we see David's version. Each dream is infused with old-movie references and big band songs performed by Cybill Shepherd, and perfectly aligns with the character of the leads. The sequences are as different as Dave and Maddie themselves, and just as entertaining.

Debra Frank (Writer of "Dream Sequence"): Carl Sautter and I came up with the idea of going back to the forties and doing a show in black and white that dealt with an unsolved case. This was our first script together. We tailored it to every detective series that was out there. Off of a *Remington Steele* script that I sold, we were lucky enough to get various meetings for the other mystery shows that were on then. We were very young at the time, and when we pitched it to people they looked at us like, "You don't really understand TV. You can't go back in time. You can't do black and white from the forties. You're going to lose the audience." We would always get a lecture. I like to jokingly say we were kicked out of every office in Hollywood.

Glenn Gordon Caron: You've got singing and dancing, and black and white, and period. Particularly back then, people didn't do that stuff on television.

Debra Frank: When Carl and I went in to pitch to Glenn we had somewhere between three to five ideas. We thought, "We'll start with the black-and-white show and then he'll tell us we don't know how television works, and then we'll move on." So we went in, pitched the idea to him, and there was this long pause. Glenn said, "OK, you know what we can do? We can do Maddie's part as an MGM glossy version and then do David's like Warner Bros. film noir. It will be grainy." Carl and I were stunned. We were just so expecting to be rejected that we sat there dumbfounded.

Glenn Gordon Caron: Debra and Carl were a team. They wrote the Christmas episode ["It's a Wonderful Job"] and the black-and-white episode, which are two of my favorite episodes. I liked them both enormously. Carl has since passed away.

Debra Frank: In the opening, the owner of the club tells them about the murders and that they both claimed to be innocent and that they were set up by the other one, and they both went to their death claiming that it was the other person who did it. So right from that setup, it's not really going to be solved. When David and Maddie get in the car, their argument is two different points of view. Maddie thinks he took advantage of a woman. David's was that she manipulated him. Then, when you went into the dream sequence, that was exactly what you saw.

Jay Daniel: I loved the script when it came in. When you're doing a series, you're filming an episode, you're prepping the next episode, and you're cutting the episode you shot before. As a producer, you are involved in three different episodes at the same time. I knew it was going to be a challenge.

Sheryl Main: I remember reading the script for "Dream Sequence" and thinking I had never read anything like that before.

Peter Werner (Director of "Dream Sequence"): While we were out on a location scout, Glenn slipped me the "Dream Sequence" script to read because I was going to be directing it. I just remember reading that script on the bus and saying, "How did I get so lucky?"

Debra Frank: It was like, "I can't believe this is happening." Not only did Glenn respond and get it, he was adding to it. He was excited about the idea. He couldn't wait to jump in and do it. It was one of the best days ever.

Jay Daniel: We actually moved up the black-and-white episode. We shut down the show that would become "My Fair David." We had to shut down because we were out of scripts. So we started prep on "Dream

Sequence." We came back from the shutdown to start shooting the black-and-white episode on August 7, 1985.

Neil Mandelberg (Editor for "Dream Sequence"): I wish we had done more of what we did on "Dream Sequence." Cybill had tons of fun when she didn't have to play Maddie every day. She was wonderful in that episode.

Cybill Shepherd: My first film, *The Last Picture Show*, was the first black-and-white film for a long time—that was kind of revolutionary—and then I got to do the black-and-white episode for *Moonlighting*. It was kind of thrilling.

Debra Frank: We didn't select the songs. I think it was Cybill that selected "I Told Ya I Love You, Now Get Out." I think that was a negotiation between Cybill and Glenn. He wanted "Blue Moon." I don't think she cared for "Blue Moon" that much. So it was like, "Well, if you do my song, I'll do your song."

Cybill Shepherd: I talked to Leonard Feather about what I should sing and he suggested that song. I believe he was the jazz critic at the *LA Times*. So that is where that idea came from. I believe we recorded it at Capitol Records.

Glenn Gordon Caron: My recollection is that on this one Cybill was excited, because she likes to sing. She had put out a bunch of albums. She loves that period. There's a song in the second half called "I Told Ya I Love You, Now Get Out," and I wanna say that's a song she brought to me. "Blue Moon" was my idea.

Peter Werner: *Of course* she should sing "Blue Moon." [Music supervisor] Alf Clausen did the arrangements. We went into some great recording studio one day and Cybill sang. She has style, and she's got a great voice. Then we used the playback on the day that she sang. It was just a big day on the set, with all these extras and everybody dressed to the gills in tuxedos.

Jay Daniel: We had to find time to get Cybill time to rehearse. She had to learn the songs and rehearse. That all took time and money. The actual scene was filmed at the Aquarius Theater. It had that huge revolving stage. She was great in that number.

Debra Frank: Nowadays, everybody does a musical episode, but then, it had not been done before. That was the most expensive show that had ever been done on television. It was pretty outrageous—until "Atomic Shakespeare," and then that became the most expensive.

Peter Werner: The musical section of the episode was the MGM musical and the detective part was the Warner Bros./James Cagney type. I'd seen fifty MGM Judy Garland melodramas. And I'd seen many of the Warner Bros. Paul Muni, detective/bad guy stuff. Those were the two styles that we were very consciously trying to emulate in terms of montages when Bruce is walking with all the signs over his head and stuff like that. It was a little bit of parody/satire on top of homage.

Debra Frank: Once Glenn liked the idea, we went to Blockbuster and rented all the MGM and Warner Bros. movies and just listened to the cadence. It was like *Dial M for Murder* and all of those film noir movies. We just lifted all of the great bits—the voice-overs, the walking with the signs over his head, the newspaper spinning. We used every gimmick from those movies. Glenn had always said that the series was this screwball comedy from the forties. He had Maddie and David's character set up that way. We just added these other two genres.

Peter Werner: My favorite genre is screwball comedy. My favorite movies are *It Happened One Night* and Preston Sturges films. I was doing what I always dreamed of doing with my life.

Neil Mandelberg: Peter Werner did such a beautiful job. I enjoyed every bit of that episode. I didn't want to go home. I also enjoyed, even though it was really early on, Bruce and Cybill being somebody else in the episode. I've always loved the old thirties and forties movies. I just love the way it was designed.

Man with a Horn: In the second half of the episode, we see Addison's version.

Allan Arkush (Director): I learned from watching Peter Werner. He was the guy doing most of the directing at that point. His visual style was what I was picking up on.

Debra Frank: The network wanted to film it in color and then take the color out. Glenn knew if they filmed it in color, the network would never air it in black and white. He really fought for that. We had to get special cameras and special lighting to do everything in black and white. They had to track down the cameras and people who could develop the film.

Glenn Gordon Caron: No one developed black and white. We literally couldn't find a lab to do it, and they were scared of the liability if there were problems, because they didn't do it on a regular basis.

Debra Frank: Carl and I were oblivious to all of this. We didn't think about the fact that no one could develop the film. A writer doesn't realize the headaches they cause for the production staff.

Suzanne Gangursky: Instead of actually shooting in black and white, there was a less expensive way they could have filmed it called decolorization. I think Glenn was like, "No, it's going to be done this way because we want it to have a certain feel."

Peter Werner: ABC wanted to shoot it color and then take the black and white out, which is a very different look. Jerry Finnerman was raised in the old school of hard lights. So we had the perfect DP for black and white. It took time that really made a difference. Everybody knowing that you're doing it the right way affects the content, and performance.

Cybill Shepherd: Jerry was really an amazing person. He gave me a gift where you can look at the brightest of lights and it won't harm your vision. He inscribed it to "C.S. from G.P.F.," and it is one of the most precious things to me. (See photos below.)

PHOTOS COURTESY OF CYBILL SHEPHERD

Cybill Shepherd shared these photos to illustrate how a DP can view a scene without the light affecting the view.

Glenn Gordon Caron: Jerry was sort of a classic motion picture cinematographer, and I think a big part of the episode's success was his familiarity with how to light for black and white, because back then, remember, we had no monitors, we had no playback. There was no video. You shot and you went to dailies the next day and hoped it worked out.

Neil Mandelberg: We were on film, so if a director printed over an hour of dailies in the day, there was a phone call made because of the cost. So he had to make his decisions and choose what to print as he went through, which sometimes helped me and sometimes hindered me. Peter really did a tremendous job making decisions.

Jay Daniel: The wardrobe people, Bob Turturice and his group, would get charged up when you do something like that. If you do a show like the black-and-white show, you start the prep on wardrobe even earlier. But we didn't have the script earlier, not on *Moonlighting*.

Peter Werner: In those days, you had cranes. It wasn't all operated by somebody on the ground and you just look over their shoulder. So the director actually had to sit on a crane as the camera moved in or swooped out. That was such a joy.

Cybill Shepherd: We filmed this episode at the old Cocoanut Grove at the Ambassador Hotel. The episode looks like a movie. It was incredible that it was a television show.

Sheryl Main: It was so beautiful. I was on set quite a bit for that one because we all felt like something was being created that was really groundbreaking for TV. Even though we all weren't sure how it would turn out—except for Glenn. He always had the confidence in his cast and crew, which was pretty awesome.

Jay Daniel: I think the network had come to trust us. For some reason, they went hook, line, and sinker for it.

Debra Frank: Glenn would sometimes add certain things. We might have written Bruce playing all the instruments in the big band. I think that was ours. I know Glenn added at the very end when David's being executed and his final request is for the long version of "Stairway to Heaven." That was Glenn.

Peter Werner: By the time I was directing a script, Glenn was doing the rewrites. So I had very little to do with the writers. If I worked with anybody, it was Glenn.

Debra Frank: When we came out of Maddie's dream sequence and she called David, Glenn wrote a scene where David was in bed with another woman when he gets the call from Maddie. Carl and I were so against that. We went to him and said, "No, no, no!" I mean, this whole episode is about getting Maddie and David together in a fantasy for the first time. Having him in bed with another woman just ruins it.

Mel Harris (Actress): I was going to be the first person that Bruce Willis's character slept with. This was a big deal for me. I went to the audition and I got the job.

Debra Frank: We had this discussion. We were adamant about it. In any other episode you could have him in bed with someone else, but not this particular episode because this is about their love affair. The subtext of everything is their love affair. We were in his office over and over again, fighting for that. Then at one point Glenn said, "OK, it was a good scene, but it just wasn't in the right place." So finally he took it out.

Mel Harris: I showed up for work. I'm in hair and makeup and Glenn Gordon Caron walks in and says, "We're not gonna film this scene. I love you. I loved your audition. I just have come to think it's not the right time for him to be sleeping with someone." It was the best job that I ever got and never filmed. The fact that I had been hired for *Moonlighting* was a great selling point for my agents. I can't remember which episode it was, but it may have been the black-and-white episode.

Glenn Gordon Caron: It is absolutely true. I felt terrible about having

led Mel down the garden path, but Debra and Carl were right. Once they got me to see it, I realized it would have been a mistake.

Debra Frank: The mystery of who did it really didn't matter. It wasn't important who killed her husband. We were using that as a device to have Dave and Maddie play these characters. In each of their versions, they were the victims. It was really *Rashomon*, where you see it from two different sides. What mattered was getting to see the actors play these different characters. It was just a projection of their feelings. The main thing was that it played on the sexual tension and that you actually got to see them kiss.

Peter Werner: The scene where they actually kiss was filmed in the back alley at the 20th Century Fox lot. We just found a little kind of doorway. It was a really big deal. Oh my Bruce Willis and Cybill Shepherd are finally going to kiss on camera!

Debra Frank: When you come back at the end of the episode, you still have the sexual tension. They slept together, but they didn't sleep together. But in both of their minds, they had slept with the other person. It was just all about the characters and the emotion and the undercurrent of their love story.

Allyce Beasley: That was the episode when we brought in the gentleman who became Bruce's permanent makeup artist. He was an older gentleman; I know he has since passed. He was a black-and-white expert. He had a very old makeup box with little wooden trays in it. Bruce liked him so much that they kept him as the makeup person from that episode forward. How that relates to me is that I had to share a makeup artist with Bruce. What he knew how to do was how to put on pancake with chalk, basically like something that you would cement between bricks. Bruce loved him, and I was like, "Somebody help me!" [Laughs.] Every time he would put my makeup on, I would go and wipe half of it off. It was way too heavy and not right for me. And again, a lovely man, Bruce adored him, but what did Bruce need? He needed powder.

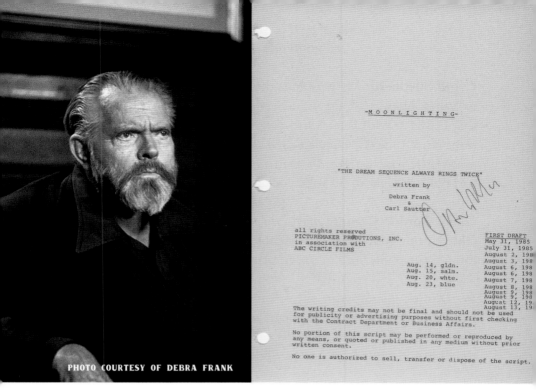

The great Orson Welles, and his signature on Debra Frank's script

Jay Daniel: The black-and-white episode did a 19.4 overnight, which was very good.

Debra Frank: They had Orson Welles come in at the very last moment to shoot that little promo saying that twelve minutes into the show it will turn black and white, and there's nothing wrong with your TV set—just so people understood.

Roger Director: I'm sure Cybill and her relationship with Bogdanovich might have helped. Whoever called Orson Welles, by this point the show certainly had buzz.

Jay Daniel: Cybill knew Orson through director Peter Bogdanovich. Orson actually lived with Bogdanovich for a time, and Orson and Cybill got fairly close. Glenn had the idea that this needed a cold open. He thought, "How about somebody like Orson Welles?" Cybill said, "Yeah, I'll ask."

Cybill Shepherd: My granddaughter is named after Orson. Her name is Welles. He was a huge influence to me. Often at the house in Bel Air that I lived at with Peter, Orson was a guest of ours—on and off for like three years. One day I had smelled smoke and I knocked on his door and asked if he was all right. He said, "Yes, everything is taken care of." He had put a lit cigar in his robe pocket and it caught on fire.

Glenn Gordon Caron: I may have gone to her and asked for his number and just not gotten it. I can't remember who gave it to me, but I called him on the phone and to my surprise he answered.

Jay Daniel: Glenn wrote the opening. We went to an empty stage. We wanted to do this separately, apart from the sets. He came up in a limo right to the stage door. They opened those big stage doors. He got out of the limo and came in; the stage door closed behind him.

Melissa Gelineau: It was pretty incredible, which is one of the reasons why I think I can't remember specifics—just that I wanted to be on that set to see Orson Welles. We'd literally studied him in school, and he's an icon.

Jay Daniel: We set up a very small unit with a set behind him. He arrived on time. Glenn asked, "Do you have any questions?" He said, "No, I think it's fairly self-explanatory." We said, "Shall we rehearse one?" Orson said, "Why don't we shoot the rehearsal?"

Roger Director: Glenn directed that little segment of his intro. He was so taken in by the fact that he was going to be directing Orson Welles I think he forgot to say action.

Peter Werner: It's one of the little bitter pills, because Glenn shouldn't have directed Orson. That would be a Directors Guild violation in this day and age, and he didn't tell me that it was happening. I came to work one day and everybody was like, "Oh, we came in an hour early; we did this great thing with Orson Welles." And it's like, why? So I felt a little bad about that. Because I'd have been the last person to direct Orson

Welles. But Glenn did that.

Jay Daniel: Glenn said "Action" to *Orson Welles*. [Laughs.] I think Glenn was about to say, "That was great." Orson said, "Shall we do it again?" Orson felt he could do it a little better. I think we ended up doing three takes. The only direction he got was "Action." Each time there was never a stumble. He just went through it quite beautifully.

Sheryl Main: It was amazing having him there. He was enjoying himself as much as we were enjoying having Orson Welles in the house.

Jay Daniel: It was just that little crew and Orson, except when I turned around that totally empty huge stage was full of people. They were in the greens. They were standing way in the background.

Debra Frank was the only one who brought a camera, and each of these writers told me that they still have this photo. From left to right: Ron Osborn, Debra Frank (background), Orson Welles, Jeff Reno, and Roger Director on a day to be remembered by all who were there.

Glenn Gordon Caron: The soundstage was filled with people—there were like three hundred people watching.

Jay Daniel: They had silently come in because they had heard that Orson Welles was on the lot, and they watched. We NEVER knew they were there. It was crew people and secretaries from other shows. Somehow the word got out that he was on the lot shooting something. There were quite a number of people there. It made me tear up.

Debra Frank: I had my script and I got him to autograph it.

Jay Daniel: Cybill had known him for a number of years, but she didn't come to say hi, which I thought she might. I think she was actually working on another set. I can't remember now. We kept it as quiet as we could. But word got out somehow. He was just so easy and professional and willing to take a picture and all of that.

Roger Director: I have a picture of Orson Welles with the writing staff from when he came to shoot that. It's a very prized possession.

Debra Frank: I brought the camera to the set because I wanted to get a picture with Orson. It was just going to be a picture with Orson and myself at first, and I handed the camera to somebody to take the picture. When I went back, all the writers and everyone fluttered around to get into the picture. I'm in the back, like on my tippy toes trying to get my face into the shot.

Melissa Gelineau: I was on the set. It's funny because my husband has a picture of me on the set. Either in front of me or behind me is Orson Welles. I was there, saw him, watched the scene, but I did not engage with him.

Jay Daniel: We took some photographs, and we showed him to the door. The limo was waiting. He got in the limo and drove away.

Debra Frank: I don't remember him being in a limo. What stood out to me is that a friend drove him to the studio in an old, beat-up green car from the sixties. I was stunned. Here is an icon of a man and he wasn't getting into a limo, and he was wearing a suit jacket, pants, and flip-flops.

Sheryl Main: I got to meet *Orson Welles*! We were all like, "Oh my God, Orson Welles." It was just one of those moments. We were all on set that day to watch him film. We were afraid that we killed him. [Laughs.]

Jay Daniel: When we got word that he had passed, I couldn't believe it, because he did not seem infirm in any way. It was really a shock. Orson Welles passed away one week after he did the show. We filmed him on October 3. And he died October 10, 1985. *Moonlighting* was the last thing he ever shot. The episode aired on October 15.

Glenn Gordon Caron: He was in horrible shape. But he was Orson Welles. You just assumed he was invulnerable. I certainly didn't think, "He'll be gone in a week."

Neil Mandelberg: The day before he passed, I was aware that I was cutting the cold open with a man who was so important to our industry. He looked so very much alive the day I met him. It was really upsetting for all of us to have lost him. Orson was the biggest man I'd ever met. I don't mean just in stature. We only talked for like ten seconds.

Debra Frank: Just this morning, I remembered that I have that autograph of Orson Welles on my script. Well, last year when there were the California fires and I had to evacuate, I thought, "Shit. I didn't take my script with Orson's signature on it." Next time I have to evacuate, I need to take that with me!

Jay Daniel: We didn't advertise that Orson would be introducing the episode at all. Today, it would be advertised everywhere. I think it was a lovely surprise for people. That's one of those things you bring to your memory bank and say, "Wow, I'm glad I experienced that. I got to meet that man." It was an honor. He honored us by doing it.

Debra Frank: That was the episode that brought about the sixteen Emmy nominations. So that was very exciting. When I say, "I wrote on *Moonlighting*," people say, "Oh, I love that show." And if I tell them I wrote the black-and-white episode, they say, "No way!" It turned out to be a classic episode. I'm so fortunate to have been a part of it.

Neil Mandelberg: I chose to put the "Dream Sequence" episode up for Emmy consideration because I got to cut that episode entirely by myself, and I won.

Debra Frank: Chic Eglee started writing for *Moonlighting* right after the black-and-white episode. He came from *St. Elsewhere*. Someone from that show called and said, "We liked that. We think we are going to do one as well." Both the black-and-white episodes were nominated against each other, and *theirs* won.

Peter Werner: I think, to be honest, the legacy is that it's been voted one of the top fifty episodes of all time, and of course it's awfully nice to be connected with something like that.

Debra Frank: No, I *absolutely* will not tell which character actually committed the Flamingo Cove murder. No way!

DAMN, I TRIED. I guess file this one in the same folder as the Anselmo case. Another mystery goes unsolved.

Chapter 6
The Talk of the Series

After the-black-and-white episode aired, *Moonlighting* became a critical and popular hit. The episode catapulted the series into the top ten, where it stayed for over the next year and a half. More importantly, it emboldened the writers to try to be even more creative. During the time period covered in this chapter, there were no "theme" episodes, but the writers fine-tuned the style the show would be remembered for. They began breaking the fourth wall and doing more cold opens, and crazy chase scenes to bring the mysteries to a close. At the same time, the cases began to directly reflect the friction between Maddie and Dave. This sometimes caused the characters to speak (yell?) at the same time. This was not how other television characters behaved. Certain MTM-produced shows, most notably *Hill Street Blues*, may have used overlapping dialogue, but on most series characters politely waited for one another to stop talking before opening their mouths.

The series also bolstered its all-star writing staff. While there was no doubt that Glenn was still taking a pass at every script, the staff was starting to come together. Debra Frank, Carl Sautter, and Roger Director had already joined. At this point, a writing team that had made its name on *Night Court* joined the staff. The limbo bar was lowered (or should it be raised?) with the addition of Jeff Reno and Ron Osborn.

"KNOWING HER"

Jay Daniel: The Season 2 premiere aired on September 24, 1985. It got a thirty-one share. It beat a two hour *A-Team*. It looked like we were going to be a hit. On September 25, we had to pull the plug because we didn't have anything to shoot. We shut down until October 3 to get the scripts ready. We started shooting "Knowing Her," which was the episode with Dana Delany.

Jeff Reno (Writer): The writing staff was Roger, Debra and Carl, Ron and I. Chic Eglee was brought in at the end of the second season. Kerry Ehrin and her partner, Ali Matheson, wrote a freelance episode for Glenn the first season. Kerry came on staff for probably the third season.

Ron Osborn (Writer): Kerry wrote a spec script for us on her own. We said, "We've got to get this person on staff." She was terrific. Here's a show about a male/female relationship, and at the time, Debra was the only female on staff. You think we would have half and half, but it wasn't the case.

Debra Frank: John Wells [*China Beach*, *ER*, *The West Wing*] came in and pitched to us. He was this new kid on the block. He hadn't started his career yet. He would bring Mrs. Fields cookies in. He would describe the shot exactly. I remember thinking, "This guy's amazing." Roger and I were talking about how Glenn should hire this guy. But nothing ever happened with that.

Jeff Reno: Ron and I wrote the limbo scene for "Knowing Her" originally. We started out with that. Glenn needed a first act for the episode before ours, "My Fair David." I remember my first line I wrote for the show. David said, "Do math majors multiply? Do eggs get laid?" I bet it's in the first act of "My Fair David." We had to come up with a new first act for "Knowing Her," so I think Maddie gets stuck in the rain.

Suzanne Gangursky: Like most scripts, they'll go through new colors every time there's a revision. On several of them, I counted twenty different rewrites on one script. That gives you some idea of how quickly things were changing. One of the scripts with twenty colors was called "Blast from the Past" and opened with the tops of umbrellas, water puddles, and the song "Singin' in the Rain." It became "Knowing Her."

Ron Osborn: Jeff and I were new writers, and we were having kind of a hard time figuring it out. Roger Director had been there before us. The three of us would bounce ideas off each other until Glenn came in and said "yes."

Jeff Reno: We had written one detective pilot that Glenn saw, and that made him want us on *Moonlighting*.

Ron Osborn: This was Glenn's first show as a showrunner, and it was not, to put it politely, a well-oiled machine. Part of it was because Glenn didn't delegate as well as he could have. Showrunners need to hire people that they can trust to go edit and develop stories while they run the show. He sat in on almost all the casting. Glenn was in the editing room quite a bit. In fairness to Glenn, he was developing the style of this show. It was hard for him to communicate that it was a really heightened reality.

Neil Mandelberg: The editors would make a pass, and then Jay would come up and make a pass, and then we showed it to Glenn. We tried to find a way to minimize Glenn's involvement, because every word on the screen went through Glenn. He spent less time in the editing room as we got better at the show and all understood it.

Suzanne Gangursky: Many times I would get a call saying, "We have nothing left to shoot here. In two hours, we're out of stuff. We thought we were supposed to get pages, when are they coming? We're going to have a crew sitting around wasting all this money." Glenn would say, "Oh, yeah, don't worry, I'm coming in. I'm going to write those." [Laughs.] This was often the way it was.

Allyce Beasley: So much about the show that was crazy was just the nature of that show. Could Glenn have been otherwise than he was? I would not expect that of anybody. Could he have written things on time and got them to us sooner? I don't know. That's just not the way it was. That's the animal that it was.

Glenn Gordon Caron: If I had a great idea, and I got it in the middle of the night, and we were supposed to shoot something that morning, I had no compunction about saying, "Wait, here's a better version." None. Part of it was that I didn't know any better.

Jay Daniel: The one piece of casting that I have always been fond of is Dana Delany in "Knowing Her." I didn't really know her work at that time. I just thought she was wonderful in the episode.

Ron Osborn: It's kind of a *Double Identity* story. Dana Delany comes back from David's past and basically sets him up to witness what David thinks is his ex-girlfriend being attacked by her husband.

Debra Frank: Alf Clausen told me a story about the episode with Dana Delany. He wrote a theme song for both Cybill's and Dana's characters, and outside the cemetery, when they confronted each other, he played the dueling theme songs. Alf was so important to the show.

Jay Daniel: We hired a director that had to drop out because of an illness or something. So we hired a replacement director, whose name I won't tell you. We had to fire him. The original thing that he shot just didn't work at all. It was the scene with Dana hanging from the balcony in her apartment and the scene between Bruce and Dana. I ended up having to reshoot it. The original scene dismissed any kind of magnetism between the two characters completely. There wasn't a stunt double for Dana involved in that balcony stunt. Dana did that. Our stunt coordinator, Chris Howe, had a strong wire on her. She couldn't have fallen. She actually said, "Oh, yeah, I'll do that." I really enjoyed working with her. The two of them really had some nice chemistry.

Dana Delany guest starred and created the first triangle on the series.

Dana Delany (Guest Star, Jillian Armstrong): Bruce was a bartender at the bar I used to hang out in New York, so I knew him before he was acting. It was sort of a fun thing. That is not why I got the job; I still had to audition. But Bruce didn't intimidate me. Cybill was another story.

Jay Daniel: I was pleased to be able to direct Dana. It was just one of those things that happened. There was no griping about, "Oh, we have to reshoot this thing." They both knew that it just didn't work the first time. After having to shut down the production just before this episode, we were not starting off on the best foot in terms of getting things running smoothly. But the episode ultimately turned out to be quite good. Peter Werner stepped in to direct it for us.

Peter Werner: I think they had shot a day or two. I come in and they say, "Here's the script. Action!" And for me, it was like, "OK, I know how to do this. These people trust me; let's go." It's kind of a wonderful confidence builder that you could get some of your best work in the moment of collaboration with some extremely talented people.

Dana Delany: The episode meant a lot to Bruce because it was an old girlfriend of his. He chose the use of "This Old Heart of Mine" in that famous scene in the park. That was all Bruce.

Jeff Reno: In "Knowing Her," we had written the scene where they play "This Old Heart of Mine" on the car radio. It's Bruce and Dana just kind of dancing. We had written the scene with them talking back and forth. It had them getting together right before the murder happens. Glenn said, "No, lets lose all the words." Which really surprised us, because it was a pretty wordy show. He put the song over it and it worked beautifully. It just reminded us to find new ways to do things, and even in a comedy show to not forget to do warm and emotional things.

Jay Daniel: I actually shot that sequence, as well as the apartment scenes, with a B unit. The first unit was on daylight, and to take them into night and get them into day the next day would have been impossible and expensive.

Peter Werner: I remember shooting scenes with Dana Delany. She was such a phenomenal actress. The chemistry between her and Bruce was amazing. It was just so much fun. We really did try to push the TV envelope with the show in general. I remember thinking that the scene with Dana and "This Old Heart of Mine" was pretty cinematic.

Jay Daniel: That's the only thing I've ever done with Dana, but when I saw her at award ceremonies and talked to her about the episode, she gushed about doing it. It meant the world to her.

Peter Werner: John Sacret Young [cocreator and executive producer of *China Beach*] talked to me about directing the pilot for *China Beach*. To my regret I passed, but I told him, "I just worked with this actress who I think you really should read. She would be fantastic."

Dana Delany: I had grown up watching Cybill. I was a huge fan of *The Last Picture Show* and *Taxi Driver*. This was when they were not getting along. They had just started to have problems. I didn't have a lot of interaction with her.

Ron Osborn: In a romantic comedy the best thing you can do is bring in a third person. Our favorite all-time comedy is *His Girl Friday*. It was a very short step to bring in an old flame and see how Maddie reacts. Nothing puts a relationship under a microscope better than watching the other half of the relationship interact with someone who knows him better than they do.

Peter Werner: If you're not going to bring Maddie and Dave together, you need obstacles—emotional, physical, sexual. Here you have two people who are mad for each other, who adore each other, and who can't be with each other. Now bring in somebody who the other one is attracted to. It's a great idea. Then it's a question of can you cast somebody who really is a rival? When you cast Dana Delany or Mark Harmon, it's just a great dramatic situation.

Reaction Shot: Jillian (Delany) and Addison come across what they believe to be a murder.

THE BANTER

GOOD. GOOD. FINE! Fine! Door slams. Just about every office scene ended that way when Maddie and David were fighting. It was exciting to see the two of them go at it spewing out a hundred words a minute. But recording that dialogue was a new thing for television.

Will Mackenzie: On other television shows, we were never allowed to do overlapping dialogue. Cybill and Bruce both had body mics, as well as there was a boom man. But if somebody was off camera they had a mic, as well as the person who was on camera. So that Cybill, Bruce, or Allyce could always overlap, just the way we do in real life.

Glenn Gordon Caron: Maybe we'd have a substitute soundman and he'd say, "You can't talk at the same time." Technically you're not supposed to do that. It's very hard to edit. But I was never afraid of that. I like the energy of it, the combustibility of it, the reality of it.

Cybill Shepherd: We were doing these scenes like in *His Girl Friday*, and we would have these two characters talking and overlapping and moving around in a brisk, not predictable way. When we first started we were doing those incredibly long days, and then I was asked to overlap dialogue because they thought that if you did a close-up you couldn't overlap. In the master shot we would overlap. The sound engineers wanted to get your audio lines separate in the close-up. We had to keep firing sound engineers because that just wasn't done back then. I think I tried at eleven o'clock at night to overlap something, and they finally got a sound engineer that could do it so we didn't have to loop. When you try to do just your part, it is really hard.

Jay Daniel: We would use two cameras, do a master and a close-up. We would have it lit for both. We tried to shoot their coverage at the same time. We got to where we could do that pretty well.

David Patrick Kelly (Guest Star on "Somewhere Under the

Rainbow"): They had to explain to me their dialogue style, which was kind of revolutionary at that time. People weren't doing that, even though Robert Altman had done it and Spencer Tracy and Katharine Hepburn had developed that style of talking over one another. I remember jamming with Bruce. He played his harmonica and I played my mandolin on the set. Bruce and I are huge James Cagney fans. I thought I was an expert, and Bruce thought he was. Bruce and I got into it a little bit. We kind of alarmed Cybill. We thought we were being tough guys with each other. So we made a bet about a catchphrase of Cagney's: "That's the kind of hairpin I am." Cagney said that in one of his movies. I thought it was *Public Enemy*. Bruce said it was *Strawberry Blonde*. We did *Moonlighting* in 1985. Twelve years later, when we did *Last Man Standing*, the first thing I did was walk up to Bruce and give him five dollars. He remembered exactly why I was doing it. He took that five dollars and put it in his pocket.

MYSTERIES AND THE FOURTH WALL

TV GUIDE **DESCRIBED** *Moonlighting* as a detective show, so mysteries, murders, and mayhem were a part of the weekly recipe. But they were never more important than the relationship between the two leads. Viewers weren't investing in how they did it; it was more when would they do it. The show started to let the seriousness of the investigation scenes slip away and even let David comment on their unimportance directly to the audience.

Roger Director: Most cases served as a framework and a scaffold in which we could play out David and Maddie's relationship. We worked very hard to come up with cases that would have twists and turns.

Glenn Gordon Caron: At the height of *Moonlighting* mania, I was invited to dinner with Billy Wilder. He recognized that I was trying to do anarchy. He said, "I bet you that you start with a really strong story, because it doesn't work otherwise." You need that story so you can throw it away. You use it as a hanger to hang all the character stuff on. He said, "*Some Like It Hot* begins with the Saint Valentine's Day Massacre death. These men will die, which is what allows them to put on ladies' clothes." The cases always function as sort of the narrative engine. We would have it. We always had to figure out how to solve it. I made everybody go through all that arduous work, and then we just stomped all over it. That's how the show worked best.

Roger Director: We were constantly being challenged to come up with new cases, new ideas, new show concepts, because Glenn had a wish list of elements that he wanted to see in shows for the first couple of years. He wanted to do a prizefighting show, and we worked to get that in.

Debra Frank: On "Portrait of Maddie," we watched the dailies and thought, "All right, so we've killed *this* person off. We've killed *that* person. So who's left to be the killer?"

Jeff Reno: Dan Lauria [*The Wonder Years*] had been playing the police detective, and we couldn't figure out who the murderer was. So we decided to make it him. He had played the first three acts on screen not knowing at all that he was going to be the murderer. For the actor, it was a complete surprise. He could hide it pretty well. That was the kind of thing that happened because we got to things late.

Peter Werner (Director of "Portrait of Maddie"): The episode begins with a Hitchcockian kind of murder. There was no script. There literally was only a first act when we started shooting. The first day, one of the actors came up to me and said, "I just don't know, am I the good guy here?" and I didn't know. We shot Act 1 without knowing what the rest of the show was. This was insane, because we would go to the locations and only have one scene to shoot. We made the company move, we shot the scene, we packed up, and we moved to someplace else and shot another scene. Then Act 2 comes out. We have another scene back in the first location. I've never directed something where you basically shoot it in chronological order, and you don't know what's going to happen. So you really had to do the scene as it is. It was a marvelous experience for me. I've never had that experience again. It's just fantastic fun to discover the story along with the characters.

Neil Mandelberg: There was at least one episode that we shot linear. He was writing it from the get-go. The first morning the first couple of scenes came out, then the next couple scenes. We actually cut a show linear. I had never done that before, and I haven't done it since.

Roger Director: As long as the reality of the case that the detectives were working on was established, then we could use the fourth act to springboard out of the reality that we sort of set up and do something a little wacky, and have it be fun. And people accepted that.

Jeff Reno: We got to the fourth act of "The Bride of Tupperman" and there was a hospital room scene. We didn't know what the solution was going to be.

Ron Osborn: We were writing as they were filming. We finally figured out how the mystery was going to be solved and we are just starting the fourth act. We just didn't have time to find the shoe, the button in the box, the receipt from a store, or whatever clues it would take to solve the mystery.

Jeff Reno: So David lays out what happened to Maddie and she says, "When did you figure that out?" He responds, "During the commercial." That was one of those fourth wall moments. It was so freeing to be able to do that. We had no time. We had no room in the script to figure it out or find a way to make sense of it. We could throw it away with one line.

Ron Osborn: We put it in the script and it flew. Glenn had already had David look in the camera before. That wasn't the first time it was done. Even the characters acknowledged that there was an audience out there.

Roger Director: *Moonlighting* was not the first time the fourth wall was broken. I could be wrong about this, but in one of Betty White's earliest TV shows [*Life with Elizabeth*] she occasionally would talk to the camera.

Glenn Gordon Caron: When we started breaking the fourth wall people said, "Oh my God, what an innovation." I was embarrassed. I'd say, "When I was a little kid, I would see *The George Burns and Gracie Allen Show* and they did it all the time." If you look at Bob Hope and Bing Crosby in the road movies, Bob Hope was turning to the camera and making jokes about Paramount Pictures. It just felt to me like I was stealing really good stuff. It was stuff that had existed in a different way before.

Jay Daniel: It was always the characters breaking the fourth wall to talk to the people that were watching their lives.

Roger Director: I don't know that David Addison and Maddie Hayes understanding that they were on a TV show was an absolute revolutionary thing, but at that time, I don't think anyone was doing that. It could not have been done by just any actor. It had to be done by someone who actually could *be* David Addison, who had the cheek to be able to break away from the scene, look into the camera, and deliver comments and make it be funny, and then go right back to the scene and zip up the fourth wall.

Neil Mandelberg: Bruce was so good at those moments. That's what really helped make it work. And the audience loved it. Every time we did something different, they loved it more. A number of the cold openings were written for length. But the style was something that Glenn wanted to do anyway. Also, sometimes we needed to set up our episode a little better than the episode itself.

Jay Daniel: Today on television, an episode begins and then you get credits. But that wasn't happening when *Moonlighting* was on. I guess it was, in its way, groundbreaking.

Neil Mandelberg: Whenever we stepped outside of reality, Glenn had a blast. He was a master at breaking the fourth wall. The moments he chose to do it were beyond brilliant. It was just unbelievable to have the balls to do that.

Roger Director: If we wanted to break the fourth wall, that was an executive decision. We'd have to go get Glenn. We did not have a blank check to break the fourth wall. We tried to do it sparingly.

Peter Werner: Glenn found new ways to break the fourth wall. One of my favorite scenes is in the office at the very end of "Twas the Episode Before Christmas." Dave and Maddie hear caroling, and then they walk out the door, down the hallway, and then off the set. There's the whole crew singing. My first wife and children were in that shot.

Jay Daniel: It was a lovely thing and really touching. It was really nice to meet a bunch of the crew's families. Glenn had his kids there.

Sheryl Main: We were singing a Christmas carol and snow was coming down. It was fun for all of us because we're standing on stage singing. We really were a family on *Moonlighting*. I made friends on that show, like Melissa, who is one of my dearest friends to this day.

Melissa Gelineau: I'm in the Christmas episode, but I don't know if you can see me, but I am definitely in that one.

Neil Mandelberg (Editor): I wrote a note on the wall in production that said, "Anybody who wants to be seen in the Christmas show, twenty-five bucks to me."

Allyce Beasley: Vincent, my then husband, is next to me. My whole family was back in New York. That was so great because I loved everybody so much that was involved with the show, just like Ms. Dipesto would feel, with my loyalty to Glenn and Jay. I was crazy about Jay and his wife, and Artie, and Neil, and everybody!

Neil Mandelberg: My kids were there that day. Glenn had the crew bring in their family. It really was a big family.

Allyce Beasley: I remember Glenn saying, "We've just written a scene and you're going to love it. It's going to be you and a new baby under the Christmas tree." Glenn was so supportive. I knew he loved my work. I knew it was him who gave me the opportunity to really do a little something. He was thrilled with the shot. It was a nice moment for Cybill and I too. She was into it too.

Allan Arkush (Director): I had a meeting with Glenn and Jay to start directing on *Moonlighting*. I had to come after work on *St. Elsewhere*. I drove over to the *Moonlighting* set, and these guys are sitting in their office. It must be 7:30 at night, and they're completely relaxed. The cast was still on stage shooting the Christmas episode. On *St. Elsewhere*, you started at 7:30 a.m. and you wrapped at 7:15 p.m. If you were going to go one minute over, you had to call [executive producer] Bruce Paltrow and explain why. Glenn and Jay are totally relaxed. The production manager comes in and asks, "Well, we've got another two hours. Should we just plow through or take a second meal?" And they say like it's *nothing*, "Oh, take a second meal." I'm thinking, "What the heck?" On *Fame*, they'd beat the shit out of you to finish on time!

DIPESTO EPISODES

THROUGHOUT THE SERIES, writers would focus occasional episodes on Ms. Dipesto (Allyce Beasley). It gave her a chance to take on a case and step to the forefront once a season. The Season 2 episode was called "North by North Dipesto."

Jay Daniel: Dipesto episodes were just like any other episode. They were created just the same way with the same respect. Allyce didn't wait in her trailer to be called to the set. During those shows, she was on the set. You know, like a lot of actors are when they do a show. When you have somebody that's totally prepared and is ready to hit their mark, the shows just go faster. It's really that simple.

Allyce Beasley: I didn't know where my character was going. All I did is say something on the phone, and then I didn't have anything to do with the rest of the episode. So I asked Glenn out to lunch. I said, "What do you think Ms. Dipesto wants to be when she grows up? I think she wants to be a detective. I think she wants to be an equal partner with Maddie and Dave." He said, "No, I don't think she wants to do that. I think she just wants to be happy. She wants everybody else to be happy. She is the emotional Geiger counter between Maddie and David." So that was convenient for everybody else. [Laughs.]

Debra Frank (Writer of "North by North Dipesto"): Glenn told Carl and I, "We're approaching the holidays. I need to give Cybill and Bruce time off because they're in every scene. So I'm giving them a week off. So you're going to have them for only one or two days. Then it's going to be all Ms. Dipesto." I felt like, "OK, that will be a nice challenge." It didn't bother me at all. I thought Allyce was sweet, cute, and fun.

Need someone to fill in for an episode? Allyce Beasley's got it in the bag. This is a shot from the chase scene in "North by North Dipesto."

Allyce Beasley: The only reason that they started to write Dipesto episodes, including the first one, was because Bruce and Cybill wanted to have some time off. Now in all fairness, they were in just about every shot of every episode. ABC considered it a two-person show. It was a runaway hit in terms of them being stars.

Jay Daniel: I think the network understood that giving Cybill and Bruce a break would not be a bad idea.

Debra Frank: To acknowledge to the viewers that we knew what happened, we threw in the line at the end for Maddie which is "I'm going to go talk to the writers and make sure we have bigger parts in next week's episode." A lot of people were like, "What happened to Maddie and David? Are they going to be in the next episode?"

Allyce Beasley: They would film the Dipesto episodes during Christmas so that Bruce and Cybill could have a vacation. I was really excited to do it, but that's really how it came about.

Debra Frank: We were sent to the laundromat to write the chase scene, and then a couple days later they filmed it. There wasn't much time. We were actually just at the location saying, "OK, we'll zip her in here, and then we'll put her in that laundry basket. We could do this. That'll be fun."

Jay Daniel: That laundry sequence took some time to choreograph. We did quite a few days on that.

THE ATHEIST

FOR ALL THE ways that *Moonlighting* was pushing television into new territory creatively, the fact that the writers made Maddie an atheist in a 1986 episode should really be at the top of the list. America in general, and on television especially, had only one religion, and it was Christianity.

TV was there to tell you that if you were good and you prayed everything would turn out just right. Here Glenn took a major character, who was on the cover of every magazine, and had her say, "I don't believe."

Ron Osborn: An outside writer pitched an episode where a client says, "My husband died and I want you to guard the body. I cheated on him, and he promised he was going to come back and haunt me." We asked, "What's the emotional undercurrent of the story? How does that reflect back on David and Maddie and their relationship?" I'm not sure how we got to it—clearly it wasn't me—but it gets into the afterlife.

Maddie Hayes smiles and shines like a glimpse of the heaven she doesn't believe in. Glenn Gordon Caron decided that Maddie would be the one to not believe in an afterlife.

Cybill Shepherd: "In God We Strongly Suspect" is compelling because it brings up a subject that isn't discussed much. Who is gonna be on what side of faith? Which one will believe and which one won't?

Glenn Gordon Caron: I started to wonder how they felt about faith. My quick response was that David's an atheist and Maddie must be fairly religious. The more I thought about it, the more I realized it's quite the opposite. Then the provocateur in me got excited.

Jeff Reno: Isn't that great? I remember the conversation in the room. I don't remember who said it first. I do know that Glenn at least had to OK it. It wasn't that we were just having one of them say they were an atheist. It was that we were flipping the audience's expectations. That was a big deal at the time. If we were gonna talk about religion, and that was something we specifically wanted to do in that episode, the fun of it was going to be "Oh, David believes and Maddie doesn't." That is not at all how audiences would assume it was gonna turn out, because David was such a counterculture kind of guy.

Glenn Gordon Caron: It just made great sense to me that David would be the one to say, "Even if you don't believe, don't say it—cover your bet." She would be the one to say, "Well, that's silly. That's a fairy tale." Because she's such a pragmatist. I'm not sure it's a dialogue that had ever happened on American television, and that just amused the heck out of me. At the same time, I thought it was important and got to some interesting truths.

Jay Daniel: I remember absolutely nothing from the network about them being concerned about Maddie being an atheist, which is somewhat surprising. I think they trusted us because we were starting to get really good numbers. We were in the top ten during the season. ABC didn't have a whole lot that was successful. We were their tentpole at the time. When they saw numbers like this coming from the show, they just had to trust us.

Cybill Shepherd: Sometimes the nature of the show was such a strong, driven show. Between Bruce, Glenn, Jay, and I, it was a very intense group of people who wanted to do something good that said something. You don't get those chances too often on television. With *Moonlighting*, we couldn't help but be on the edge of everything. The glamorous woman was supposed to be a certain way and the rough guy was supposed to be a certain way, but we didn't do that.

Glenn Gordon Caron: One of my great frustrations at the time was Cybill was clearly vexed because she believed very strongly that Maddie was a weak female character. She felt that she was participating in some way in something that didn't give the character agency. I kept trying to reason with her. I'd say, "That's not what's going on here." Plus, here's Bruce, who nobody's ever heard of, and he's making a lot of noise. The audience is really responding, but they're responding to the duet. I think that all of that, at the time, very much frustrated her. Since I was the author of a lot of that, her focus fell on me.

Suzanne Gangursky: We would have walkie-talkies and you would hear them say, "We are ready for Bruce or Cybill on set." Then you would hear, "Is Bruce on set yet?" Then, "Is Cybill on set yet?" There was a lot of "I'm not waiting for the other one." They would eat certain directors alive with that. I'm not saying they were right or wrong; just saying they were getting tired of it all and had different reasons, and there was friction between them as well. So things were changing behind the scenes.

Peter Werner: I felt I had done the work that I could do, and that I couldn't contribute that much new to the show. At that moment, I was doing a lot of TV movies. I also really did not like the energy between Bruce and Cybill at that point. Getting them to the set and going back and forth and stuff like that. The crew is coming in, they're working their ass off, and they're getting the thing ready as fast as they can, and then they sit around. Then it's two hours of overtime. There were a lot of bad vibes between them at that point. And I was close to both of them. At some point, it was like, "Choose me." I just didn't. It lost its glamour and joy. Why take an experience that was so joyful and suddenly just make money off of grinding it out?

Jay Daniel: Season 2 was not the easiest, because of some of the tensions and the lateness of the scripts. But because the show somehow, someway stayed pretty damn good, I think we came away thinking, "Well, we got through this and we're going to have time to take a breath and come back." [Laughs.] Season 3 was the best work that we did, and the most difficult season we ever went through. Well, I guess we'll talk about what happens next time. . . .

Season 2 ended with Dave and Maddie waving and saying goodbye to each other. Lots of drama would be awaiting them in Season 3.

Chapter 7

It Happened One Season

Jay Daniel: We went back on July 1 to start Season 3, but we had to keep pushing it back because the script wasn't ready. On July 21, we finally started shooting "The Son Also Rises." So we pushed it back twenty days just to get the first script going. We finally finished that on the thirty-first. It took ten days to shoot it.

Glenn Gordon Caron: We did a cold open to start Season 3. It was right after we lost all the Emmys. It was a Sunday night. I remember saying that we have to speak to this on the upcoming Tuesday show. So I got up at five o'clock Monday morning. I wrote this thing with Dave and Maddie sitting on the desk before the show starts and Maddie says, "How's your mother?" He says, "Mom's not doing good. The doctor says if I could give her some good news it might make a real difference." She says, "Did you tell her about the Emmys?" He picks up the phone and says, "Mom, sixteen Emmys. We are gonna win. It's in the bag." And then there's a card that says: "This program is dedicated to the memory of Irma Addison Nov. 2, 1922 - Sept. 21, 1986."

Jay Daniel: We got sixteen Emmy nominations, and we only won one, for editing, but sixteen Emmy nominations ain't bad. I remember the day that we announced the nominations on set. Stage 20 was not that far from the office, and everybody was cheering. I was walking back to the office and I started to cry. I thought, "Maybe all this work was worth it." People recognized that we were doing some pretty good work here. The nominations mean something because they come from the industry. They know, the people that do the same work, and they appreciate the kind of work you're doing in their field.

Cybill Shepherd: I was nominated for an Emmy but I never won. The show was an usual combination of a detective show and a love story. It was a hard show to put in the right category.

WHILE THE TELEVISION Academy was giving Emmys to other series, the *Moonlighting* team was looking to the future. Season 3 opened with "The Son Also Rises." I must enter a note in the Anselmo case file that this episode is the most underrated episode of *Moonlighting*. It's most likely forgotten by casual fans of the series because it isn't a theme episode. It's funny, has a wonderful story, a twist ending, and the first truly standout performance from Bruce Willis (Cybill got the chance to stand out the season before in "Every Daughter's Father Is a Virgin"). But what is most interesting about this hour of television is that it's the first *Moonlighting* episode that doesn't have a case, at all. (Before you tell me I am wrong, remember that "Every Daughter's Father Is a Virgin" does have a case; it's just that Maddie is the client. They are investigating her father.) The hour begins with the aforementioned cold open about the Emmys, then goes into nine minutes of just everyone coming back from vacation. It's all shenanigans, contained in the Blue Moon offices. I dare you to watch it without smiling ear to ear. Truly feel-good television balanced with character development is rare. This opening is drenched in it. It should be taught in scriptwriting classes everywhere.

Allan Arkush (Director of "The Son Also Rises"): It's a really gutsy move to open a season with them coming back from hiatus. It's as gutsy as the opening of the second season of *Lost*.

Jeff Reno (Writer of "The Son Also Rises"): I wrote a line in that episode that I still use with my family: "Vacation never ends; it just changes location."

Allan Arkush: Cybill's in the office first and then Bruce comes in singing "La Bamba," and they see each other. They look at each other. That's the shot. Within five seconds of the two of them looking at each other. That's the magic. That's just the two of them and their ability to make those moments work.

Cybill Shepherd: If you think back to *It Happened One Night*, it has two characters that are attracted to each other, but also have some contempt for each other. I see the similarities between Clark Gable and Claudette Colbert's characters and Maddie and David.

Jeff Reno: We had a great time with that opening scene. It was a little like the limbo scene, which was the first thing we ever wrote. It was just the office having fun. You just didn't need to get the story going any more quickly than that because people had so much fun watching these guys.

Ron Osborn (Writer of "The Son Also Rises"): Glenn asked us to write the season opener. He wanted to kind of "renew the franchise," is how he put it. The territory of this series was love. We came in with an idea about David's father getting married and the son trying to grapple with it. Usually, it's the other way around. The parents wonder why their kids are marrying that person. For once, David's playing the conservative parent.

Jeff Reno: I think that "Every Father's Daughter" paved the way a little bit because it was so much about family and the emotion of family. If Glenn struggled with the network about there being no case, he didn't tell us. Things were happening very fast on the show, even at the beginning of the season. This was a movie idea that I thought of like two weeks before we started writing the episode. It was this thing that I was kicking around—the son and father finding out that they were dating the same woman. I just thought that's something I'll work on one day when I'm off the show. I just moved it over to the show. At that point, ABC wasn't really arguing with anything that we wanted to try. They were pretty happy with whatever. Glenn liked it very much.

Glenn Gordon Caron: I believed very strongly that no one was tuning in for the cases. I remember it was a revelation to me. I would watch a Marx Brothers movie, and it seemed like anarchy. I thought, "How do you do anarchy?"

Allan Arkush: That was a very smart move on the part of Glenn, and I don't think it was calculated. I don't know what was going through his head. I don't think about the lack of a mystery in that episode. I think about the relationships in that episode.

AFTER DAVE AND Maddie reunite with the viewers (and each other), David gets a message that his father has been trying to reach him. He tries to avoid making the call, but his father, played perfectly by guest star Paul Sorvino (*Goodfellas*), shows up in David's office. His father has something to tell Dave. There is a jump cut to Maddie's office, and David bursts in full of excitement and tells Maddie that his father is engaged. This is a perfect example of great writing and understanding the essence of the series you are writing for. They do not waste time on the elder Addison telling his son he is getting married. Viewers want to see Dave and Maddie bantering. So the scene of Mr. Addison telling David the news is skipped, to be replaced with dialogue between the two stars. The same thing happens at the end of the episode: the wedding, a staple of television programming, is never even shown. Why waste time on scenes that don't involve Dave or Maddie?

Jeff Reno: I don't remember conversations saying, "Let's skip showing the action and get them talking." My guess would be it's instinctual. Our preference, to a fault in the beginning, was to write them talking. That kind of dialogue was always my favorite thing to write.

Allan Arkush: I don't think I even noticed. I didn't think about it.

Ron Osborn: There was a scene that was filmed. We realized in the cut: we just didn't need it. We could go right to David. So it was lifted.

Jeff Reno: We wanted to see Dave and Maddie talk to each other. Therefore the audience would too. That is the opposite of most shows. Most times when you go on a TV show, people above will tell you, "Don't tell me about it, let's see it." That was a nice kind of flip that we were able to do, where people would rather hear you tell them about something than see it happen, because their dialogue was so entertaining. I can't take full credit; I'll take partial credit. We wanted to do those scenes rather than the shoe-leather scenes. I can't remember ever saying, "Let's leave out this part in favor of this part." We chose it because the show did it so well.

Allan Arkush: Glenn once said to me, "Be careful, not every course is dessert." And that was really good advice. That was a caution about one day's dailies, and that has served me so well.

Jeff Reno: You don't want to hear it repeated by David to Maddie. You definitely want to hear David and Maddie talk about it, but you don't want to have heard it already. So that just seems like the better choice.

Allan Arkush: Paul Sorvino hadn't done *Goodfellas* yet, but he was pretty well-known. He liked to sing opera between takes. He got a little impatient waiting around as we worked through things. He was used to features where the director says, "We're going to do this now," and everyone does it. But on *Moonlighting*, it could be a bit of a negotiation. Is that a romantic way to put it?

Jay Daniel: I think Paul Sorvino was a little unhappy. He felt that he wasn't able to prepare properly.

DAVID AND MADDIE go to a party to meet Stephanie, his potential stepmom, played by Brynn Thayer. When David gets a glimpse of Stephanie, he drops to his knees in the middle of a fancy party and crawls across the floor to hide in the bathroom.

Allan Arkush: There was a little bit of pushback from Bruce because there's a lot of very broad choices in the script. He was concerned about

"Can these things work out? Can we make these believable?" He's the one who had to have all the extreme characterizations with the father and the bride. There's a lot of extreme comedic choices in seeing her at the party, and he crawls away. There were a bunch of meetings to get that scene. It was pretty broad.

Jay Daniel: I think you see more colors and that every line didn't have to be a smart-ass line. You got to see his heart a little more. Bruce played those kinds of things really well. He is really a better actor than people know. His career took him to action films, but he is a very nuanced actor.

ONCE EVERYONE ARRIVES at the church, David takes his position as best man and keeps his eye on the bride. When the minister says that command that is only ever uttered on television, "Speak now or forever hold your peace," David responds, "Oh, boy." Stephanie and David leave the ceremony and go to a room to talk.

Bruce Willis, Paul Sorvino, and Brynn Thayer stand at the altar just moments after the final script reached the set.

Allan Arkush: When you don't have those pages but you kind of know what's supposed to happen but you don't know what is going to happen, here's the directorial challenge. We're shooting the wedding scene with three cameras. We shot twenty thousand feet of film that day. And we still didn't know how the episode was going to end and what we're going to shoot tomorrow. We know David and the bride are going to go in a back room. Jay and I look around for a back room. Jay said, "We are probably gonna do three or four pages back here, and then we'll go back out to the wedding." The pages arrived three hours later. The scene has children of all ages singing "It's a Small World." And it's a ten-page scene. It's like, "Holy shit!"

Glenn Gordon Caron: Somehow we got the rights from Disney to play "It's a Small World" in the background of the episode. Everybody said, "There's no way they're gonna let you do this." I said, "We have to ask." Disney said yes. Of course, today that would never happen. That's the reason you can't see *Moonlighting* right now—because of all that music. None of it was cleared because nobody anticipated DVDs or streaming. They've asked me if we can change the music and I always say, "No, we can't change the music."

Allan Arkush: Look, it's hard enough for me to direct, but how did they cast the kids, get the rights to the song, and get the costumes? I'm thinking I got off easy. I gotta figure out how to stage a scene with fifteen people in it. It was not easy. It took a lot of time with rehearsal and blocking it, so I could cut to the kids when I needed them but still show that they were in the room. Directorially, it was a pretty complex situation.

DAVID IS ABOUT to confront Stephanie about the fact that the two of them slept together back in Jersey, but before he can, Stephanie, assuming David is confronting her about rumors that she would frequently go home with strangers, tells him that she used to pick up dumb guys at bars. It's obvious that she doesn't remember David, or that they slept together. Here is the twist that would usually come in the mystery: David was so sure he was unforgettable, and he was just the opposite.

Allan Arkush: We get to the part of the scene where Brynn Thayer tells her story. The first take is awful. And this is her big scene. She's playing it "Woe is me." It's deadly. She's playing the words instead of just playing the emotions, because that's the scene. Bruce came over and said, "You better do something here." This actress had to carry this eight-page scene. I said to her, "The reason you like David Addison's father and David Addison is that they're assholes. They're funny, but they're really assholes, and they don't take themselves seriously. You're the same as they are. That's why all this happened." She does the take, and she throws it all away. She tells it like it was a funny story. At the end of the second take, Bruce looked at me and said, "I think we got it." They were on fire. That's what's in the show. Whenever you see that two-shot, that was that moment. It was just magic at how much it changed. So when she says that line as they're walking out—"At least we never slept together"—it kills, because it so fits the mood. It was all a group effort that led to that laugh. It's one of those laughs that I'm really proud of. That scene is what I had been trying to do since film school, when I was watching all those movies that I love. That was it.

DAVID AND HIS future stepmom head back out to let the wedding resume. We do not see the ceremony, but go directly to the reception. David and Maddie share a dance as David avoids telling Maddie that the woman didn't even remember the sexual encounter with him. The episode ends in romantic fashion as they dance in a spectacularly lit scene. Director of photography Jerry Finnerman outdid himself on this shot. The depth, sparkle, and color are at a level of artfulness extraordinary for television of that time. It looks like a shot out of a classic Hollywood feature film. Jerry passed away in 2011, but his art in scenes like this will last forever.

Allan Arkush: I learned so much on *Moonlighting* from Jerry Finnerman about how to light a scene, because I spent so much time waiting for people to come out of their trailer. I learned the history of cinematography from his point of view, which was old-school Hollywood hard light. I got him to explain everything that he was doing, because it was so different. Jerry always called Cybill "Cookie." He'd say, "Don't forget, Cookie looks left." Every shot is blocked so she looks left because she was convinced that she looked best when she looked right to left. It worked in her office because the door is to the left of where she is, but his office is the other way. So she always had to cross the lens. That is as inside baseball as you're going to get! [Laughs.]

Will Mackenzie (Director): Jerry Finnerman was fabulous and knew lighting. I came on as the new guy, and he knew that I wasn't as experienced as some of the others with camerawork. Glenn and Jay did not want zoom lenses on their show. We were filming a scene that involved two goons. They said, "Film them low so they look bigger than they are in real life." Jerry said, "It would be quicker and we can get out of here sooner if we sneak in a zoom. I can't imagine they're going to suspect." I got a call that night at home from, I think from Jay, and this was my first day on *Moonlighting*, "Did you put a zoom lens in there?" I cannot tell a lie. I didn't say it was Jerry. Jay said, "I'm sorry, you're going to have to come back and shoot that scene again."

Allan Arkush: Jerry designed that shot of Dave and Maddie dancing. Normally I would have done that shot kind of on a Steadicam, but Jerry came up with the idea of doing it with a long lens with the camera in the center and panning so all the lights are out of focus and Bruce and Cybill are sharp. Jerry shot at a very high f-stop. That's how it had the rich blacks and that old-school Hollywood look. They are like thirty feet away from the camera. The reason that the lights and everything looked that way is that we're on a telephoto lens. They are moving, we are moving, and they are constantly changing places, every two or three feet. Remember Jerry had also done *Star Trek* [the original series], so all those kinds of big black shadows on the walls that you see, that's Jerry doing what his teacher Harry Stradling, Jr., taught him. Jerry actually carried these cucolorises, which are cutouts that you put in front of the lights because you can get so many different shapes out of them. They were built in the fifties. He carried silk stockings with him from France that he put in front of the lens and burned a little hole for Cybill's eyes, so her eyes twinkled. We're lining up this shot. And it's one of those mornings where they . . . How much do people say about what was really going on?

THE DANCE SCENE is one take that lasts seventy-seven seconds. In that oner, Dave and Maddie dance and talk, and Brynn Thayer enters to cut in, kisses David, and exits the scene. This scene already includes complex lighting while the actors are dancing and delivering lines; now they are upping the ante by trying to do it in one take. Allan Arkush was brought back to this moment and shared this story about getting that shot.

Allan Arkush: In order to do this dance thing in one shot [see photo above,] which was the goal, Bruce and Cybill had to pivot so that each one's lines landed on camera. Now, Cybill is nobody's fool. While they're doing it, she keeps turning Bruce so that she's on camera more and he's not. They would get into these discussions about this.

I'm trying to do a camera rehearsal. Jerry turns to me and says, "Allan, you gotta get them to do this." Because he has to lay marks for this. It's got to be perfect. They're moving, the camera's moving, it couldn't be harder. It looks easy, but it's very hard, technically. Just then, this Greek salad arrives for Cybill. We often went into meal penalties on the set.

That didn't stop them from eating in front of the crew. They didn't take the meal penalty. They just ate and forced us to wait for them. So she gets this Greek salad, which she ordered all the way from the San Fernando Valley, from her favorite Greek restaurant, called The Great Greek, and we're laying out the marks. I'm talking to them about the marks, and she goes, "I hear you. I hear you." Jerry looks at me and says, "Tell Cookie to stop eating the salad. She's got to get the marks exactly, because if we do too many takes they're going to scream." So I said, "Cybill, could you put down the salad?" She puts down the salad. I have to give them another note. I say the note and she just turns on me and says, "Don't give me notes across the stage. If you're gonna give me a note, come here." It was like a simple note. So as I'm walking across the dark stage, I see the salad is on the floor and where she put it down. So I stepped in the salad. I can feel the camera crew laughing. I said I was sorry, gave her the note, and picked up the salad. When I got back to the camera crew, they all turned their backs and said, "Man, thank you." Everyone felt that tension. Then we got the scene. We were trying to end the first episode of the season on a high degree of difficulty.

DIFFICULT OR NOT, "The Son Also Rises" is a monumental step in *Moonlighting*'s journey. The episode debuted to a forty-two share and was ranked as the number-six show for the week. The very shape of the series changed forever with this script. Before this episode, the plots were centered on outside forces. The characters reflected those outside forces. Now the show had the forces come from inside the main characters. This time there is no detective work to be done. David knows when he sees his future stepmother what her crime is, because she committed it to him and with him. In Season 4, the lack of cases will be deemed by critics as one of the reasons for the end of viewers' love affair with the show. This episode proves that the characters of Maddie and Dave were interesting enough to engage viewers for an hour of television—as long as the writing, plot, and comedy were at a high level. Bruce Willis brought a new level to his acting and a depth to the character of David Addison that wasn't quite there in Season 2. He was funny and had moments of anger in Season 2, but here he becomes a real character with multiple facets to his personality. This will be developed even further throughout this season. The comedy in the episode is as prevalent as in any Season 2 episode. The episode also had a twist, just like the cases did. The romance that fans wanted is found in the scene where they danced, as well as when Maddie admitted she missed David during her vacation. The guest stars were hugely effective. You feel Paul Sorvino's nerves at the party, as well as his disgust with David. Brynn Thayer's monologue is pitch-perfect. Even her body language is top-notch as she dismisses the Sunday school kids from singing "It's a Small World." She truly owns her acting space. She has only five minutes of screen time in the entire episode, but develops a character who can be believed and understood. Compare this with shows like *Law & Order* or *Bones*, where a guest star is just a prop to move the story along. On *Moonlighting*, guest stars are given rich, emotional monologues. The script for this episode is akin to a theater piece. Jeff Reno and Ron Osborn's writing is confident and displays great talent. This script testifies to their ability as deeply as "Atomic Shakespeare" will in a few weeks, just with less iambic pentameter. Allan Arkush and Jerry Finnerman designed wonderful scenes. Cybill shines in the scene with Bruce Willis in the bathroom at the party. The show was firing on all cylinders, and it was just getting started on Season 3.

WRITING/DIRECTING

Ron Osborn (Writer of Fourteen Episodes): "Symphony in Knocked Flat" became the episode where the writing staff really fell into place. Dale Gelineau and Pauline Turboff Miller pitched a "fun date" versus a "fine date," or that's what it became. Of course, everything goes off the rails, and they end up in a boxing match and there's going to be an assassination à la Alfred Hitchcock.

Jeff Reno (Writer of Fourteen Episodes): Pauline Miller was in postproduction, and Dale was the husband of Jay Daniel's assistant—nice people and good writers. They got a shot because they were close to the show. We were all pitching in and helping out on it.

PHOTO COURTESY OF DEBRA FRANK

The writing staff (from left): Jeff Reno, Chic Eglee, Ron Osborn, Roger
Director, Debra Frank, and Carl Sautter appear to just be hanging around,
but there was plenty of work to be completed on each script.

Ron Osborn: They handed in a draft, but we were so behind. We were
sitting in a room rewriting it. Everyone went off and wrote various parts
of the script, and we came back together. We started getting the hang of
the show and what was needed. I remember being really pleased with
what happened. By this time, we had more people on staff.

Debra Frank (Writer of Seven Episodes): You could just throw out
anything and it's not like you'd be laughed at or told "That's a stupid idea"
or "That won't work." When you were working in television at that time,
if you said a line and you thought only half the population was really
going to get this, you didn't use it. But on *Moonlighting*, if there were
eight people out there and they laughed at a joke, great. Not everybody
has to laugh. They'll get what they get. So nothing was flattened out.
That's what made it so much fun, and allowed you to watch it over and
over.

Roger Director (Writer of Fifteen Episodes): Glenn was always wondering what would be a funnier line. What would be a funnier take? All the writers were learning that stuff about the show at that point. So he had to be there, and we were generating ideas for him.

Chic Eglee (Writer of Fifteen Episodes): *Moonlighting* was getting a thirty-eight share at one point. [Former NBC chairman/CEO) Grant Tinker wrote a scathing editorial about how Glenn was irresponsible, for these wildly overbudget productions. Glenn's argument was that *Moonlighting* was the cheapest show in television to produce per ratings point.

Glenn Gordon Caron: We spent a lot of money, and ABC would get really upset about that. I said, "It's OK. You can repeat this show three times and you'll still get the same rating." They said, "You can't do that." But they would rerun them, and of course they would get the same rating. It was because there were so many jokes and so many things packed in. It was really only the beginning of people taping episodes. So if you wanted to see the show again, the only way to do it was wait for the rerun. And with the way we made shows, that rerun would come sooner rather than later.

Suzanne Gangursky: If you look at *Mad Men* or *The Sopranos*, they were only making twelve episodes a year. We were doing on *Moonlighting* what HBO and all these critically acclaimed shows started doing in just the last couple years. They never cranked out twenty-two episodes a year. I feel like we set the stage for those shows to come on later and make that kind of great television.

Karen Hall (Writer of Six Episodes): The real difference was the amount of time you had to write. On most shows the writers come back about six to eight weeks before the actors do and then try to get as many scripts written as possible. It's almost always true that at the end of the season, you're gangbanging the scripts—that's the technical term in show business. But on *Moonlighting*, it got that way faster, and we had less time to do it.

Debra Frank: Carl and I were working at one of our homes, and we worked through the night. It was like 4:30 in the morning. I drove home, and Carl dropped the script off at the studio because you physically had to deliver pages so they would be there when Glenn arrived at 7:30 for him to look it over and make any adjustments. It would go to the set to be filmed that day.

A photo from 1985 of writers Debra Frank and Carl Sautter standing in the doorway of Blue Moon Investigations.

Will Mackenzie: Glenn is one of those people who is so bright, but I'm sure he studied for his exams in college the night before. Whereas most of us spent more than a month studying for that final grade, he did it the night before, stayed up all night, and got through his exam.

Glenn Gordon Caron: When we weren't delivering episodes regularly, I wrote and shot this commercial of a guy standing on a loading dock. He's got an ABC logo on his pocket, and underneath him the text says 2:45 a.m., and my voice says, "What are you doing?" He says, "Waiting for *Moonlighting*." I said, "Oh, is there going to be a new episode?" He says, "Who knows?"

Jay Daniel: God bless Glenn, those scripts, when they came out, were great. I prepped many a show over the years where all I really had was an outline of what was gonna be. We didn't have page counts. We didn't know how long it was gonna be. I might know that there is a chase scene and it's gonna end at a park, but I don't know how complex it is.

Glenn Gordon Caron: That "morning of" thing is probably overplayed, maybe a little bit. I think more writers do it. I could be completely wrong about this, but I have to believe that almost every episode of *Mad Men* went through Matt Weiner.

Jeff Reno: It was nuts. Glenn is a wonderful writer, but he ran a very last-minute show. I don't know how much of it was because he was involving himself with other aspects, like postproduction and being on the stage, but he tended to just not get to things very quickly. It backed things up.

Ron Osborn: I knew someone who worked in standards and practices. She told me that had we been a well-run show, we might not have gotten away with as much stuff, because the scripts always came in so late. They weren't pleased about that. Here's the other thing with this show: When you go to the bank and you borrow a million dollars, you owe the bank; when you go to the bank and you borrow 100 million, they owe you. This show was the class act of ABC. We started a little before *thirtysomething*. I think the network knew there was a bit of lightning in the bottle here, and they couldn't handle this show in the way they would handle a Dick Wolf show.

Glenn Gordon Caron: I didn't get in too much trouble because while the rerun may not do as well as a brand-new episode, it did awfully well, and they've already paid for it. They would yell at me, but then it would get a twenty-eight share or a thirty-two share, which is an unheard-of number for today. I remember once we did a show and I want to say it got about a forty-eight share. Tony Thomopoulos, who was running the network at that time, called me, and I was sort of crowing about this forty-eight share. He said to me, "That means 52 percent of the country rejected you."

Roger Director: Glenn is gonna take a look at every person, every scene, and every script. Steven Bochco, executive producer of *Hill Street*, did not spend a whole hell of a lot of time on the set. He sent the script down to the set, and if any actor has any questions about it, it better be a damn good question. Glenn spent more time on the set. He was still working on the tone and the tenor of the show. He was making changes to some scenes and doing rewrites and starting to sort of get into the flow of making this thing right. He saw that it had to be right to work for these two actors.

Glenn Gordon Caron: While we worked on *Tyrant*, [executive producer] Howard Gordon once said to me, "You, more than anyone I've ever met, really believe in the power of inspiration." I used to say that on *Moonlighting*. They'd go, "What's going on?" I'd say, "I'm waiting for the truth." Which is like the most pretentious answer, and I knew it at the time, but I didn't know any other way to say it. Sometimes the truth didn't arrive until the morning of the shoot. The great thing was Bruce, at that moment in his life, could memorize a three-page monologue. He would look at it for twenty minutes and be word-perfect.

Cybill Shepherd: Bruce and I would have our lines taped to the dashboard, and the cameras were set up so that you didn't see that. We'd have seven pages and we'd film that and then come back and get the other eight pages for the scene.

Jay Daniel: Bruce was a very quick study. I've watched him get three or four pages and look at them and say, "OK, let's go." He was very quick. Cybill was not so quick. But she, got it done. She wouldn't come out of her trailer until she had it all in her head. And we waited a lot. That was not the best circumstances, but the results, because they had gone through Glenn's typewriter, never failed. He wouldn't send them until they were right.

Cybill Shepherd: There is a lot of trust in that. We tried to stay true to our characters. If I ever wondered how I was going to be able to do this, then I wouldn't have been able to do any of it. That was the most important thing. Don't ever ask yourself how you are going to do it. Just do it.

Allan Arkush (Director of Twelve Episodes): I showed up for prep and there was no script. I showed up for thirteen more days and there was no script. What I did was just hang out on the set and watch. There was nothing else to do as the script was being written. We did a couple of scouts because Glenn knew where the stuff would take place, and he filled us in with some ideas. I watched the chemistry of what was going on on set. I watched when the directors succeeded and when the director failed with those two.

Chris Leitch (Director of One Episode): In those days, most network television directors were old men that were coming out of seventies and sixties TV. They were just doing sort of cop shows, detective shows. Glenn was looking for someone different. And I think he found it.

Will Mackenzie (Director of Four Episodes): We were paid to come in for a week of prep. I remember just going off to lunch a lot of times. He'd send us away because he didn't want us sitting around the office going, "Where's the pages?" He got annoyed by that.

Dennis Dugan (Director of Five Episodes): There was a lot of getting the pages the night before and then trying to figure out what you're going to do the next day. I would get to the set early so I could do my shot sheets, which is all stuff that I took with me for the rest of my career.

Peter Werner (Director of Seven Episodes): ABC was not so happy about the extra days and the extra hours. So then you are the director that was caught between not having a scene and then having to shoot another scene at double pace and still be criticized if you don't have the coverage. That really was not joyful.

Jay Daniel (Director of Four Episodes): Lack of preparation was pretty much something any director that worked on the show had to deal with because the script was not normally there. I directed "A Womb with a

View," and the script was done on that one. That was a pleasure to direct because I had the time to get it done right. I ended up getting to direct "Blonde on Blonde" because another director fell out. So that is how I got my directing debut. It was tough to direct and take on my producer responsibilities.

Suzanne Gangursky: Glenn liked the directors that brought the artistic value. But it was a juggling act for Jay to get the pages that needed to be shot that day.

Karen Hall: Most shows get seven days of prep, and there was no prep for directors, as we were never finished with the scripts. So they were always just flying by the seat of their pants.

Roger Director: If you don't have a script, that just starts to kill you. You don't want to be in the situation where a director comes in to prep a script and all you can say to the director is "I think it's going to be about this. Now go out and scout a location." That is so unfair to the director.

Dennis Dugan: Right now somebody could walk into my office and say, "Hey, we are shooting outside and the director just dropped dead, and we only have the location for the next six hours. Can you come and direct?" I would say, "Great. What's the scene?" Whatever thing I needed to do, I could do it in two seconds. And that was all because of *Moonlighting*, because you always had to be thinking on your feet as fast as you possibly could.

Allan Arkush: I would give Cybill notes, and then she'd stop me because I could not talk to her when she was putting on her lipstick. And that was the last thing that she did. Our makeup person did not put it on. He held the mirror and she did her lipstick and looked at herself in the mirror. And you could see her thinking about what she was going to do. It was like a moment of meditation. And then she put it down. And she'd looked at me like, "I got it." When the lipstick came out, I knew I had said enough. She went out and did something that was spectacular. She was great.

Cybill Shepherd: You've already done the work. You are ready, and you have to let it go for a moment. I don't remember it having anything to do with my lipstick, but it was like having a blank mind and being ready. There is a moment where you step back from your actors and see what they are bringing to the table before you tell them what to bring to the table. It's like getting the oil in the machine and letting them get rolling.

Chris Leitch: Glenn was very supportive, but at the same time, if it didn't quite click for him, we would reshoot it. I think we reshot the opening argument in my episode. He literally rewrote the entire scene and said, "Let's do it like this." We went back in and we shot it over.

Neil Mandelberg: Glenn would write the episodes day to day. So the directors didn't have a real timing on the episode when they shot it. Your script supervisor will give you a timing so you get an idea as to where you're at as you're shooting. We didn't have that luxury, because no episode was fully written when we started shooting it.

Allan Arkush: The editing was done by Neil and Artie Mandelberg. They would be going all week with Glenn, just going from editor to editor to have it on air on Tuesday. They would start locking stuff before they locked the whole show, which is unheard-of. So Alf Clausen could then start scoring.

Sheryl Main: Alf always made time to score the episode. He always made it happen. When you look back, you go, "Well, how did they do that?" We just did it. I know there was a time when there was a deadline that was so tight that we were actually sending the episode to New York to air at nine o'clock hot off the press. These shows were really ambitious, and they were always able to pull it off. The timing was a little rough, but you know what? The editors, the guys who colored it, timed it, made it happen. That's just the way it was. Nobody questioned it. We just did it.

Melissa Gelineau: It's what you do. That's why you get into this business. It's not a nine-to five job, and I was always amazed at some of those—who will remain nameless—who literally wanted to work nine to five.

Even though we had newer assistants, they would all be gone, and I would end up working eighteen-hour days, but that's what you do. That's what production is.

Roger Director: Every show I've ever worked at, from the first meeting of the year with the writers and the producers, it was always hard. Every show I ever worked at was a twenty-four-hour, seven-day-a-week enterprise. I've heard others say they were on shows that weren't that way; I was never on one.

Neil Mandelberg: We would work long hours that whole week leading up to the tight schedules. So the director, if he was available, and producers would get a look at most of the scenes. Then the last couple of days began the gang bang. The last step would go through me so we could be sure we're on time and that everything was still in-line and synced.

Allan Arkush: When they locked the whole show, they would time it and realized that they were long. To get it on time, they would then run the whole film through a film chain that would speed it up, like 3 percent. You wouldn't notice it. That's one of the reasons it plays so fast.

Neil Mandelberg: At least six times a year I went to work on Friday and came home on Sunday afternoon. We took turns sleeping in the editing room. They would wrap the show either on Thursday or Friday. We kept the lab open to do whatever we needed to do. We would send sequences to Alf Clausen to score as we were cutting new sequences. Alf would have a conversation with Glenn. We were like a chain. Producers were going from room to room.

Allan Arkush: Imagine the pressure Sheryl Main was under to get those shows finished? How they got them color timed and done?

Sheryl Main: You can ask any editor: when you're doing a show, you have to be prepared to work long hours. Once you get the film, it's always challenging. Not much has changed in the movie world in terms of long hours.

Neil Mandelberg: One of the things that unfortunately happened in *Moonlighting* was our schedules became so tight I stopped having time with my directors. It went right to the producers because we had to get them on the air.

Will Mackenzie: "When will I see the director's cut?" I asked. Glenn said, "You'll see it on Tuesday night on ABC." There was no director's cut. He'd say, "If you want to come in and spend all weekend with me, fine." But I never did. After the first one turned out so well, I trusted him.

Allan Arkush: You just didn't get a cut because you finished on Thursday night. Then there would be a bunch of the second-unit shots. So you'd wrap on stage at about eight. Then you could stay on or go to B unit, who would stay up all night, picking up everything that you didn't get. They edited all weekend and mixed it. Glenn could only edit like he wrote, which is from beginning to end. That's why you never got a cut. They basically would mix it on Sunday or Monday as they were scoring it. I don't know how they did that! The network would see it on Tuesday morning and it would air Tuesday night. That's what I observed.

Neil Mandelberg: The director normally gets a certain amount of days per episode per their contract. But we'd only have three days from wrap to air. You can't give the director those days. So the director would acquiesce and accept. Depending on who the director was, they would be up in the screening room with the producers and us, the editors, or they wouldn't. It really depended on whether they were involved in something else.

Allan Arkush: The Directors Guild called me up one time and said, "We've gotten a lot of complaints from directors on *Moonlighting* about not getting the director's cut." At that point, I was there a lot. I didn't want to rock the boat too much. They said, "When do you see the editor's cut?" I said, "Tuesday nights at nine with the rest of the country."

Neil Mandelberg: The DGA had conversations with the network and our producers, because they want to protect the directors and directors want to protect themselves, as they should. Glenn included them in any way he could. We never really got to a proper scheduling for *Moonlighting*. People really wanted to see shows, and no matter how early we started to film them, it was so hard to get shows on every week because of the amount of pages to shoot, and it was on film. We could have done that job without the crazy—well, without as many crazy—hours had it been digital at that point.

Dennis Dugan: It was always fun working on that set because it was so chaotic. A lot of it was last-minute because most of the time you didn't get the script until the night before. So preparation was last-minute and chaotic. Everybody in the crew knew it, the actors knew it, I knew it. You just flowed with the chaos. It was structured chaos, and that's what was great about the show.

Will Mackenzie: I remember my first day very well in that Cybill worked for three or four hours in the morning. As she was leaving the set, she passed Bruce coming in to do his scene. She whispered, "I think you're gonna really like this guy." That was enough; that just made me feel good.

Chic Eglee: Will Mackenzie once said, because that show was—well, I'm sure you've heard all the stories, and they are all true and then some— but Will was the one with the famous quote: "One does not direct *Moonlighting*. One hosts *Moonlighting*."

ENTER HERBERT VIOLA

IN THE FOURTH episode of Season 3, Curtis Armstrong joined the cast as Herbert Viola, a love interest for Ms. Dipesto. He was brought in for a multiepisode arc and ended up staying until the end of the series.

Curtis Armstrong (Herbert Viola): I had not done television before. I had three auditions in a day, which has never happened before or since. One was for a movie which starred Ed Asner, and the other was a movie

with Kevin Bacon and John Hughes. Both of those jobs were the ones I thought I had a chance of getting. The last one was for *Moonlighting*, which friends had been telling me that I needed to see. I went in and read with [casting director] Karen Vice. The *Moonlighting* thing had been pitched to me as being the love interest of one of the stars. I have a very low regard of myself as a love interest. They called me back the next day to read for Glenn and Jay and everybody who was there.

Glenn Gordon Caron: I was always just a fan of Curtis. I saw *Risky Business* and *Revenge of the Nerds*. His name was on a list and I went, "OOH!" He came in to audition and I went, "Would you really do this show?" I just loved Curtis. He's become a writer of some repute.

Curtis Armstrong: Glenn called Jon Avnet, the producer of *Risky Business*, when he was thinking about offering me the show because he wanted to find out from Jon's perspective whether I was trouble or not.

Because he didn't need any more of that, I guess. He needed somebody who was easy to get along with and professional. Jon said, "Oh, yes," and thank God he did. It was Jon's recommendation that clinched getting the job.

Jay Daniel: Having another character there allowed us to have Allyce play more scenes with someone that didn't involve Bruce or Cybill. We just needed another character.

Curtis Armstrong: They wanted somebody in there to work with Allyce because even then it was becoming harder and harder to get Cybill and Bruce together all the time. As time went on, Bruce was doing movies and their complicated relationship made it necessary that they get another, alternate storyline going that would fill in the cracks with the David-and-Maddie story. Roger Director was the one who created Viola as a character, but it was still evolving.

Roger Director: Glenn saw the need for a fourth hand and envisioned Bert as the person in the office pool stepping out from behind a keyboard with way more going on inside than you imagined. All the writers poured different colors into Bert. He was a shameless kiss up to Addison; he had grandiose fantasies; he was sincere, overly earnest, and surprising.

Glenn Gordon Caron: I really counted on Curtis and Allyce. I mean, I needed people. I couldn't do just Bruce and Cybill. First of all, Cybill wouldn't show up. [Laughs.] You can't do a show with one person. You just can't. It's physically impossible. People don't understand that it's a very glamorous business, but the business of being an actor on a television show means it's a minimum twelve-hour day, and usually closer to fourteen to sixteen hours.

Curtis Armstrong: It was not like there was any preparation for the role. I got the job the day of the callback. I had to go out to 20th Century Fox for the costume fitting because I was going to be shooting the next morning. I was pretty ragged by the time I got there for the actual shooting. We always had very early calls. Allyce said, "Can we get half an hour? Can we get forty minutes where we can just sit and talk?"

Allyce Beasley: Everything just went at such a speed and in such an out-of-control way. OK, now Ms. Dipesto has this boyfriend, and the first scene that we have with each other is us rolling around on the desk and knocking things on the floor.

Curtis Armstrong: I got the impression that she didn't ask for much. So they gave her that, and we sat in her trailer eating bagels, as I remember, and did some talking. I knew her husband at the time, Vincent Schiavelli, who had been in *Better Off Dead*. So we were able to start with that, and that's where she opened up that Vincent wanted to have the part of Viola.

Allyce Beasley: My husband actually flipped out, and he was really upset. I don't think Curtis and I had done a lot of love scenes in our life, and I think Curtis and I are both very private people in that way. I was just really happy for the half-hour, to just take a look at his face before we had to roll around on the desk together.

Curtis Armstrong and Allyce Beasley had to just "jump into" their on-screen relationship. Their first scene was a make-out session.

Curtis Armstrong: When it comes to chemistry, that's something which is just not doable. You don't create that. It's flukish. If it hadn't been exactly the way it was, they were prepared—according to my contract—for this to be a one-off. I would have done the episode and then never be seen again. I didn't know right away that they were going to pick me up. It was a recurring role that first season that I was on the show. It just sort of crept up on me. Suddenly I was there all the time.

Jeff Reno: Roger Director wrote the show where Viola was introduced. He came on as a love interest for Dipesto. That was sort of his purpose. I don't think MacGillicuddy [played by Jack Blessing] was ever going to rise to what Curtis did with Herbert. When we saw how good he was, and got to know him a little bit, we just figured he could do it. We all loved the character, and Curtis. He really is a terrific actor.

Sheryl Main: Curtis was one of my favorites on the show. Just a good guy. Professional and always stepped up. Allyce and him were just darling people to work with.

Chic Eglee: What I loved about Herbert was he was just so tightly wound. This is Booger from *Revenge of the Nerds*, and he just wants to be David Addison. David is the coolest guy in the universe to Herbert Viola. That character was straight from the mind of Roger Director.

Jay Daniel: Curtis was a willing participant in the shenanigans. I liked him very much.

Chapter 8

The Barkleys of Mulberry St.

The episode "Big Man on Mulberry Street" is full of extremes. While the series is known for fast-paced back-and-forth banter, this episode is constructed around three monologues and one long dance sequence. There is either continuous talking or none at all. This is the second script of *Moonlighting* to contain no case. But it contains plenty of mystery. David gets the news that a friend died in New York City and has to return to the city for the funeral. As Maddie inquires about the friend, she discovers that the deceased is David's ex-brother-in-law. He was married? The bomb has been dropped. Left to her own devices, and with a shortage of information, Maddie goes home, pours herself a glass of wine, and starts wondering. She dreams up a ballet of sorts, set to the 1986 Billy Joel song "Big Man on Mulberry Street," from Joel's then-current album, *The Bridge*. The song is a big band/jazzy tune that is brash and loud, and demands attention. The lyrics describe someone who is struggling with his position in life ("Now I ain't a bad guy. So tell me, what am I trying to prove?") and just can't seem to behave ("Why is it every time I go out I always seem to get in trouble?").[1] Sound like any Addison you know?

---

[1]   Joel, Billy. "Big Man on Mulberry Street". *The Bridge*. 1986.

This scene isn't comic dancers doing a silly kickline and lip-synching to "Uptown Girl." This is an *actual* story told through dance. The sequence was directed by movie-musical icon Stanley Donen [*Singin' in the Rain*] and choreographed by Bill and Jacqui Landrum, and featured Golden Globe winner and Bob Fosse protégé Sandahl Bergman. For six and a half minutes of screen time, the story of David and Tess Addison's courtship is told through movement. Bruce Willis dances alongside Bergman, who portrays Tess in Maddie's fantasy. The couple fall in love at a bar, get married, and soon a male dancer sashays in between them and dances away with her. Alone, David finishes up his work at the bar when Maddie bursts through the door and kisses David hard on the mouth. Maddie wakes up. The best part of all? It's all a lie.

That alone would tick off enough boxes for the episode to qualify as groundbreaking television, but—as was typical for *Moonlighting*—there was more dazzling creativity to come, making "Big Man" one of the best hours of television ever. Following this dialogueless segment, the episode mutates into a Mamet-like play containing three major monologues. The show, known for featuring two characters who can't possibly wait for the other person to finish their sentence before they disagree, allows Maddie to talk and David to listen, and vice versa. Cybill Shepherd, with all due respect to her movie work, gives the performance of her career in this episode. Maddie flies to New York to surprise David. When he opens the door to his hotel room, she is sitting inside, her coat still on, bathed in a deep-blue light that only Jerry Finnerman could have crafted. Maddie gives a two-and-a-half-minute monologue about why she came. She hits all the right emotional notes. Cybill and Maddie open themselves up, displaying vulnerability but not weakness. The writers had tended to lean toward making Maddie shrill and unrelatable, rather than letting the viewer understand her position. There isn't a person who wouldn't understand why she flew to New York after this monologue. This is the deepest glimpse that viewers are ever given into who Maddie Hayes is inside. It should be noted that this episode was written by a female. Karen Hall wrote this monologue. This is, amazingly, her first script for the series.

A scene later, it's Bruce's turn to shine. Bruce Willis delivers a four-minute monologue that tells the story of his first marriage. This monologue, as you will learn below, was written by Glenn Gordon Caron. It has the comedy we expect from Addison, but also some brilliant moments of dramatic acting. Watch Willis's eyes as he describes the first time he met his future wife, Tess, and then watch them as he reveals that she got pregnant and lost the baby. The details in the monologue are incredibly specific and memorable—like when David describes the name tag he fears he will have to wear as he works the rest of his life at a gas station because of foolish choices made in his youth. Consequences that every teenager knows can happen when they let lust override what they know from science. These two monologues almost equal the run time of the "Big Man" sequence, as if the series had to make up for the missed dialogue. It does so and then some. But there is one more monologue left for the viewer. There also is the truth.

Maddie attends the funeral, against David's request, only to find that he never shows up. She learns from Tess Addison that what actually happened wasn't what was depicted in the dance sequence or in the monologues. It was not another man David found his wife with, but another woman. Everything viewers had been led to believe in the dance number was just a red herring, a misdirection to trick them into believing something that wasn't true. This revelation—that David's wife had left him for another woman—was astounding television in 1986. David Addison was the prototypical manly man for his time. The idea that a woman had left him for another man was, for viewers, already a shocking blow to the character's ego. But for her to have left him for another woman turns all the sexist and chauvinist comments he had made over the previous two years upside down. The episode may have not contained a traditional detective mystery, but it certainly solved a few long-running questions.

The final monologue is handed to Bruce Willis, just like the Emmy he would receive months later for his performance in this episode. His two-minute speech in a taxi cab, talking "to the driver" but looking into the camera to speak directly with viewers, gives us another look deep inside David. He says, "A person in bed with your wife is a person in bed with your wife. Gender is not the main issue"—an expression of tolerance at a time when the US government wouldn't even mention AIDS or homosexuality. This Addison is not performing his story and displaying his feelings, like he did with Maddie. This is a raw, "just the facts" monologue covering all the thoughts and emotions that this episode stirred up for him. Willis does a fantastic job of not overacting. The scene also packs an unintended additional punch for viewers now with an establishing shot of the cab under the Manhattan Bridge, the Twin Towers looming in the distance. Just like the Twin Towers, this kind of television making is long gone.

The mystery, the monologues, and the "Mulberry Street" dance sequence combined to make this episode a fan favorite. Bruce Willis's Emmy for best actor in a drama series in 1987 was the only win the episode picked up—although choreographers Bill and Jacqui Landrum were nominated. Cybill was nominated for this episode, but she did not win. The episode should be studied for its writing, creativity, character development, acting, and most certainly lighting. While the dance sequence is directed by filmmaker Stanley Donen, the dramatic part of the episode is helmed by Christian Nyby. In doing research for the book, I also discovered that it was the episode that would forever change the relationships on and off the set.

Jay Daniel: We were in the middle of a five-day hiatus that cost us $135,000 to shut down because we had no scripts. At the same time, we got a forty-one share when Episode 2, "The Man Who Cried Wife," aired. So all was forgiven. ABC said, "Keep doing what you are doing." ABC Circle was very supportive, because they were liking what they were seeing with the ratings and the Emmy nominations. That allowed us to shut down without being beaten down. We used that time to be able to rehearse with Bruce and Cybill for "Big Man." We also had time to practice the boxing scene for "Symphony in Knocked Flat."

Glenn Gordon Caron: Phil Ramone, an amazing record producer who produced Simon & Garfunkel and all of Billy Joel's classic albums, called me. We had never met. He said, "Billy Joel wrote a song for your show." I said, "Really?" He said, "Yeah, I'd love to bring it over and play it for you. I have no idea how you would want to use it or if you'd want to use it." I am an enormous Billy Joel fan. I grew up in Oceanside, New York. Billy grew up on Long Island. He's a couple years older than me, but I felt the songs he sang were things that I understood. Phil came over and played "Big Man on Mulberry Street." I was blown away by it.

Billy Joel: There's a song called "Big Man on Mulberry Street" which came from a picture I had of this guy. I had a writing studio down in Soho. I would go in there and work in one little corner. But sometimes I would leave the building and walk down to Little Italy, get a little food, wine, a little espresso. And the walk I took was on Mulberry Street. And I just kind of invented this character who thought he was Mr. Cool. The character is really kind of a nebbish, but in his own mind he's king—king of Mulberry Street. I just had fun writing that song. It was just one of those things I invented.[2]

Karen Hall (writer of "Big Man on Mulberry Street"): On *Moonlighting*, we got a lot of stuff that was rare, because people loved the show. That was the first episode that I wrote. The beginning of that episode was Glenn giving me a cassette of that song, saying that he wanted to use it in the show. I guess he already knew that Billy Joel had said he could use the song. I put the song in my car for a while and tried to figure out what it inspired. The song made me understand David Addison better. I'm from the South; I've been to New York, but I have not hung out on Mulberry Street.

Glenn Gordon Caron: I'd always wanted to do storytelling through dance and tried to find an excuse to do it on the show. I heard this song and I thought, "This is it." We needed to come up with a story, and then we needed to stop for seven minutes and do this dance number.

Jay Daniel: One of the things that Glenn and I talked about was him wanting Maddie to dream about David's ex-wife. He said, "I wonder if we turned that into a dance number." We knew we would have to plan ahead because you can't shoot that like a regular episode. Since we had to shut down, that gave us a little time to work.

---

2   Torgoff, Martin. "Interview," *The Bridge* piano book. Hal Leonard. 1986.

Glenn Gordon Caron: I called Stanley Donen. At the time, I did not know that Stanley Donen had directed *Singin' in the Rain* when he was twenty-eight years old. He went on to direct an amazing group of musical movies, including *On the Town* and *Seven Brides for Seven Brothers*. I called him and said, "We're going to do this musical thing. Would you come and direct it?" He said, "No." I said, "Why not?" He said, "Well, first of all, you can't afford me." I said, "Well, that's true. I have no money at all. But would you come and direct it anyway?" He said, "No, I'm sure you don't have enough time." I said, "Well, I think we would probably have to do it in two days." He said, "That's insane. You can't do that in two days. You have to choreograph it, you have to rehearse it, and it's seven minutes long." But ultimately I persuaded him to come and do it.

Melissa Gelineau: It was the height of *Moonlighting*. Everybody wanted to be a part of it. I was not part of the creative meetings, but from what I recall, Stanley brought in the Landrums.

Bill Landrum (Cochoreographer of "Big Man" Sequence): The music was given to us, and we read the script. So we had an idea, but they already knew what they wanted. They gave us two minutes of music. Jacqui and I go, we choreograph. They absolutely fall in love with what we're doing—the whole opening with her leg on the table and Bruce coming through and that whole opening. Then suddenly we ended it. They said, "Well, what happens next?" We said, "There's no more music." They said, "Call Billy Joel." So they called Billy Joel in New York and said, "We need more music." Twice they did this.

Jay Daniel: I think it was Alf Clausen that did the extended middle part, because throughout the show that theme recurs, and that was all Alf.

Bill Landrum: I loved the song. So it was not difficult to listen to it ten thousand times in rehearsal. What we found that we had to do—because the body language required to keep going forward—the whole point is what happens next, taking it more and more forward. We had to use the music as a river that we floated on, rather than respecting any kind of integrity of lyrics.

SCOTT RYAN

Jay Daniel: On August 25, 1986, we took a look at what Stanley and the choreographers had for the dance sequence for "Big Man." We got the rights for the song early on, and they were rehearsing it. It was just a matter of showing what it was going to be like with dancers.

Karen Hall: The dance and Stanley Donen were great. Anytime somebody wants to make me look really great on a show with my name on it, that's wonderful.

Jay Daniel: Once Stanley locked down the choreography, we started to get Bruce and Cybill down there to rehearse. When there was a scene that featured only Cybill, Bruce would rehearse. He got in a number of rehearsals. He had never had a dance lesson in his life. But he pulled it off. Cybill did too.

Bill Landrum: Working with Bruce every day, as a nondancer, it was constant repetition. My wife must have done that pas de deux with him ten thousand times before Sandahl Bergman's first rehearsal. We wanted him to know everything precisely before we brought Sandahl in, who is genius. We had to have him really know how to support a body and how to spin. That's how we approached those weeks with Bruce.

Glenn Gordon Caron: We brought in Sandahl Bergman, who was at that time, I think, one of the most celebrated dancers. She was the lead dancer in *All That Jazz*, the movie that Bob Fosse directed. She was amazing.

Bill Landrum: When Stanley offered us this job, he said, "There's one request. You can hire all the dancers you want, but I would like to request that you use Sandahl Bergman. I think she would be perfect for this. I feel like I want to present her, and this would be a good presentation." We said, "Are you kidding? We're more than happy to work with Sandahl."

Sandahl Bergman (Tess Addison/Dancer): I got the call and the Landrums said, "Do you want to do this number?" I said yes, because I had the utmost respect for them. And I was always a fan of *Moonlighting*.

My question was, "How are we going to get Bruce Willis to rehearse it?" Bottom line, I just trusted Jacqui and Bill.

Karen Hall: The thing that was on my mind was how hard Bruce worked on that sequence. He came in when it was his lunch hour. He just went way above and beyond for that sequence, and that always stuck with me.

Melissa Gelineau: Bruce is very New York. He had that sort of vibe, but I just remember everyone being so impressed with how well he moved. He did a great job.

Bill Landrum: Stanley would come and watch rehearsal. He was endearing. Occasionally, as a director he would say, "Let's make this moment a bit clearer." For the intro, we had the camera catch just the calves in the high heels, walking through those windows, then stop, a little brush with the top of the shoe on the leg, and then boom, burst through those doors. That is all Stanley. That's how he opened the shot. [See photo below.]

Sandahl Bergman: It was pretty extraordinary, because if you look at that number, he's lifting me, and it was a very long number. But the fact is that Bruce Willis is a musical guy. I remember when we were rehearsing, he'd go with his band afterward and perform. The guy's obviously got musical chops. So that was good. But in some ways, when I look at it, I'm kind of dancing for two people. When he was off-balance, I could adjust and do something. But bottom line, he was so willing and was excited to do it.

Sheryl Main: There was something so different about "Big Man." It felt like we were doing something unique. That's what I was attracted to. It was a big production. You had all kinds of stuff going on. Watching Sandahl Bergman was like, "Oh my goodness." I don't know any other shows that were doing that.

Sandahl Bergman: The icing on the cake was the fact that they brought in Stanley Donen to direct, which was for me extraordinary because I had done Gene Kelly's show in Las Vegas when I was nineteen and then I did *Xanadu* with him. Dance is very hard to shoot any way. People don't do it that well. So it was great that he came in and directed that number.

Melissa Gelineau: Stanley would tell us Gene Kelly stories. And he's just an icon to me. I just remember him being really lovely. There were certain people that you have such a respect for that you had to go to be a part of it.

Neil Mandelberg: "Big Man" was what *Moonlighting* was all about. That series was able to take any atmosphere you put on it and enhanced it.

Sandahl Bergman: What I loved about "Big Man" was Vince Paterson was one of the dancers in that number. After that, he actually directed and choreographed Madonna's Blond Ambition tour. Jerry Mitchell, who was phenomenal in the dance, is a huge theater choreographer, director. He directed and choreographed *Kinky Boots* on Broadway.

Peter Werner: Glenn specifically offered me that episode to direct, and I couldn't do it. I actually came down to the set just because I'm such a fan of Stanley Donen. I watched him do the dance sequence.

Allan Arkush: I remember I was working over at *LA Law* and would visit the set when they were doing the Donen episode. I was on the set watching that a lot.

Sandahl Bergman: Bruce was so funny in rehearsal. If I could speak the dancers' language: there's lifts that are involved, which, when you do a lift, it's all about timing. It's not about lifting dead weight. At one point Bruce wasn't getting it, and he goes, "OK, I'm done." I said, "Bruce, you know what, we have to do this over and over and over again to get the timing of what's happening." They put a red wig on me, because Cybill Shepherd was blond. They didn't want me blond.

Jay Daniel: We shot the dance number on October 10, 1986, on Stage 15.

Bill Landrum: I think that for two and a half minutes there isn't one camera cut, not one edit. The old MGM way—one camera just followed the action all the way through and back down before there was ever an edit. That was the beauty of the piece too, because we had Stanley.

Sandahl Bergman: Stanley didn't do close shots. He shot like in the old days, like they used to do in a movie. They shot the whole scene that was going on—not a tight shot to Bruce, not a tight shot to me. He sort of shot the number in its entirety so it told the story. That's what I like so much about it.

Neil Mandelberg: I don't remember having direct contact with Stanley. I think we were in a screening room together. It might have been one of our crazy schedules. But it was shot very specifically. So there really weren't a lot of other choices. He just made that era of that scene look exactly as it should.

Sandahl Bergman: The camera traveled and went from point A to point

B, up to C, to me entering. So that's why we all had to be pretty good, because you couldn't make a mistake. The only problem—which I still look at this and laugh at—was when they put me on the banister for me to slide down. I wasn't able to slide. We always had a little bit of a problem with that, trying to figure out how it can look like me sliding down. I forget how we did it. It wasn't smooth, but I still got down there. [See photo below.]

Glenn Gordon Caron: Bruce had never danced before. But what was great about Bruce was that he was just game for anything.

Cybill Shepherd: What is fun about it to me is that Bruce works wonderfully well because he isn't a trained dancer. You see Sandahl as the perfection and then you see Bruce as raw. That is what makes it fun, that Bruce isn't that perfect and contrasts are always great. It's just so cool.

Sandahl Bergman: He was having the time of his life. That number does

have a lot of humor. We're both sort of smiling and laughing in it quite a bit. I love that, because a lot of times in a dancer's head, if you're thinking about what you're supposed to do, you're not present in the moment.

Bill Landrum: It was Stanley's idea to do the special effects with the seven different Bruces. He brought that technology—which was new at the time—into everybody. We were all excited. It was the first time people had really worked with it.

Cybill Shepherd: That is like a shot in Orson Welles's *The Lady from Shanghai* where you see all the reflections in the mirror of Rita Hayworth.

Jay Daniel: We shot it "one Bruce at a time," with a locked-off camera. That is how we did F/X in the old days. Bruce did that dance move seven times, and then it was all narrated in post on film. It was well before the days of computers. We had no choice but to do it seven different times. We filmed that one shot for an entire day on the last day of the shoot, on October 14.

Bill Landrum: When it came to the end of that number, Stanley wanted to recapture that same walk-through moment that we started with, but with Cybill. It would be Maddie's idea of her being there.

Jay Daniel: Cybill wasn't sure if she was gonna be able to do it. Even on the day of shooting, Cybill was saying, "I can only do this one time."

Glenn Gordon Caron: I mean, in a perfect world you would want the dance of "Big Man on Mulberry Street" to be about Maddie and Dave. I knew I couldn't go to Cybill and say, "We're going to do this dance that is seven minutes long." She would have said, "Not me." I couldn't have done that. So we had to sort of redesign everything. Sandahl Bergman could be the person that Bruce danced with and then bring Cybill in at the very end, which is what we did. Stanley Donen was truly one of the great treats of my life. I want to say it took about three days, and when we got to the third day, it was Cybill's part, and she literally came in, walked down some steps, Bruce threw her over his shoulder, I think it was one shot, and the great Stanley Donen said, "Cut. I need another." Cybill said, "That was good for me." We were all sort of appalled.

Bill Landrum: If you wanted another take of something, you had to tell her that the lighting was bad and we have to relight, and then she would do it again. So we didn't always have the choice of getting good footage of her.

Glenn Gordon Caron: Stanley turned to look at me and said, "I've never been here before. How does this work?" I went to Cybill and said, "That's Stanley Donen. Could you please do it again?" She said, "No." Luckily a camera operator bailed me out and said, "I lost focus halfway down." And she begrudgingly agreed to do it again.

Jay Daniel: We talked her into doing another. Once she had done it once, and the crew applauded, she was willing to do it again. It took some gentle persuasion to do it more than once.

Cybill Shepherd: Seems like I didn't get along with Stanley Donen, but I am not exactly sure why. I don't know how I did that dance back then. But I am glad I don't have to do it today, let's just put it that way.

Sandahl Bergman: I want to say it probably, in its entirety, with Cybill Shepherd coming on board at the end, took probably a week. Which was a long time for episodic television. Whereas now they shoot something in a heartbeat, and good or not, it's on there. But I think they spent the time with that number because it was a long number, and Stanley Donen was on board to direct it. So he's going to get it right. He's not going to get it wrong. And he didn't get it wrong; he got it. I mean, he captured dance. Dance is one of the hardest things to film.

Bill Landrum: Everybody was saying, "Will it get past the censors?" There is a little moment with Sandahl and the crotch, and in those days people were sensitive. It was scandalous enough that everybody was talking about it the next day.

Sandahl Bergman: As an actor and as a performer my whole life, there's always a couple of projects that you really love. And for me, it was *All That Jazz, Conan the Barbarian*, and then it was *Moonlighting*. Those are the three things I'm the most proud of.

Glenn Gordon Caron: I don't think Sandahl's right about that, but I think that's very sweet. She has done so many amazing things in her career.

Jay Daniel: I recently rewatched the episode, and I was proud of it. I think it holds up. I don't know if all of our episodes would hold up today. The dance number was something that you don't expect. I was proud of how we worked with Stanley. But the thing I was really aware of is how attractive Bruce and Cybill were and how much fun it was to watch. Yet there was a deeper story being told in that episode. I think they both did some of their best acting in that episode.

Glenn Gordon Caron: The fact that people would say to me, "Well, that's absurd, you can't do that" had no effect on me. The bad side of it was I didn't understand the discipline that was expected of you to make, particularly back then, a weekly TV show. In fact, I held TV in contempt. The good news was I felt I made some very ambitious, very special hours of television. The bad news was they were a little more expensive than they should have been and took longer to make. As a result, we didn't have twenty-two episodes a year. But I didn't care. I felt if the viewer sat down at nine o'clock and turned on their TV and they saw something good, then they would reward you with their faithfulness. The only thing that would break that contract was if you gave them something that was unworthy of their time. That was honestly my approach to it. And I thought, "I'm either going to live by that or die by that."

Karen Hall: I worked hard on that script. I was new to the show, and I wanted them to think my first script was really good. The lesbian story was completely Glenn's idea. I can take no credit for that. I really liked it as a plot twist. I was a little nervous about writing it, but it just kind of wrote itself when I got there.

Glenn Gordon Caron: I don't actually remember the development of the story. I remember really loving the idea of this revelation that David's been married before and that she'd left him. I loved that it sort of inverted everything you thought about—every expectation you have of him. Because that has been my experience in life. We meet people, we assess people, we think we understand who these people are, and then invariably we are surprised to discover the truth.

Jeff Reno: "Big Man" is one of the few scripts that Ron and I actually didn't work on. We had a little bit of story input, but I don't know much about it. Karen Hall wrote the original draft.

Glenn Gordon Caron: I was so proud of it. I found the story around it really, really moving—the story about this other woman that he'd been married to and who left him for a woman. This was complicated, adult, evocative, and interesting.

Jay Daniel: Amazingly enough, I don't remember us getting any grief from the network about the reveal. And they did get the scripts as they came out . . . but they may have come out in pieces. [Laughs.]

Karen Hall: I do remember that I wrote Maddie's monologue, when she first arrived in New York. It might have just been wanting to try to do a monologue over them bantering because we knew the power of a monologue. It was something that we hadn't done. When I wrote the monologue, I just thought, "What would she be thinking and saying?" Because I've been the female who was known to chase a guy in my day. I kind of felt like I understood her combination of being horrified by what she's done but wanting to defend it as well.

Cybill Shepherd: Karen's lines for Maddie in that episode felt like I was saying them as a human being. It wasn't a character. It was just "Let the words have their power. Don't try to decide to land on a certain word so that the dialogue can flow; just be natural." People can forget what you look like or what facial expression you are making. "Don't put a lot of scribble on your face." I think Hitchcock said that.

Monologue 1: Maddie explains why she flew to New York. Notice the exquisite lighting by Jerry Finnerman.

Jay Daniel: I think the written words brought that performance out of Cybill. She just nailed it. Cybill is capable of some wonderful work. You've got to hand it to someone who performs a scene like that bedroom monologue. It's a remarkable feat. She handled it just beautifully. Christian Nyby directed the episode and is a wonderful director, but he is not someone who pulls a performance out of an actress—not to take anything away from him. I give her full credit for it. It was an opportunity that she grabbed ahold of. I also give credit to Jerry for the way it was lit. It all worked.

Cybill Shepherd: What a fantastic scene. How lucky was I? It was one of the best things I have ever done. I think it was the simplicity of it. I didn't overact it. Acting is in the eyes, not in the face. In my cabaret show, if I cry, then the audience doesn't cry. My job was not to cry, and get out of the way so that the songs can be about them and what they are feeling. That applies to this scene, because I am not thinking about what I look like as I say it. I am almost embarrassed to look directly at David. That wasn't planned. I kind of hide my face. I don't even look at Bruce.

Karen Hall: Cybill was very happy that there was a Southern female suddenly writing for her. When I wrote that scene I wasn't thinking North and South. I was just thinking, "This woman has done this, and how does she feel now that she has done this idiotic thing?" I wrote a version of David's first monologue, but Glenn threw that out and rewrote it. [Laughs.] Which needed to happen.

Glenn Gordon Caron: I'd been writing monologues for Bruce for a long time, but they were comedic monologues. I was really pleased with that episode. There was an audacity and truthfulness to it that I liked.

Karen Hall: That third monologue, the long speech to the cab driver who doesn't understand what David's saying, I think was my idea. I can't be positive. I just needed a scene there, and I didn't know what it could

Monologue 2: David tells his version of the story. Another example of Finnerman's blanc-noir lighting of Bruce Willis.

be. The audience needed to know the story. David and Maddie were not going to be together in any more scenes except on the airplane. And with her decision not to say anything, there's no way for the audience to know how David was going to react to all of this unless he tells somebody. There was nobody for him to tell. I think that's where the idea came for that monologue.

Glenn Gordon Caron: Apparently Billy Joel hated the episode. I don't think it was what he had wanted. He didn't know he was dealing with a hopeless romantic. I still love Billy Joel. It was actually Phil Ramone who broke the news to me. Phil produced the *Moonlighting* album, which is the only piece of merchandising we ever released that was associated with the show. "Big Man on Mulberry Street" wasn't on the album because of a rights issue. Billy was on Columbia records and our album was MCA.

Jay Daniel: We filmed the scene on the balcony with Cybill and the ex-wife on October 13. There was an incident that happened onstage between Cybill and Glenn. He was down there because he cared so much about the scene. Cybill wanted to react in a particular way when she saw the ex-wife for the first time and she looked her in the face. Glenn wanted something different. I can't remember the details, but it was a subtle difference. Cybill was saying she was going to do it this way, and Glenn was saying, "Can you try it that way?" Glenn, after having a very serious discussion, said something funny, and the crew laughed. They were all standing around watching this confrontation. It was a low-key confrontation. He tried to lighten it up with a little joke. I can't remember what the joke was. It made the crew laugh. Cybill took it that he had humiliated her in front of the crew and they were laughing at her. It led to her walking off the stage. I had to get my referee shirt on. I had to go chat with her and get her back on the stage to do the scene, which she did, and we went forward.

Cybill Shepherd: Hmm? I wonder what the joke was? My performance in the scene with David's ex-wife seems odd to me. There is something about my performance that seems a bit off. It seems like I am in some ways not engaged. So much of that scene is shown in profile. I feel like I am uncomfortable, but not appropriately so for the scene. This isn't my favorite scene that I play. I seem like I am not there in a way I'd like to be. Sometimes I am not at my best if there is a lot of pressure put on me. I wish that I had played the scene better. They didn't show many close-ups because I seem so kind of not there. Strange. I see why my performance would not work for the scene. I think I could have done it better, and I don't know what went on with me. I don't recall that Glenn told a joke. I'm not sure. Maybe I felt more pressure?

Jay Daniel: We finished that episode the next day, on October 14, and Bruce did his special-effect scene. On October 15 we started the next episode, "All Creatures Great and . . . Not So Great." There was a meeting with Cybill's manager and lawyer to talk to Glenn and I about her not being treated with respect. On Monday, October 20, Cybill called in ill. We shut down. We were gonna start up the next day. She called in ill. Cybill worked briefly on October 23, shooting a pickup scene. Cybill was on set shooting in the confessional booth. We were working late; it was around seven. She broke down because we were shooting so late. The reason we were working late was because she was taking so much time to get out of her trailer. Then it was late, she was complaining, but she was what made us late. On Friday the twenty-fourth, we had a 7:00 a.m. meeting with Cybill. Glenn was apologetic. We did everything we could to get her back in the game.

Cybill Shepherd: It seems like I was once late to the set. So I was told when I got to the stage to go directly to Glenn's office. In his office was my lawyer, Walter Teller, and my agent. It was a little scary.

Jay Daniel: October 27 we had to shut down because she fell ill again. She finally came back on November 5 and had another incident, with Allan, on the set.

Allan Arkush (Director of "All Creatures"): We're shooting Cybill in all one direction and it's close to lunch, and the next part of the scene is her at the window. The only thing we have left shooting in that direction is a shot of Bruce on the couch asleep. So we say, "Cybill, why don't you go to lunch and we're going to clean up the shot?" She said, "What shot?" and I said, "The shot of Bruce." She said, "You have to do my shots first." I said, "That's right, but we won't get to your shot before lunch. We'd have to take all the equipment and the furniture out to shoot you through the window." Jerry says, "Cookie, it's just a straight shot of Bruce asleep. We're here. We're lit. And you can go to lunch early." Cybill says, "No, you finish me first."

Cybill Shepherd: I don't remember that, but it is interesting to hear about. When you have really talented people together, it's like you are in a cave together. I mean, there are gonna be all kinds of emotions and flare-ups. There is a lot of pressure.

Jay Daniel: That is what happened. That is how the show was going at that time. It was November 7 until we finished that episode. The reason I tell this story is because I don't think we ever got past this moment. Cybill and Glenn were really never the same after it.

Glenn Gordon Caron: Not to contradict Jay, but we were already at loggerheads. The relationship was fractured way before "Big Man on Mulberry Street." I always liked Cybill a great deal, but she had already decided it was my turn in the box. I think she was unhappy for a long time, and I felt badly about that. I didn't know what to do with that. Cybill went through a period where she wasn't crazy about me, but we have talked since and we're on friendly terms now.

Chapter 9
Kiss Me, Shakespeare

Here is a little-known excerpt from the original text of Shakespeare's play *The Taming of the Shrew*:

> O monstrous episode, how like a swine you lie!
> Grim tales, how fun but expensive is thine hour!
> Sirs, I will explain to thee weary reader.
> What think you if we spent money galore,
> Wrapped in sweet budgets, reruns put upon our eyes,
> A most delicious idea from writers' head,
> And brave actors nearby to forge the task,
> Would not the network then forget deadlines?
>
> *Tos.*(1.1.35-43).

OK, I might have changed a few of the words, but I must admit that wasn't easy to adapt. Now imagine writing fifty minutes of that kind of prose while you pack in more jokes than an average episode of *The Simpsons*. Think of the pressures on Cybill, Bruce, Allyce, and Curtis to memorize all those lines, the production staff to create the sets, props and costumes to match the Renaissance. Compile all that together and you start to realize the undertaking that was "Atomic Shakespeare," written by Ron Osborn and Jeff Reno and directed by Will Mackenzie. And because this was *Moonlighting*, that wasn't challenging enough: they upped the ante by producing the entire episode, from first shot to actual airing at 9:00 p.m. on Tuesday, November 25, 1986, in just eighteen days. It became the most famous episode of the series and was the most expensive hour of television produced at that time. An average episode of *Game of Thrones* in 2019 cost about six million dollars. That is actually in the ballpark of how much "Atomic Shakespeare" cost in today's dollars. It was unheard-of for network television.

The episode is a retelling of the Shakespeare play *The Taming of the Shrew*, which, in 1948, was adapted into the Cole Porter musical "Kiss Me, Kate" (pointless trivia: Cybill Shepherd recorded an album of Cole Porter songs in 1976, which contains several songs from that musical). David Addison, as Petruchio, marries Katherina, played by Maddie Hayes, for her dowry. But Petruchio will be paid only if he can turn her into a dutiful and well-trained wife. The couple fight, banter, throw plates, and fall in love, just like in every other episode of *Moonlighting*. This special episode passed the singing duties to Bruce Willis, who performed the classic rock song "Good Lovin'" at the forced wedding of the two characters. In the end, it's Katherina who tames Petruchio, and all is set right in the world. That is all fine and dandy for the characters on the world's stage, but for the people who had to create this ridiculously ambitious hour of television, there was toil and trouble in the world.

Jay Daniel: We finished the "All Things Great" episode on November 6, and it aired on the eleventh. We were ranked number four that week. We started the shoot for "Shakespeare" on the seventh of November, 1986.

Glenn Gordon Caron: When I was in high school, I saw the [Franco]

154

Zeffirelli movie of *The Taming of the Shrew*, with Richard Burton and Elizabeth Taylor. In college, my wife at the time was in a production of it. So I must have seen her in that show ten times. When I graduated college and was living in New York City, I saw Meryl Streep and Raul Julia perform it in Central Park. So the bones of the idea of two people who seem incredibly attracted to each other save for the fact that they agree on nothing and have completely different worldviews—I thought that's really interesting and you don't see that very often.

Jeff Reno: I specifically remember the moment I had the idea for the episode. It just came to me—almost full on. I was driving to work on Pico Boulevard. I was trying to think of a special episode. I don't know if Glenn asked us to think of something special or we just wanted to.

Ron Osborn: Jeff came in one day and pitched the idea of doing a show in iambic pentameter, and I thought that was great. We were going to do it in present day. It was *Hamlet*.

Jeff Reno: What hit me was that there was a murder mystery in *Hamlet*: an uncle killed his brother because he was having an affair with the mom. I thought, "We could do that as a detective story." I had the idea that it would be a kid's homework and he had to do it before he could watch *Moonlighting*.

Ron Osborn: We were doing it as a modern-day episode in which the characters were speaking in iambic pentameter. We hit a conceptual snag and told Glenn. He was the one to suggest that we just do it in full-on Elizabethan period.

Jeff Reno: Ron said, "We should just do *Taming of the Shrew*—it's the show—and not worry so much about the detective part of it." That is how we got to it. It just hit our sensibilities right.

Ron Osborn: Glenn's hand slammed the table, which surprised me, and he said, "That's it!" Even with how long that script is, it was one of the easier ones to write because you had Shakespeare going for you and you could do very obvious jokes, like when Petruchio rides in on a horse and the horse is wearing sunglasses and has the BMW insignia on the blanket.

Jeff Reno: Probably because Ron and I came from comedy and this episode was a little closer to sketch comedy than the rest of the series was, and possibly because we were just having so much fun, we didn't have as much trouble writing this episode as we did other episodes.

Karen Hall: I have to brag on Jeff and Ron because that was almost a first draft that they shot. They had something like three or four days to write it. I always thought what they did was just miraculous. How do you go into your office in three days and write a perfect script in iambic pentameter?

Curtis Armstrong: They were using actual dialogue from Shakespeare's play between David and Maddie. They just transplanted the "What, with my tongue in your tail?"—that exchange. The network tried to cut that because it was too sexual. Glenn went back to them and said, "It's five hundred years old. This is Shakespeare." He eventually won that fight.

Jay Daniel: I don't think Glenn touched it. Jeff and Ron wrote it. Glenn loved it. We filmed it. It was a huge help to have the script.

Cybill Shepherd: When Glenn pitched it to me I said, "Who's gonna play the shrew?" I said it just like a shrew.

Melissa Gelineau: The Shakespeare show is one of my favorites. I love the black-and-white episode, but the Shakespeare episode was brilliant. It was the one episode that did not go through Glenn's typewriter. I think Glenn didn't want to touch it because of all the iambic pentameter, but it was very much Jeff and Ron.

Jeff Reno: Every word of that script is a first draft. It went through no rewrites, no changes. The show started shooting after we had only finished three acts. I remember writing just ahead of the camera.

Jay Daniel: It really was an undertaking. We knew a few weeks earlier that we were going to do the Shakespeare episode, so wardrobe and props, while they were working on the various episodes that led up to it, were also working on the wardrobe for that episode.

Suzanne Gangursky: That was just massive—the entire scale. From my end, it was hiring practically every additional talent in town for wardrobe and hair. It was done on such a massive scale. You felt like you were walking onto a major motion picture set. You didn't feel like you were walking on a weekly TV show set.

Curtis Armstrong: We were working at the Court of Miracles on Universal's back lot, instead of our home studio at Fox. We were doing interiors in one place and exteriors in another, which again felt very much like a feature film rather than a TV show.

Will Mackenzie (Director of "Atomic Shakespeare"): My mother was the Shakespeare professor at Wheaton College. I, for some reason, had mentioned this to Glenn, and he remembered that I'd done a lot of Shakespeare in college. Glenn called and said, "If you're interested, I'm trying to get you out of directing your new series, *The Popcorn Kid*, because we're doing an episode called 'Atomic Shakespeare.'" I read the script and loved it. So they got a guy to replace me for two or three episodes and I just left. I was given a week of prep, which was great. We were able to prep it all on the back lot at Universal. They gave us a humongous budget. They never told me exactly, but I think it was close to $500,000.

Suzanne Gangursky: I would say the average episodes that were being made around then were around $900,000 for a one-hour episode. It probably cost 2 to 2.5 million, I am sure. It was easily double whatever anyone else had spent on an hour of television.

Jeff Reno: I think it was around $3.5 million. I am not sure if that is correct, but I think it was in that area. Which was a ton back then.

Ron Osborn: We were told $3.5 million, at a time when an hour-long show was about a million and a half. When you think of *Hill Street Blues* being made for a million with the cast they had, and we had basically a cast of two, it was crazy.

Neil Mandelberg: As I remember, I could be wrong, but I remember hearing somewhere in the vicinity of $4 million.

Jay Daniel: I hesitate to even throw a number out. I can't tell you. It would be at least double a normal episode—at least.

Glenn Gordon Caron: I don't know. I *do* know it was the most expensive hour of television at that time.

Suzanne Gangursky: The amount of extras, the costume designers, the extra crew that we needed, I think we went into golden time for the crew. When people are getting paid more because they are not getting enough turnaround time between shifts, it gets really expensive because of union rules. Add in sets, customs, cast, crew, it jacked everything up.

Jay Daniel: This was the most difficult show we did in all the seasons from a cost and production standpoint. I look back on it and I don't know how we did it.

Suzanne Gangursky: I am sure there were fears that we were not gonna be able to pull it off.

Jeff Reno: TV series usually have an A unit and a B unit. The A unit shoots the main stuff, and the B unit grabs the stunts or actions and the extra stuff. This episode had two A units. A lot of people assume it was the sets and costumes that made the episode cost so much. I am sure that added to it. It was because there were two A units filming last minute. That affects a lot of things, like location scouting and a ton of stuff that the director can't prep for.

Melissa Gelineau: It was a great education in terms of learning production, but it was also an education on maybe not the best way to do production.

Jeff Reno: That was just because things were being run last minute. That was how it was. We were handing in pages to them as the thing was being shot. [Laughs.]

Will Mackenzie: Brandon Stoddard was a huge fan of *Moonlighting* and ran ABC [Entertainment] at the time. They were winning awards, and they were getting ratings. And that's all they care about. I can't remember how many days we had, but I'm sure we had thirteen or fourteen days. We had a wonderful second unit that Jay directed.

Jay Daniel: We shot the show in eleven days, but included in those days were five days of B unit. The B unit, which I directed, really was another A unit. I shot the big scenes around the fountain. There were quite a few scenes shot there. We *started* on the back lot of Universal, which contained the fountain scenes, on November 21, for an airdate of November 25. At the same time, the A unit, with Will Mackenzie, was shooting at the church with Bruce. We would then shuffle Bruce and Cybill back and forth between the church and the back lot. It got very complicated. It was crazy how we did it. But somehow we pulled it together. We had to shoot cutaways, over the shoulders, and use doubles. When you add the days of B unit to the total of A unit, it really took sixteen days to shoot it.

Neil Mandelberg: That's twice the amount of a normal episode—twice the normal amount of a television episode. Not a *Moonlighting* episode.

Glenn Gordon Caron: We were literally shooting units simultaneously. We had horses, we had a gazillion extras, and all that Elizabethan dress.

Ron Osborn: We didn't shoot any of it on our existing sets, which is also why it was so expensive. We had to rent other sets out. It was also the biggest cast, biggest extras, the biggest use of animals. [Laughs.]

Jay Daniel: Cybill really got into that episode. She was OK. We didn't have any of the issues. It was like she was back. Maybe it was the excitement of doing something different. Even with the elaborate wardrobe she had to deal with.

Cybill Shepherd: Those costumes must have weighed thirty pounds, and they itched. I pretty much faced every challenge in that episode. I've always loved a challenge.

Will Mackenzie: That was one of our delays, that she hated the costume. The first day, she was in the first scene—she was in most everything—we had to wait while they put moleskine into all of her outfits because it was so itchy, and so heavy. The wardrobe people had to line her outfit.

Jeff Reno: In *Taming of the Shrew*, Kate had a real strength; that is why she was considered impossible to wed, because her temper was impenetrable. It was those characteristics that comment on Maddie and Dave. The

"I see thee in me" line is a way to say, "You don't see the similarities on the surface because of the way the characters are played." They each understood that they did have something in common, not only loving each other, but a romantic look at life. Underneath all the huffing and puffing, Dave and Maddie did find that connection.

Neil Mandelberg: Cybill was having a blast on set. She was a wonderful actress when she's having fun. That's what we found out. When she's having fun, she's on. And she loved playing that role. With Bruce, it didn't matter. Just put anything on him. He had no discomfort. He would walk around in short underwear if we asked him to.

Will Mackenzie: My wife is a choreographer and a dancer. She helped with Bruce's "Good Lovin'" scene and gave me some hand gestures for the kids in the chorus. We wanted to hire people who not only could wear the Elizabethan garb, but could do what we call finger choreography.

Jay Daniel: I think Bruce sang "Good Lovin'" live. I think it was to a synced track. He wasn't lip-synching. He was doing it live.

Once again Cybill Shepherd was tied up on the set, much to her displeasure.

Will Mackenzie: Bruce played the harmonica. He played it live. He played in a band, and he had his little group. We decided that he should play the harmonica. So I'm sure we popped in for a single on him or the camera went in on him.

Curtis Armstrong: No, I think he was lip-synching. I don't see how they could have done that live. I can't imagine that.

Jay Daniel: There may have been some work done on the song in post. Everything was going so fast. I don't think we had the time to refine that in post. I don't remember.

Will Mackenzie: We had so little postproduction time that I'm wondering whether he sang that live. I feel like we had a prerecorded version. I know we did the playback. But I feel like he played the harmonica live and sang live. But maybe not.

Curtis Armstrong: All I was doing in "Good Lovin'" was being silly. I remember it was late at night and Bruce had a hideous fever. He had a terrible flu of some kind, and his temperature was like 103 or something. He should have been in a hospital. Instead, that's how he's spending his night after filming all day. That's the one thing that I was sort of dazzled about: that as tired as I was, at least I wasn't sick on top of it.

Jeff Reno: We needed Bruce to have a sidekick in the episode, someone who would marry Bianca. Curtis just worked out perfectly. It was also the parallel of Dipesto being Bianca and Herbert would be romancing her.

Curtis Armstrong: Do I really play any form of Viola at all there? They were still trying to figure out who he was. From a character standpoint, it doesn't really tell you anything. Viola, if anything, when it came to David would be taking everything much more seriously. He did tend to take everything that David said as being gospel. He looked up to him so much.

Allyce Beasley: I was Bianca as played by Ms. Dipesto. It was like doing it in a theater where Ms. Dipesto was cast as Bianca. I was allowed to look pretty and romantic in that episode. In most episodes I didn't get a chance to have that kind of lighting and makeup, as Ms. Dipesto.

Curtis Armstrong: It was like Bruce said later: he referred to *Moonlighting* as a master class in directing because not only was it shot like a feature film, but it was shot like a different style of feature film every week. "Atomic Shakespeare" is a great example of that. To have that kind of freedom, where suddenly you're doing this or you're doing a golden-era musical or you're doing a haunted-house movie—it was just whatever genre helped tell the story. It was written for people who would appreciate that. You couldn't do that now. But at the time you were still doing shows that were done in a style that was recognizable to an audience which was more brought up on classic Hollywood.

Suzanne Gangursky: I have worked on series where one show might be expensive but then you tried to make that up on another episode and go underbudget to even it out. I don't think Glenn ever thought about that. He thought, "We are gonna write what we are gonna write and do what we need to do to make it the best episode."

Will Mackenzie: We knew Bruce and Cybill had never done Shakespeare before and they were terrified, but they're both so talented. Bruce took to that rhyming and iambic pentameter so easily. Curtis Armstrong had done Shakespeare. I think he's the only one of the four principals that had.

Curtis Armstrong: I think I was the only actor—aside from Ken McMillan [Katherina's father, Baptista] and a very well-known character actor, Colm Meaney [*Star Trek: The Next Generation* and *Deep Space Nine*, and *Mystery, Alaska*]—who had actually done Shakespeare. I had played the character from *Taming of the Shrew* that was being sent up in this episode. I felt very comfortable with it.

Bruce Willis and Curtis Armstrong have their first comic pairing in this episode. The partnership will grow in the upcoming seasons.

SCOTT RYAN

Will Mackenzie: Colm Meaney was also in that episode. He played a bit part. He's one of the henchmen in the opening scene and fights Bruce Willis. Colm came in as almost an extra, and he was so good we gave him three or four lines. A few months ago in Los Angeles I ran into him in the theater. I said, "We worked together on a *Moonlighting* thirty years ago." He remembered it, which was great.

Curtis Armstrong: I was still unsure about how long this job was going to last. I'd been offered a Shakespeare play back East. I was trying to figure out whether I was going to be on *Moonlighting* anymore so I could say yes or no to the play. I turned the play down. I had mentioned this to Jay, and he said, "Well, you may get to do your Shakespeare after all." I thought, "Oh, great, now I'm gonna get fired." It turned out it was "Atomic Shakespeare."

Jay Daniel: I am up on a crane, and all of these extras are in Elizabethan garb, and I am going, "Holy moly, what are we doing here?" We had to find Curtis in the crowd and pan in, and then he sees Allyce. Just before we rolled, I said, "Wish me luck, Will." And I was talking to Mackenzie and Shakespeare.

Will Mackenzie: I think the hardest parts were the scenes between Bruce and Cybill. There's a scene of them walking around a table. It was hard getting them comfortable. I'm pretty sure that was the first scene we did. Getting them comfortable with the dialogue and making it as natural as David and Maddie—to me, as a director, that was the hardest part. The thing that I admired—and they were getting along—was that they wanted it to be good. I think we all left there thinking, "This is going to be either the worst show we've ever done or one of the best." They worked hard. They learned their lines. They came in prepared. I don't have any bad memories. I feel like I got out of there before the real shit hit the fan.

Jay Daniel: Cybill's performance as Kate was really quite good. She loved doing that episode, which was nice, because we'd gone through some stuff with her. It was a pleasure. She was ready, willing, and able to

165

go for that episode.

Neil Mandelberg: Roger Bondelli and I were cutting the episode at the same time. So each day we split up the scenes. We showed each other what we did. We weren't really concerned about matching styles in that episode because it had its own style. Glenn would help bring that to each moment if we missed any of those rhythms as we were cutting. It took a long time to cut. After that we didn't do any more of those specialty episodes. The politics started happening.

Sheryl Main: "Atomic Shakespeare" was a very big episode for the editors. We had a lot of coordinating. There was a lot of music. There was a lot of effort on everything. Our sound editors were working like crazy. There were so many components.

Neil Mandelberg: We did sixteen episodes a year, and we still worked for ten and a half months for the season. Half of that extra time is about it being film and not digital. The other half is that to shoot those sixteen episodes, we spent more time than most people spent to shoot twenty-two.

Ron Osborn: The ratings for that episode dropped down to the high teens. I think whenever you say "Shakespeare" to TV viewers . . .

Jay Daniel: The show didn't get big numbers. I can't really tell you why. I don't remember what it was up against. It was the Tuesday before Thanksgiving. It probably had something to do with that. It didn't do terribly. We were ranked number sixteen and got a twenty-nine share. "It's a Wonderful Job" aired on the sixteenth of December, and it was ranked number five. So we were right back up.

Jeff Reno: We were up for a Writers Guild of America Award and an Emmy, but lost both of them. I believe Debra and Carl might have won the WGA for "It's a Wonderful Job." I think we lost the Emmy to a *Cagney & Lacey* episode about alcoholism. We always had to decide to be drama or comedy. That was before the lines were blurred. We always entered in drama because it was an hour and it was shot like one. We were up against alcoholism and cancer. We got nominated, but we didn't win. They didn't know how to give a drama Emmy to something that was so broadly funny. We always suffered from that. We did get a lot of notices and recognition, but no wins.

Will Mackenzie: I won the Directors Guild Award for that episode. My mom and dad flew out for the dinner. Glenn and Jay were there, and I got a big table. I got to thank my mother in front of my peers. I got to thank my family, the crew, and Jay, who helped so much on that episode. I always give the credit to the script. Jeff and Ron really did their homework.

Allyce Beasley: My favorite director on the series was Will Mackenzie. I worked with him a lot on a Dipesto episode, and I just loved him.

Will Mackenzie: Every once in a while I will get a letter from somebody saying, "We saw this really neat, hip episode of *Taming Of the Shrew*."

Curtis Armstrong: It wound up being one of the most famous episodes, mainly because teachers used it as a gateway into teaching Shakespeare to middle and high school students. A lot of people can remember the Shakespeare show probably as an individual show more than any of the others.

Glenn Gordon Caron: I've always adored it. Truthfully, that's probably the script I touched the least. Ron and Jeff just did a fantastic job with it. Will did a fantastic job directing. Again, there were a lot of units Jay directed. Everybody directed some of it. But Will was the mastermind. I don't watch my movies very often, but I just watched it probably a month ago. It's still really funny.

Ron Osborn: Obviously we weren't going to do the ending that Shakespeare did. We wanted to make ours about equals. That was a very conscious choice. As funny and great as that play is—and it's one of my favorites—in the end, Shakespeare is not very woke.

Chapter 10
The Mark the Merrier

Moonlighting began 1987 as big and bright as a full moon. Season 3 was half done and contained one milestone episode after another. "Big Man" and "Shakespeare" were followed by a Christmas episode that won Debra Frank and Carl Sautter a Writers Guild Award. Next was a clip show built around the joke that they rarely do new episodes and rumors of the stars not getting along. This was followed by that season's Dipesto episode. Bruce Willis and Cybill Shepherd both picked up Golden Globe Awards in January. The world awaited their next surprising move. That's when Glenn Caron came up with an idea that would have a lasting impact on how television series handles romantic storylines. To put it in the show's vernacular: Glenn decided that Maddie and Dave would finally boink.

For the first time in its history, *Moonlighting* aired a four-part story arc. It kicked off with "Blonde on Blonde," in which David admits his feelings for Maddie to himself and heads to her house in the middle of the night to tell her the news, only to find a strange man opening the door, thereby shutting the door on the hopes and dreams of viewers. The door was opened by Mark Harmon, about twenty years before the premiere of *NCIS*. This episode is followed by "Sam & Dave," which centers on David meeting Sam (Harmon), who is Maddie's old friend and new love interest. The third episode is "Maddie's Turn to Cry," which has Dave and

Maddie admitting their feelings to each other. The arc wraps with "I Am Curious . . . Maddie," in which, well, they boink.

Glenn Gordon Caron: It was a constant refrain in every newspaper: when are they going to get together? I thought, "How long can we do this dance?"

Jay Daniel: On January 7 we started to shoot "Blonde on Blonde." I directed the episode. It was a really good experience for me. Bruce and Cybill were back to work and in good moods and rested. I finished it in nine days. I finished on schedule because they were on very good behavior and we had a script.

Roger Director: "Atomic Shakespeare" took an enormous amount of time to shoot, and we really got backed up. So we had to start turning out pages. It seemed like each of us writing an act would be helpful. Karen Hall and I had worked at *Hill Street Blues*, and Chic worked at *St. Elsewhere*. We were comfortable enough doing that. So we were able to turn out the scripts more efficiently and more successfully. It didn't mean that it didn't need a lot of work, because someone had to sew it all together. I'm not going to say that I was the genesis of that way of working, but maybe I was.

Jeff Reno: I remember "Blonde on Blonde," which introduced Mark, was really a backed-up situation. Glenn was very rarely in the room for the beating out of the story parts, but all the staff was in there. Kerry Ehrin was writing the episode, and she came in with a lot of great stuff. But we were having the hardest time breaking that episode. I remember having the idea of Maddie meeting the Donna Dixon character in the bathroom and exchanging jackets with her. So David's following the wrong person when she comes out of the bathroom. That solved the episode and allowed Maddie to free herself and end up with Mark.

Ron Osborn: It's almost like a *Vertigo* fascination with a woman, Donna Dixon, who looks like the woman you're really in love with.

Curtis Armstrong: There was a line given to Viola that was so misogynistic that it went to a place that I literally could not do. It felt like that "David Addison misogyny"—which, at the time, I think everyone thought was terribly charming. In "Blonde on Blonde" where they're following Maddie and they wind up in the bar, it's like this is the best day of Viola's life—that he gets to drive around with Mr. Addison and go to a bar! There's some encounter with a woman who is serving them. I can't remember what it is, but it deflates him in front of Dave. Again, if he was trying to impress Mr. Addison, then I could sort of make it work. But this kind of misogynistic insult, when it would come out of Viola, it bothered me. I asked to change the line. Whenever you wanted to change a line, you had to talk to the first [assistant director] and you had to talk to the director, but the director didn't really have a say in it. Then the word would go up to Glenn.

It happened with Bruce too. I remember a time he complained about a line and they had to send it up the flagpole. And the word came back, "No, you're to do the line as it is." So it wasn't just the secondary actors. They had gone up to Glenn and said, "Curtis has a problem with a line." Which is just hysterical to begin with—that I would be complaining—it was ridiculous. So I'm down on the set, and they say, "Glenn's on the phone." I go to the set phone. Glenn says, "What's the problem?" I said, "It's just this line; it's soulless. I can't say it. It just feels mean, and it feels like what David would say. Is there any way that we can make it less offensive?" He said, "You're right." I think they just cut it out, never filmed it. It probably would have been fine to the network. It was a personal thing of my own. But that was the one time where I had become either comfortable enough with who Viola was or I was beginning to get a sense that I had some needs as well.

Jay Daniel: There was a lot of night work on "Blonde on Blonde." It was draining. By the time we finished that episode we were all tired. We built an exterior on Stage 11 at Fox of Maddie's house to do the rain scene of "Since I Fell for You," where David knocks on the door and Sam answers.

Glenn Gordon Caron: I didn't bring Al Jarreau back to record "Since I Fell for You." He had recorded it already, and I just licensed it. I ended up using the song again in *Clean and Sober*, but a different version of it. There are certain songs that work really well in film. You can use them over and over. "Since I Fell for You" is one of those songs.

Chic Eglee: Mark Harmon was a friend of mine from *St. Elsewhere*. We started talking about the astronaut character, and it was like, "What about Mark Harmon?"

Glenn Gordon Caron: A huge tip of the hat to Chic. He knew Mark Harmon and got him for *Moonlighting*. A lot of it was very serendipitous.

Roger Director: Mark was one of the heartthrobs. He was *People* magazine's Sexiest Man Alive, or something like that, at the time. Bruce and Mark were very evenly matched. It was great casting.

Glenn Gordon Caron: The initial idea was inspired by a movie called *Blume in Love*. George Segal discovers that his ex-wife is dating Kris Kristofferson and that he likes him. That idea amused me. I thought, "Maddie ought to date somebody, and he ought to be the ideal man." In 1987, the ideal man, at least in my mind, was that he's an astronaut.

Melissa Gelineau: Mark Harmon was so nice. When he first came, it was sort of like—and this is gonna sound girly—but I remember all of us like, "Oh my God!" He was even better looking in person.

Jay Daniel: We needed somebody that was good-looking enough to go up against Bruce. There were times in future shows where he hung in like a pro when there was stuff going on.

Allan Arkush: Mark Harmon had a cutoff date, which no one considered seriously when we started the arc. He had to be out of there in like two months. Now normally, in a TV series, a month is like ten years.

Roger Director: In this case, the decision had been made to begin focusing on David and Maddie's relationship. I always trusted Glenn. I know people feel that this was a turning point. I think the feeling was at that point, what else were we going to do? We had given so much foreplay. It was either do it or forget it.

Jeff Reno: It kind of heated things to a point where you had to do something. If we would have come out of that season still teasing, all of us just felt like we would just be frustrated as hell. You knew how David felt at this point. He couldn't stand watching this happen.

Jay Daniel: Mark Harmon was so good as Sam that it made you wonder if she wasn't better off with him instead of Dave.

Chic Eglee: Sam absolutely is better for Maddie than Dave. He's heroic. The guy is Mark Harmon! He's a famous college quarterback. Here is this really good-looking astronaut. He's got all kinds of engineering degrees, and then David Addison shows up. David is like, "Do bears, bear? Do bees bee?" But the thing about Maddie is that she is drawn to her opposite.

Jeff Reno: Once Mark Harmon came in and we decided to do a kind of a triangle, it just became the right time because of David's jealousy. I remember sitting in the room with Glenn. We were just talking about it. We always tried to kind of go against expectations. The idea that we were going to tease forever was never our plan. I don't think it was that much of an intellectual decision.

Glenn Gordon Caron: Here's a guy that actually rivaled David in a completely different way. Because whereas David is bombastic, Sam is sort of quiet and more intense.

Allan Arkush: Those four episodes never aired back-to-back. At that point, the show was gigantic. The show was on every magazine cover. While we were shooting, the press would be across the street trying to take pictures. I would get phone calls from reporters wanting to know if there was a fight on the set. A reporter even started to date Cybill's costume designer to get information. It was ugly.

Melissa Gelineau: Fans were getting irritated. If ABC wanted the show, they sort of had no choice but to deal with the delays. After the season of eighteen episodes, we never even came close to that. This is what always boggled me, because it's like, "Come on, network, you kind of know the schedule." Yet every year they would pick it up for twenty-two episodes. Pay or play. They had to pay a lot of money—to certain people—for episodes that weren't done.

Allan Arkush: I tell people that we never made more than fourteen episodes in a season, which meant missing eight airdates. They ask, "What do you mean?" I said, "We were not on the air. We never finished an episode. Eight times."

Ron Osborn: Things were getting very, very tight. Well, they always were, but this was more so than usual, just in terms of never turning out a season of twenty-two episodes.

Allan Arkush: We had an ABC executive who would be there a lot at the beginning because of the cost of the show, and eventually they stopped showing up because there was nothing they could do.

Chic Eglee: I don't particularly remember the specifics of how those four episodes were written. When you get slammed, everybody is writing stuff, and then it all gets stitched together. One of my assignments on that show was to divide up the credits on the episodes so that everybody got the same money. So "written by" is the whole script; then, if you break it up into its component parts, there is "teleplay by" and "story by." You can split each one of those credits. You can have two people on "story by," two people on "teleplay by," because the Writers Guild will never pay anybody less than 50 percent of the amount. So a lot of times people's credits will just be moved around to keep the money right.

Karen Hall: We all just got along great. Chic is hysterical. On the rare occasion that we could, we'd all go out to lunch together and have a good time. We used to joke: if we were one day ahead, that would call for a three-hour lunch.

Ron Osborn: The staff was just on fire. We were breaking the scripts up. I don't know if I should say this, but we just sat in the room and said, "OK, who wants credit on this one? Who wants screenplay and who wants story?" This matters for the residuals. You really just sit there and divide up the credits because everyone was working on it. Jeff and I were even writing scenes separately by this point. We couldn't afford the time to put two people on one scene.

Jeff Reno: We were a band. I'd do a little air guitar. Ron tended to be playing drums, and Roger was on saxophone. It became this thing between the staff like we were jamming. It was backed up all the time. It seemed to become the way that Glenn ran the show. In some ways we thrived doing it that way. In some ways, it was really hard.

Ron Osborn: I remember that being kind of an adrenalized period and a lot of fun. Because we were basically doing a high-wire act and yet it was working. We were working very late in the offices at 20th Century Fox.

Jay Daniel: "Blonde on Blonde" aired February 3 and got a forty share and was ranked number eight. On February 3, Cybill was ill and we shot on the fourth and fifth with just Mark and Bruce. We finished the "Sam & Dave" episode on February 6. Cybill was not 100 percent. On the ninth we started "Maddie's Turn to Cry."

Allan Arkush: They were way behind when I came in to direct "Maddie's Turn to Cry" and "I Am Curious." It was the day that we were shooting the bowling alley chase scene and near the end of the shoot—there was a lot going on because there was a mad dash to finish that episode—the chase scene is why it came up: Cybill had to make an announcement and say that she was pregnant.

Jay Daniel: It was February 17, 1987, that we found out Cybill was pregnant.

Allan Arkush: At this point, the tension between Bruce and Cybill was pretty much unbearable. This is the end of the season, everyone's tired, and everything is building. The press is everywhere. We're doing the scene when they come out at a bowling alley, and it's supposed to be dawn. It was actually late in the afternoon. What you can't see is that off camera, the entire sidewalk is lined with people watching us or taking pictures.

Glenn Gordon Caron: Cybill came to us and said, "I'm pregnant." We were happy for her, but you have to understand Cybill was always coming up with a reason why she couldn't work. [Laughs.] She just pulled an inarguable excuse. It wasn't "My dog ate my homework." It wasn't "There were all red lights all the way to school." This was "I'm pregnant." The whole pregnancy plot grew out of it. It was the mother of necessity. At the same time, Bruce was committing to film *Die Hard*.

Allan Arkush: I was happy that she's gonna have a baby, and then it sort of dawned on everyone that they'd have to rewrite through all this. Bruce had an out date because he was going to do *Die Hard*. Mark Harmon had an out date. Cybill goes to the doctor and finds out that she is pregnant with twins.

Jay Daniel: I wrote in my notes: "Congratulations." I was genuinely happy for Cybill and for her family. I also wrote: "Is this the beginning of the end?" Like any medical leave, it brings up all kinds of production problems, on a series that *already* had all kinds of production problems. Two days later she called in sick. We were all happy for her, of course. But we also knew it was going to really complicate things. On the twenty-sixth, we found out she was having twins. On the twenty-seventh, she was too ill to work.

Cybill Shepherd: I didn't find out I was going to have twins right away. I went to four different ob-gyns. The first one just thought I was further along than I thought I was. Once I knew it was twins, I chose a doctor very carefully.

Melissa Gelineau: I just remember we—the assistants—would have bets on if she was going to show, what time she was gonna show. This is when she was pregnant. Obviously there are a lot of issues with having twins. But it was sort of frustrating because it ties your hands even further, and you certainly can't do your best work when your hands are tied and you don't know what you're filming. You would have crews waiting on the set. And you would have to regroup.

Roger Director: People were pissed off at Cybill, and I wasn't. When I was working with her I made that clear. I didn't hold it against her, and she thanked me for that.

Allan Arkush: When you would film a scene, sometimes Bruce and Cybill would actually not be there for each other. It happened very rarely at first; then it became more often. Then it started to be where even in over-the-shoulder shots they used a double. We were trying to get this episode done. We have to make this airdate. We are filming in the office. We say, "OK, we're fine, Cybill. We don't need you." She had a big trailer; he had a big trailer. When she got to her trailer, she would take her belt off because the belt was really tight. She was pregnant and uncomfortable. She'd take off her costume. She'd lie down in the back, which we called "the back forty." So if she is in the back forty, it'll be forty-five minutes because she had to get the costume back on. Jerry Finnerman says, "There's a hair in the gate. We have to do one more take."

I say, "What? We sent her to the trailer. Stop her!" Skip Beaudine, an AD, takes off like a rocket, and everyone is going, "This is gonna be bad." Skip's gotta get her back. He knocks on her trailer, throws the door open, and she's walking toward the back. Skip goes in and gets down on his knees and says, "Miss Cybill, don't go to the back forty!" She started to laugh, and she put her belt back on, and we got her back for the last take.

Jay Daniel: On March 1, I was driving to work, and I heard on the radio that Bruce Willis broke his collarbone skiing. That same day Cybill got married. I knew we weren't filming. He didn't come back to work till March 9.

Allan Arkush: Cybill had a lot of morning sickness, Bruce breaks his collarbone, and I gotta get Mark Harmon out because now his hard out is getting seriously close. I had to figure out how to stage a whole fight scene with the three of them in the parking garage. And remember, this is not a script that I'm sitting with for a month. Usually I'd have no more than a couple hours to figure out how to do it and lay out my shots. I had them on separate days and had to work with doubles. I had to walk through the whole thing, figure out where I needed them really, and where I had to have at least two of them at the same time for the shortest period of time. And that's how that fight scene was done.

Jay Daniel: Mark was such a pro. He would come over to me and say, "You do this every week?" [Laughs.] We had to move some scheduling around so that we could get him out by his drop date. I think we got him out on the last day.

Neil Mandelberg: It was a little more challenging when we saw the dailies and we only had part of the fight scene in the garage. We were so busy cutting other things. For me it was like, "OK, that's incomplete. I'll come back when I have the rest of it."

Jay Daniel: We went back to that garage four times to get that one scene. We would shoot over one actor's shoulder to get the close-up and then a week or two later do the reverse. It was amazingly difficult. When you watch it, you aren't aware of it. I ended up shooting some second unit for that scene. We actually storyboarded it to make sure we got the coverage that we needed. It was . . . a *challenge*. [Laughs.]

1. Willis is there, but Harmon is not. 2. Harmon is there, but Willis is hurt with a broken collarbone. 3. Cybill Shepherd couldn't run, so that is a double. 4. Bruce and Cybill are together for the two-shot, but Mark Harmon is gone.

Neil Mandelberg: Just a simple thing like Cybill would move her head when she talked and her hair would be moving. Well, when you jumped into an "over behind her" shot and the double is standing perfectly still, it affected the patterns that we wanted to use. I don't care how good an actor is, if you're talking to a double, it's different than if you're talking to the actual actor. But the biggest problem in shooting two different times will be the framing and the light.

Jay Daniel: Cybill is here shooting her scene in the garage; Bruce is shooting a scene that doesn't involve her.

Allan Arkush: The scene when Mark Harmon goes to Bruce's apartment and confronts him in the bedroom, we rehearsed the scene and Bruce said, "Can you have Glenn come down here?" So Glenn comes down to the set. Bruce says, "I shouldn't say anything." I said, "But you have to say *something*." Bruce says, "I think I can say it all with my body." It made the scene twice as good as it could be. It's a wonderful thing, and that was a great choice.

Jay Daniel: We finished Mark Harmon on March 11. We had to go on hiatus after that because Bruce couldn't work because he was in too much pain from his injury. Bruce and Cybill came back on March 16.

Glenn Gordon Caron: Cybill was pregnant. It was clear that we were gonna have to incorporate that pregnancy in the show in some way. These characters had been together for two and a half years. Them having sex kind of came out of a confluence of all of that.

Karen Hall: I was not in favor of it. I thought, "That'll be the death of the show." But it wasn't my show. I think that the dramatic tension was the two of them. Once they're just a normal couple, it just wasn't there.

Sheryl Main: They have that connection. They both brought something out in the other that wasn't there, but never kind of revealed before. I liked it better when they weren't romantically involved.

Melissa Gelineau: I just remember my gut, "This is not good." Because then where do you go? Then it becomes something different.

Ron Osborn: That sexual tension was what made everyone tune in. The minute you consummate it, it becomes something else.

Jay Daniel: Glenn's point was that you can't carry on this unrequited thing. They had kissed while playing other characters; it had to happen at some point. I had some doubts, but I got the point that how they dealt with them getting together could be very interesting.

Glenn Gordon Caron: It was something people wanted. And in my egomania, I thought, "I can do this; I can make this work." I don't think these people are any less interesting if they have a child or if they get pregnant. I think they're more interesting. I never got to prove that because of what happened later on.

BEFORE "WHAT HAPPENED later on" could happen and before Maddie's pregnancy could play out on screen, they still had to film THE SCENE. Directed by Allan Arkush, the final ten minutes of "I Am Curious . . . Maddie" contains one of the most famous love scenes of all time. Viewers knew it would happen that evening, but not how. Putting aside the plot points of the four-parter, and the fact that part four didn't even air until twenty-eight days *after* part three, the real drama was how to stage a raucous sex scene while Cybill was pregnant with twins and Bruce was recovering from a broken collarbone. Sam leaves without saying goodbye to Maddie. Dave, waiting for her to return home, crawls into her bed and falls asleep. Maddie arrives and delivers a monologue to whom she thinks is Sam about wanting one more night with him. She undresses and then discovers it's David, not Sam, in bed. Dave and Maddie fight. He calls her a bitch. She calls him a bastard. She slaps him. She slaps again. It's as if those slaps are the first smacks on the drums of the Ronettes' 1963 classic "Be My Baby." Those slaps echo in the drums as the song kicks up. They kiss and tear up Maddie's place with physical and destructive lovemaking. Even the script caused a little drama among the writers.

Karen Hall: I have mellowed a lot in my old age, but I absolutely despised the scene where David gets in her bed and she thinks it's Sam. I just felt like, "You're getting intimate with someone under completely false pretenses." Maybe people would agree more in the #MeToo era, but it just seemed very wrong to me.

Jeff Reno: In my draft, I had David asleep on the couch downstairs when Maddie comes in and talks to him. Glenn had not really been rewriting Ron and I very much at all. He would do that early-morning thing and take a pass at a script sometimes, but our stuff he didn't really

The writers argued about whether David should be waiting in bed, but the final decision was made by Glenn Gordon Caron.

play with. But he did take that scene and put David up in her bed and had David being a little more aggressive than I had written.

Karen Hall: Yeah, that was Glenn's decision. I remember I got into it with him over it. I remember that it really upset me then. She didn't know who she was in bed with. And David was OK with her not knowing.

Allan Arkush (Director of "I Am Curious"): I thought the scene in the bed was not going to work. I had a hard time believing that she wouldn't know it was David.

Jay Daniel: Is it a hard buy that Bruce is in bed there? Maybe for a half a second, but then they explain it all. That starts an argument that leads them to not being able to keep their hands off each other.

Jeff Reno: Having him down on the couch waiting for her wasn't quite the same as being upstairs. In my version, he did let her do the speech. He did let her get all that out. And then they sort of made their way to the bed. But Glenn just put them right there. I think a lot of people like it, but it was an ounce too strong for me. I still think it worked. It was a great moment.

Allan Arkush: There was a ton of tension on the set at that point. We were under pressure to finish this thing. Bruce's collarbone was broken, and she can only work a couple hours. I agreed that having them in the bedroom was problematic. In terms of the intimacy of it, it seemed wrong. And in terms of how long that scene goes on before she figures out that it's not Mark Harmon. And the actual blocking of the scene. That was where the problem was. But at that point, I'm just going along.

Jeff Reno: I had written a lot of the banter and the surprise of it not being Mark Harmon. I think I wrote "bitch" and "bastard." But Glenn put him upstairs. Because I had done the central part of it and he had done some work on this one, he and I shared "teleplay by," and the other guys shared "story."

Karen Hall: Yeah, and I remember that either Jeff or Ron was on my side. Maybe it's a female thing, but I feel like that would be a real violation of trust, if nothing else. I remember I made my case to Glenn as strong as I was capable of making it, but he really wanted to do it that way. And you know, when you're the showrunner—because since then I've been the showrunner—your neck is in the noose, and if you are gonna die, you want to die on your own decision.

Roger Director: If Glenn wanted to do this, that was the way it was going to get done. When you're executive producer of the show, you've got to make decisions. I didn't have too many misgivings about it. I probably in the back of my mind thought, "Well, I don't know exactly where we're going from here."

Allan Arkush: *TV Guide* was there that day. And so everyone was on their best behavior and laughing and having a good time. You don't want to rock the boat too much on that day. We got all the bedroom stuff done.

Jay Daniel: At the time, I thought it was a great scene. I was aware that there was a lot of discussion of how it was going to happen. I didn't have any problem with it. I thought it was clever and unexpected in the way it was done.

Allan Arkush: Where my real troubles began was once they went out the bedroom door, because I don't have the pages, but I know they're going down those spiral stairs. I find out, at the end of the day when I get the pages, that they *will* have dialogue as they go down the stairs. It's too late to ask for a crane, because that would be the right way to film it. I needed a minute to think about it. We start to do the rehearsal. The gloves are off for what I'm going to tell you. She's in a terrible mood. She does not want to go up and down the stairs. She's really feeling pregnant. She says, "I'm only going down those stairs once. And that's when we're going to film it." So I ask, "Will you do one rehearsal?" She says "No, you play me." So I walk up the stairs with Bruce and we kind of look at each other. Bruce and I are standing at the top of the stairs. He turns to me and says, "Put your helmet on. This can be a rough game." Bruce and I go down the stairs and she is saying the lines from a chair while I'm walking with Bruce. She yells, "Stop! Face him! That's where I'm gonna stop and say this line, and then we'll keep going."

She asks, "How are you gonna shoot it?" Jerry Finnerman's voice rings out from across the stage. "Cookie, it looks great from back here in one big, beautiful wide shot, and then we'll move in at the end when you stop." And that's what's in the show. There's no coverage as they come down the stairs. It stays as a big, gorgeous wide shot, which is exactly what's needed because it lets the pace and the energy stay. Because you've been in that little bedroom. And then comes the slapping.

Chic Eglee: Every romantic comedy always logically ends at the altar. This was a deconstructed romantic comedy. Screwball comedies proceed from that basic misunderstanding of two people who barely like each other, but they make some wrong assumption based on some miscommunication and then spend the whole story being neurotically mad at the person they secretly like, and it always ends with the altar. This was also infused with a whole lot of real life. At the end of the day, you'd begin to wonder if Dave and Maddie actually even liked each other. Which, of course, in real life, they really didn't.

Allan Arkush: Today you couldn't slap. You really shouldn't have been able to slap then. I always thought that was too far.

Roger Director: It was sort of an explosive sex encounter. I wish it had been more erotic, because certain allowances had to be made to shoot that scene because of the fact that Cybill was pregnant.

Neil Mandelberg: We didn't expect much because we were on national network television at nine o'clock at night. It was really a matter of how do you make it *feel*. People were waiting for this for so damn long.

Glenn Gordon Caron: Bruce couldn't put any weight on his shoulder. So now we had to come up with another way of filming their sex scene.

Allan Arkush: They are supposed to roll around on the floor, and neither of them could do that because of the injury and the pregnancy. So I spent hours shooting doubles, doing it from every possible angle and blocking it without them. We had to shoot them on the floor kissing. Who's going to be on top? Credit where credit is due. Jerry says, "Get me a large sheet of plywood."

Jay Daniel: All the close-ups of Bruce were him on a four-by-eight piece of plywood that he leaned on. The rest were all doubles. It's the biggest moment ever. They finally do it and it's a photo double. [Laughs.]

Allan Arkush: Jerry puts a rug over the wood, and he has it lean just a little bit back. They put stands on it to hold it in place. He said, "We're going to put the camera straight out here, and it's going to look like we're filming you from above." It was the perfect solution. I said, "You'll do the scene standing on your feet. And then I want you to roll around and we'll put the bed standing up. And you'll roll into the bed." This is genius. I said to Jerry, "The only thing is that their hair is not going to be the part of gravity." Jerry said, "Don't answer those letters."

Glenn Gordon Caron: It was purely utilitarian and served two things. It keeps her comfortable, but also, when you lay human beings down their physiology changes. You don't have that if they are standing up.

Cybill Shepherd: We weren't lying down, but you can't tell. Jerry didn't want our faces to sag, especially my face because I was pregnant and I am older than Bruce.

Jeff Reno: Glenn picked the song "Be My Baby." He might have picked it before we wrote the scene. I think I wrote the song choice in the script.

Sheryl Main: "Be My Baby" was genius. How perfect was that song? It's become kind of iconic. Glenn had a real knack for finding the right music.

Glenn Gordon Caron: In the case of "Be My Baby," we called and asked. Phil Spector literally brought over the master himself because they didn't want it out of sight. So we used it and gave it right back. Back then it was unusual for people to use contemporary music on television.

Allan Arkush: I went to look at dailies. I go to the room, and Glenn and everyone are in there. He said, "This is your scene. Come and sit down." I had not seen any of the footage. The slaps come and "Be My Baby" kicks in. Glenn has it rocked way up. I got chills. He goes, "What do you think?" I said, "Fuck, I don't know who directed that, but it sure works." It never again played as well as it did that day.

Suzanne Gangursky: There was always a speculation that this would kill the series. I didn't know if it would, but to keep avoiding it didn't seem real to me. It's a tricky thing.

Sheryl Main: I liked the sexual tension between them. I thought it added a very interesting element to their relationship. So once that happened, they kind of took that away. And for me, I would have preferred that they not. But I liked the way that Glenn did it. I know he thought about it quite a bit.

Roger Director: It had to do with a lot of different things. If anyone had said to Glenn, "Excuse me, here's an alternative to that," he would have listened to it. How much more could we have milked that?

Chic Eglee: It was the death of the show to let them finally get together. Yet, on the other hand, one of the games you have to play, because the romance was so foregrounded, it's really what the meat and potatoes of the show was. If they don't get together, and you try to keep them apart, you start hearing the typing. It's a whole lot of neurotic behavior to keep them separate. So there's a certain inevitability to it, but once it happens, well, then that's it.

Allan Arkush: I was all for it. I thought it was a good idea. And it seemed inevitable. It totally fit in with my concept of romantic comedy. I never really thought about the ramifications of it. I didn't realize that the making of those four episodes would be as fraught as it was.

It appears to be all smiles in bed, but in reality they are standing on a piece of plywood rather than lying down, thanks to the ingenuity of Jerry Finnerman.

Ron Osborn: I thought we had a wonderful four-episode arc. But then real life intruded in Cybill not being able to work because of a pregnancy. Then suddenly we had a show without our leads.

Neil Mandelberg: For me, it shouldn't have happened. We all took our votes constantly, and Glenn made the decision with the network. But I was afraid that things would change on the show as soon as that occurred. And they did.

Melissa Gelineau: It was too soon. Absolutely. No question.

Jeff Reno: The problem was the audience loved David and Maddie so much. I think people assume that once they slept together, that's the reason the show started going downhill. I don't think that's it at all. Ron, Glenn, and I had some really good ideas about what we were going to do with them after they slept together and how we could maintain the show at the same level, but Cybill got pregnant.

Allan Arkush: On the night the episode aired, I ran home, grabbed my wife, and we went to a local pizza restaurant. It's seven thirty and our waiter comes over and we say, "We really want to eat quickly." The waiter says, "Because you want to get home in time to see *Moonlighting*. So does that table, that table, and that table." That's when you know you've hit it big.

Jay Daniel: It aired on March 31. We got a forty-nine share and were ranked number three. That was the highest-rated show we ever did. The following episode was ranked number four, and it was a rerun.

Neil Mandelberg: The first three years of the show were very special. And the next two years became very challenging.

Allan Arkush: And I got an Emmy nomination for surviving that episode.

Chapter 11
Some Like It Not

From the moment Maddie Hayes walked into the detective agency and stood in David Addison's office, *Moonlighting* viewers wanted only one thing. They wanted these two attractive and combustible personalities to get it on. They wanted it and they didn't want to wait for it. The way that television normally works is simple. Don't give audiences what they want and they will continue to watch. Over the years, I have coined this type of television as "punishment television." A writer creates characters you love and then punishes you for caring about them by keeping them apart or keeping them miserable. Think Luke and Lorelai on *Gilmore Girls* or Matthew and Mary on *Downton Abbey*. Glenn and his team of writers never followed the conventional rules of television. In fact, their plan was to use those conventions to make viewers lean to one side so that they could zap them from the opposite side. After making viewers wait just thirty-eight episodes for the big moment, Glenn pulled the trigger and had his characters consummate their relationship. That is a drop in the bucket compared with the way most series handle that kind of sexual tension. Whether that was truly a good idea or not will never really be known. Pundits will say the verdict is already in, but the truth is there isn't enough information to make the call. Fact: Dave and Maddie slept together. Fact: the ratings slowly dropped from that point on. But that doesn't mean you can directly link those two facts. As in any accurate scientific experiment, one must account for all factors before drawing a conclusion. For a study to have a valid conclusion, the theories have to be tested in a controlled experiment. There was nothing controlled about the set of *Moonlighting*.

The confluence of events that occurred "the morning after" couldn't have been calculated by Albert Einstein, let alone television journalists back when entertainment wasn't covered like it is now. There wasn't twenty-four-hour-a-day, in-depth coverage, tweeting, or blogging about popular television shows. What *actually* happened wasn't covered at all. Journalists just wrote that now that the characters had sex, the show lost its mojo. The *Moonlighting* Curse was born. It's actually listed in the Urban Dictionary as "When the will-they-won't-they couple on a TV show finally gets together . . . and it ruins the show." Part of the problem with this theory is that even the participants don't really remember what happened. So many of the people whom I interviewed couldn't accurately say how Season 3 ended and how Season 4 began. It was a blur. To plot out all the elements, I had to turn my office into a scene from *The Wire*, with multiple colored strings stretched from episode titles to calendars to interview fragments as I pieced together bits of information to make sense of it all. After putting together the pieces from Jay Daniel's journal and interviews with Roger Director, who ran the series in Season 4, Chic Eglee, who wrote most of the episodes in that period, and Allan Arkush, who became the on-staff director, I have been able to re-create what happened from April 1987 through January 1988. I am the first person to solve this. (Take that, Viola and your Anselmo case.) Here are my findings: Wocka-Wocka! Zing. Boing. Lalalalala? Kersplat. Kerplooey!

Glenn Gordon Caron: There is no *Moonlighting* Curse. It was a confluence of events that no one could have foreseen. Cybill was pregnant. Bruce hurt his shoulder. And then because Cybill couldn't work for a certain number of months, he took the opportunity to go off and make *Die Hard*.

Jeff Reno: Here's what happened: Glenn went off to direct the Michael Keaton movie *Clean and Sober*. He asked Ron and I to run the show. But Ron and I started to get movie offers. The first one was when Bruce asked us to write *Hudson Hawk*. He had a one-liner idea for that movie. The movie is not ours anymore, so I can't take any credit for it.

Ron Osborn: After the Shakespeare episode, we thought we might want to explore greener pastures. Glenn made too good an offer, so we had to stay. He said we could write the first episode and last episode of Season 4 and just help break stories. Bruce at the time had an idea he wanted written, and Glenn would throw us that gig. We'd still be staying one more season—the season where Cybill wasn't on the show. I didn't watch. I can't even remember it.

Roger Director: Glenn came to me and asked if I would be the showrunner. He wrote the first episode that year, which was *The Honeymooners* episode, and then he pretty much was gone.

Ron Osborn: Glenn assembled the staff and said, "We've got a problem. Cybill is X months along, and we're going to lose her in about eight weeks." So we literally had to scramble and come up with a story arc where we could film the scenes independent of whatever episodes we're going to have that season. So we came up with her going back to Chicago to visit her parents.

Jay Daniel: It was indicative of what was going on. With Cybill pregnant, we just couldn't get much work done on a given day. It was frustrating to go so slowly for everyone to try to get an episode done.

Allan Arkush: Oh boy, you're really asking me to unpack a lot of baggage here. Now at this point, even though I was making a ton of money for this, my wife actually said to me, "You really should stop doing this show, because it's just too much strain."

STRAIN BE DAMNED, no one had much time to stop and think about what needed to be done. It just had to be done. Cybill was cleared to work a few hours a day before she was going to be put on bed rest. Despite the fact that Season 3 had *just* wrapped, the decision was made to film one more episode, which they would hold over to be the Season

4 premiere. So after filming a dance sequence, a Shakespeare episode, and the most complex story arc of the series, the *Moonlighting* team would now be filming Season 4 without a break. Glenn decided to write that episode and came up with the idea that Maddie would head to Chicago. This way Cybill could film scenes with her parents, played by Robert Webber and Eva Marie Saint, while Bruce was off filming *Die Hard*. How many days did Glenn have to ponder this idea? Three days! Season 3's finale wrapped on April 10, 1987, and filming on Season 4's premiere, "A Trip to the Moon," started on April 13. This quick decision would have a lasting effect on the series.

In the midst of prepping for his directorial debut, *Clean and Sober*, Glenn wrote "A Trip to the Moon" to set up the separation story arc for Season 4. So before everyone could go off and work on their side projects, they had to channel *The Honeymooners*. Though filming was in April, the episode wouldn't air until September. Glenn wasn't about to use all these excuses to just do a standard episode. He wanted to do another theme episode. They spoofed a *Honeymooners* episode, shot like an old sitcom, with three cameras and in black and white. David Addison played Ralph Kramden, Maddie Hayes played Alice, Richard Addison (the late Charles Rocket) was Norton, and Ms. Dipesto was Trixie. *The Honeymooners* skit begins and ends the episode. In between Dave and Maddie wonder if getting together was a good idea, and then they dance in a laundromat. They discuss their doubts with guest stars in separate scenes. The great rhythm-and-blues artist Ray Charles sings about it in a scene with Bruce Willis, while Cybill Shepherd has a therapy session with TV psychologist Dr. Joyce Brothers. But even with all the fun, the episode still ends by separating the hottest couple on television as Maddie boards a plane and heads to Chicago.

Allan Arkush: Jerry Finnerman and I studied a lot of *Honeymooners* episodes. When Cybill started watching them, she hated them. It's interesting, because she was not wrong. You can't show *The Honeymooners* to millennials. This guy is threatening to hit his wife all the time. This is like the most sexist show. Alice does get the final word, but it's the fifties at its worst. Bruce adored it, loved it. Actually, when you watch the episode, Cybill is fantastic in it. Allyce and Charles Rocket were good.

Bruce worshiped Ralph Kramden too much. We should have taken a couple of days and worked it all out. But we shot it all in one day.

Cybill Shepherd: I will always miss Charlie Rocket. I am so sorry how his life ended. That was devastating when he killed himself. It was horrifying. Charlie was very funny. They couldn't have cast anyone funnier or better for the part.

Jay Daniel: We shot *The Honeymooners* on April 20 in one day on Stage 10. It was a separate shoot. We used multiple cameras so that it looked like *The Honeymooners*. It's a much easier way to shoot stuff.

Allyce Beasley: I was pregnant in that episode. I had a big ol' bathrobe on. I was a *Honeymooners* fan. I loved getting to do that. When you are working twelve to fourteen hours a day, it goes so fast. You don't have time to appreciate things like that.

Debra Frank: Allyce and I were pregnant at the same time. She was a little further along. I have a picture of us putting our tummies together. It's "Everybody got pregnant at the same time, and everything fell apart." I didn't want to deal with the stress, and left the show at that point.

PHOTO COURTESY OF DEBRA FRANK

Neil Mandelberg: I don't remember cutting this episode during the summer. I probably cut it when we returned after the summer break. I don't remember working any of the short summers I had. I remember getting a month or so off every year; otherwise I would have died. I would think that we had the apprentices prepping the film so that they could screen it and see what they had.

Jeff Reno: There was a scene that was cut for time in the Shakespeare episode that we couldn't film. It's kind of a *Honeymooners* version of Petruchio and Kate—after they've married and moved in together. I don't know if that's where Glenn ended up getting the idea for that episode.

Sheryl Main: I don't ever remember going on hiatus. I was always working on the show, because I worked in the executive office. I don't recall having a break.

Allan Arkush: I think what was happening is that we were all shell-shocked. We had been through a whole season already. So even though we had done only fourteen episodes, we still did the work of a twenty-two-episode season.

Jay Daniel: God, no, I didn't get a break. I mean we had our wrap party for Season 3 on April 23, and on the twenty-fourth we shot with Dr. Joyce Brothers for the Season 4 premiere.

Allan Arkush: That scene is an interesting technical problem, because Cybill had to look at herself in the mirror. That's where we put Dr. Joyce Brothers, and it was really hard for her to see herself acting. I remember we had to cover the mirror. And then the Ray Charles day! See, that's the thing. I can say this was really stressful, right? But when it's a Ray Charles day, you know? And the Raelettes are there? And the whole orchestra is there? Come on!

Curtis Armstrong: Ray Charles—that was a big one. I didn't have a scene with him. All of his scenes were with David, but I actually came in the day he was there because I wanted to meet him.

Ray Charles serenades David Addison (but doesn't lip-synch).

Allan Arkush: We found out that Ray did not lip-synch. He would have the orchestra and the Raelettes perform, and we recorded them, and that would be in an ear wig. Then he would do his piano and vocals live to that track. So in the room you didn't hear anything but Ray singing unless you had the ear wigs in, which I did. They brought Ray in, and he sat down on the piano bench. He had a silver cup right next to him, and the icy silver cup was full of gin. Now, his manager would water it down, but basically he drank gin all day. Bruce never left the set. We're sitting there at one point, and Bruce and I are bursting. Bruce says, "Ray, I gotta say, growing up with my mom, she was a single mother, and every night she played Ray Charles's *Modern Sounds in Country and Western Music.* 'You Don't Know Me' is like her favorite all-time song." All of a sudden, Ray starts playing the chords for "You Don't Know Me." It's like one of those shots from an old movie where everybody just stops and there's no movement but Ray Charles singing "You Don't Know Me" to Bruce Willis on the set. When it's done, the place bursts into applause, and Bruce leans to me and says, "Not bad for two guys from Jersey."

Jay Daniel: Allan had a demeanor that worked. He was a good director. There were a lot of directors who had done the show who just didn't want to direct it anymore. They couldn't count on a start date or a finish date. It was just too much disruption to their lives. The episode might be scheduled to go eight days, but it might go twelve, and you can't get another job. A lot of directors just thought it was too difficult.

Roger Director: Allan is a personal favorite of mine because he always had this slightly wild look in his eye, and was up for anything.

Allan Arkush: Jay called my agent and wanted to book me for what they knew was going to be the big series of episodes. My agent said, "He's probably going to get a pilot." So they came back with this offer that they would have me for all of pilot season and they would pay the full freight of my salary with normal rate plus a boost, and for every episode that was rerun I would get double the rate.

Jay Daniel: Allan was willing to do it and an excellent director. He got along with the cast. We just went with him. Glenn agreed that it was a good choice.

Allan Arkush: So I was there the whole time. That's why I just kept directing. I did the next season as well, because we couldn't stop because she was pregnant. So we shot the scene in the laundromat. We shot it day for night. It was so hot in that laundromat, with all the windows blacked in. At that point the bloom was totally off the rose. Those were not my favorite scenes to shoot. But we got through that, and we said goodbye to Bruce, and then we just kept shooting with Cybill.

Cybill Shepherd: Glenn didn't want Bruce to do *Die Hard* for some reason. But since my pregnancy took me out of *Moonlighting* for three months, Glenn couldn't really stop Bruce doing *Die Hard*, which was a very great thing for Bruce. And Bruce went on to do very great performances in movies, and that is hard to admit, something like that, especially with the relationship that Dave and Maddie had. I wish I had the option to do action films too.

Jay Daniel: Bruce's last day was April 22. We finished their dance at the laundromat. He was supposed to have finished on April 10. He left to go make *Die Hard*. I was working on *Clean and Sober* as the coproducer of that movie. While Glenn was writing and casting the movie, I was spending most of that time doing *Moonlighting*. After we finished "A Trip to the Moon," I went with him to scout locations in Philadelphia for *Clean and Sober*, from May 6 to May 11.

Glenn Gordon Caron: ABC was changing hands. It had been sold to Cap Cities. The gentlemen I'd been dealing with, Tony Thomopoulos and Lou Ehrlich, weren't there anymore. Suddenly there were these new people running it. Brandon Stoddard was the new guy. Brandon had done a lot of fantastic things I really admired. He basically was sort of the father of the miniseries, but he didn't like me. He just didn't, and he wasn't shy about it. Mostly he felt that I was undisciplined. He wouldn't have been wrong about that, by the way. Certainly, our process was undisciplined, and so he didn't have much sympathy for "Oh, wow, your leading lady is pregnant and unable to work? Your leading man has an opportunity to be in a movie and you're going to go direct a movie?"

Allan Arkush: Then we had shut down for two weeks and started up again. I think the writers were just trying to figure out how they were going to meld this stuff.

SO OVER THE month of June, while Bruce Willis was running around with no shoes on at Nakatomi Plaza, Cybill shot her scenes, which would be edited into the first eight episodes of Season 4. There was no time to think about the decision or consider a better plan. The first episode was filmed. It couldn't be changed. These plot points—Maddie's trip to Chicago and her relationship with her parents—were used over the next eight episodes, which aired over the next nine months. (No pun intended.) Roger Director was now the showrunner. He was in charge of the impossible task of producing a romantic comedy without its two leads. Over the month of May they worked out the Chicago storyline. When Gillian Anderson got pregnant during *The X-Files*, they didn't film her calling Mulder on the phone and then edit her into a bunch of episodes. They just had her be abducted by aliens. That idea might have been more appealing to *Moonlighting* viewers. The problem with the Chicago idea was that—yes, both Cybill and Bruce appeared in the episodes, but viewers wondered why they weren't together in scenes. In 1987, television viewers were not as savvy or informed as they are now. They didn't know those scenes were filmed from two to six months apart. It appeared that the writers were doing the ultimate in "punishment television." What viewers didn't know was that it was punishment for the writers as well.

Roger Director: Those episodes were different *Moonlighting* episodes. They won't necessarily be on anyone's list of memorable episodes, but I'm fairly proud of a lot of the things in those episodes.

Ron Osborn: We were writing a specific amount of pages. We knew how many pages we could shoot because of doctor's orders, and you couldn't go against that. Then, when we started putting the stories together for that season, we literally had to go, "OK, well, here's where we can put that phone call, and here's where we can show the parents."

Allan Arkush: That's when I met Robert Webber and Eva Marie Saint. The first scene I did—because they were still building their house on stage—was Eva and Cybill in a car coming from the airport. Normally we would go out and take the BMW and mount cameras on it and drive around and shoot. At a certain point, they didn't want to do that anymore. So we did rear-screen projection, which is the old way of running a film behind them. This is just like *North by Northwest*. Here is Eva Marie using rear projection. All I'm thinking of is that for these two hours I'm just like Alfred Hitchcock!

Cybill Shepherd: Eva Marie Saint played my mother. Jerry Finnerman put so much diffusion on the camera for her. I think she would have been nominated for best guest star if you could have seen her more clearly, but that was the old-fashioned way of filming. The older you get, the more they put on the lens to soften everything up.

Curtis Armstrong: When you're talking about people who are sort of heroes, people who were on the show, I would say Eva Marie Saint was a big one, even though I didn't have any scenes with her. But I was on the set with her, and that was sufficient.

Roger Director: Robert Webber is one of the all-time great actors. There is a scene between Cybill and Robert with just the two of them at night. He says, "What's on your mind? What's bothering you? I'm selfish. I want to know. I want to help you." I think that is one of the greatest scenes. I watched them do that scene. I just marveled at it. It was just a beautiful, wonderful scene that shows those two actors doing wonderful things. Glenn wrote that scene.

Robert Webber and Cybill Shepherd shine in this touching scene.

Glenn Gordon Caron: I felt this enormous obligation to write something worthy of Robert Webber. I feel that way about every actor I work with, but I especially felt that with him.

Karen Hall: Yeah, I'm pretty sure Glenn wrote that scene. Anything that was just a big, crucial scene, he wrote them because they were his characters.

Allan Arkush: Robert Webber survived for a long time because he knew how to work on set, and he's talented. When we were shooting Cybill's footage, she was pushing more and more to be in charge, because Glenn was gone. So she was dictating what we shot and when, and it got kind of really ugly that way. If we were going to do one way and cover Robert first she would say, "No, no, cover me first." Robert would say, "That's a good idea. Let's cover Cybill first." I was kind of being pushed around a lot.

Roger Director: Robert Webber is so great, and to watch the things that he does, it deepens our understanding of Maddie as a person and her relationship with her father. The scene where Eva and Robert are in bed and she says, "Get up and help me flip the mattress"—that was Chic's idea, to move the mattress around. And they get into a tussle over the sheets. I would watch them do anything.

Jay Daniel: Roger really bellied up when he had to. He and the guys tried really hard and did a really good job. They are doing half a *Moonlighting*. They had a real difficult task. I don't think anyone could have done a better job than Roger. He captured David Addison's spirit.

Karen Hall: I just felt like the show could not work with Maddie pregnant and them together. So I just was not interested in writing it anymore. I had some tense conversations with Glenn, who I adore. We get along fine now. At the time, he wanted me to stay. My sister [Barbara Hall] also had the same agent as Glenn. So she was recommended for a writing job. She would call me every night, and I would tell her why she didn't want that job. She wouldn't listen to me. She lasted about six weeks on *Moonlighting*, I think, because it was just pretty much insanity after that.

Roger Director: It was a tall order, and it had to be carefully crafted. Chic and I had some experience in doing these kinds of woven story threads working at MGM. So I think we at least had some preparation for cutting back and forth between the different story elements. There was going to be the beat where Maddie shows up, the parents wonder what's going on, they throw a party for her, she meets a doctor, and she discovers that she's pregnant.

Ron Osborn: I think a settled David Addison will not be David Addison. I don't think he would be happy. And I don't think that she would be happy. These kinds of things work best when they remain in a certain world. The minute you ground them, it becomes something else. We want to keep that romance in our minds. We want to keep that relationship forever as one of the great love stories because we never see what happens.

Jay Daniel: Bruce came back July 27, and we started filming "Come Back Little Shiksa." That is quite late to start shooting a season, and that put us well behind the eight ball.

Allan Arkush: In the world of Jews, Cybill is the definitive Shiksa Goddess. In the Philip Roth world, that would be his ideal. So we get John Goodman as a guest star in that episode, and Bruce is thrilled because they are really good friends. So that is like a big thing. That's when they decided to do the Claymation scene.

Jeff Reno (Writer of "Come Back Little Shiksa"): Ron and I weren't quite as involved. We ultimately were there. But we were a little bit torn. We were kind of moving in a lot of directions at once. It was a little bit of a different kind of season—like incredibly different. Dialoguewise, Glenn, Ron, and I had done such a huge amount of the Maddie/David stuff. We were doing less, and Glenn wasn't there to do it, and then the two weren't in scenes together. But in "Come Back Little Shiksa," I loved doing the Claymation scene. We were trying to do a Cinderella story, and I think we lost a little bit of it along the way.

Allan Arkush: In that episode, Dave is upset that Maddie left, and he destroys the BMW. Obviously we're not going to take that BMW and wreck it. They had to find one just like it. Bruce gets this idea that he wants to play "Manic Depression" by Hendrix on the radio. I think that's a fantastic idea. The next day he gets word back that the network doesn't want to pay for it. Bruce gets on the phone with Jay and says, "I hear the network doesn't want to pay for 'Manic Depression.' Because—cough, cough—I'm coming down with something. I don't think I can be at work tomorrow," when we are filming the wrecking of the car. And we got "Manic Depression."

Sheryl Main: It was one of those episodes where they had to come up with something to keep things moving. Anybody else probably would have caved. Instead, the creative team kept thinking, "OK, we can't show Cybill, so how do we do it?" They constantly came up with these creative, fun, innovative ways. They got the body language down perfectly in the Claymation.

Glenn Gordon Caron: A lot of it was about trying to be inventive. And so you work your way around that. "Can we shoot this episode without her here? Hey, I'm going to call Will Vinton up in Oregon and see if he can make me a Claymation Cybill." Those moments are all born of situations that I didn't have control over. But it was me trying to solve the problem creatively.

Allan Arkush: I think that was a way of getting them both on-screen together.

Cybill Shepherd: Twins are not just like two kids. There is only one thing harder than twins and that is triplets. It becomes a very tricky pregnancy. The doctor has to be very careful. It was very overwhelming.

Jay Daniel: We finished shooting with Cybill on July 29, 1987. It was her Claymation scene. We didn't have her again until January 4, 1988. [Cybill Shepherd gave birth on October 6, 1987.] Bruce's side of the Claymation scene was shot on July 31. I was there for a little bit of that. It was amazing what they did with the technology that they had. I think what they did is they pasted little electrodes on Bruce's face to capture his motion. It was all magic to me.

Neil Mandelberg: We edited the Claymation scene. We were involved in that, but it was farmed out. We really just kind of worked with what they gave us.

Ron Osborn: When we began to write those full episodes, part of the work was done for us. So that was the good news. The bad news was no one liked it.

FULL DISCLOSURE: I am one of the few people who actually like Season 4. It is true that those three episodes are a little clunky, but the next two are in my top-five episodes of the entire series. In the two-parter "Cool Hand Dave," David finds out Maddie is pregnant and, in a classic TV wrong-identity plot, gets thrown in prison. This episode does not bother with having Maddie on the phone or with her parents. It lets Bruce Willis take over the screen. It's full of classic *Moonlighting* gimmicks, including a scene in which the prisoners at the jailhouse sing a Gilbert and Sullivan parody on a chain gang. It also contains one of the most fun cold opens of the series. Part one ends with David being thrown in solitary confinement. Part two opens with ABC executives worried because David Addison is missing. They have to hold a casting call, where all kinds of actors audition for the part, and it really captures that fun *Moonlighting* tone that had been missing since before the four-part storyline from the previous year. Roger Director and Chic Eglee were the masterminds behind this highly engaging two-part episode. Allan Arkush directed it.

Roger Director: It was just a fabulous opening; the sequence of casting David Addison because he's missing was so tasty and funny. It was such a creative and inventive moment. I mean, can you think of another one-hour TV show since then that ever did anything like that?

Chic Eglee: The opening scene was written by Roger Director. Roger was on *Hill Street* and *Bay City Blues*, and I started over on *St. Elsewhere*, which was downstairs on the MGM lot. I remember walking down the hall, seeing the name Roger Director on his door, and then Roger had this plaque made underneath it that said, "Writer, Producer." So it read "Roger Director, Writer, Producer."

Roger Director: Chic and I were mainly responsible for that script. It wasn't the case that we wrote the script and it came out to be two hundred pages long. We were in the process of beating it out when we thought that it could be two episodes, which in some sense would sort of help us and take a little bit of pressure off things in terms of turning out episodes.

Chic Eglee: I remember writing "Cool Hand Dave" pretty vividly because I wrote that chain-gang song. It was the first song I ever wrote. It got me in ASCAP. So I pay like forty dollars in dues every year, and I get my check for eleven cents. It was a Gilbert and Sullivan song from *H.M.S. Pinafore*.

Roger Director: It was the *Moonlighting* sort of spirit. I'm not even sure whose idea it was to do a *Pirates of Penzance* parody. It could even have even been Allan Arkush's idea. We thought, "What would be a crazy thing to do in the midst of having him on a chain gang? It would be having him break out into some musical number, right?" It was blisteringly hot. It was a tough shooting day. And imagine trying to choreograph it. That number came out great. It's just a tribute to Allan.

Chic Eglee: I remember writing the line about "One niggling bother, the guy's not certain he's the baby's father." I had trouble trying to come up with a word that would fit into niggling.

Allan Arkush: I had directed a lot of dancing scenes on *Fame*, so I was very focused. I probably had more experience doing that than anyone

"Cool Hand Dave," featuring a song-and-dance scene involving Addison and his fellow convicts, stops the pouting and brings back the fun David.

else on the set except for Jerry. We saw the choreography. We came up with a battle plan based on where the light was, what we were going to shoot and when, and how to break up the number. We came up with a series of dolly shots. It was one of those days where you put your head down and you just keep going. We might have done seventy or eighty setups with two or three cameras. Bruce was really, really into it. We got everything just as the sun was setting, and you really felt like, "Yeah, this is as good as it gets."

Chic Eglee: What I liked about writing the song was there are a lot of notes in the melody and it's very staccato. It allowed for a cool kind of puzzle solving, a staccato use of language to hit all the notes and tell the story about their relationship. The song comes out of the school of premise songs that they used to have on TV—whether it's *Gilligan's Island* or *Beverly Hillbillies*, themes that set up a series. Only this was just a sort of a classier version of that. I remember being in the recording studio all night long recording it. I was so proud that they sang a song that I wrote.

Roger Director: It had to be at least one hundred degrees that day. That was not easy to do in the dirt. My appreciation has only grown for what Bruce did. He had a movie career ahead of him, his costar wasn't there, people were saying that the future of the show was in doubt, but he ran at 100 percent all the time.

Curtis Armstrong: I remember loving that episode. In fact, I might actually have mentioned it in my book, because it really stood out for me as everybody operating at their peak.

Ron Osborn: That was all Roger and Chic. They came up with it. It was a moment of inspiration in an uninspired season.

Jay Daniel: Roger and Chic understood the show. They were doing things in a *Moonlighting* way, but without Cybill the series could never have what it needed. I mourned for that. But we did the very best that we possibly could. In terms of production, this season succeeded, but the missing element of the two of them together is very hard to get past.

Roger Director: I have to give Bruce so much credit. When you see all the things that he was being asked to do in "Cool Hand Dave," all the antics, the prison stuff, and the Gilbert and Sullivan song, swinging a pickax, then playing the sort of crestfallen "Where the hell is Maddie?" He did so many things. I'm just really full of admiration for all of those people: Allyce and Curtis too.

Allyce Beasley: I was filming up to five days before I gave birth. We had to just keep shooting. Cybill was off, but I had to work up till five days before. I think I had a month guaranteed in my contract, but they asked me to come back after two weeks of giving birth. My son was born September 6.

Allan Arkush: Allyce always said, "If it's Allyce's shot, it must be Friday afternoon," because that's when we always shot Curtis and her. Cybill and Bruce would be gone. I loved Curtis, and Allyce was a lovely person and a good spirit. You had on one hand the A story, and you could have more fun with the B story.

Roger Director: Certainly we were helped by how great Curtis Armstrong was, and we could put a full load on his shoulders to do those episodes.

Curtis Armstrong: The one I remember mainly is singing "Sexual Healing." My recollection is it was pretty last-minute. I was asked if I knew the song, which of course I did. And they said, "Well, you're going to sing it. We're going to come by and pick you up in the evening, and we're going to go to a recording studio."

Allyce Beasley: I was home getting ready to go to the Emmys, because I was nominated. They called me at home and said, "Can you please come back? We have nothing to shoot." Cybill hadn't given birth yet, and they added where Curtis serenades me at my window with "Sexual Healing." They said, "If you don't come back, we can't shoot it." So I missed the Emmys.

Curtis Armstrong: I went in, and we did take after take after take. Then Roger Director showed up, and we did a version of it for him. He said, "Can you go up significantly higher?" And at that point I'm beginning to strain. I said, "That's really high. This is going to sound terrible." He said, "Well, that's kind of the idea."

Roger Director: Technically speaking, Viola was my crazy creation. And we couldn't have possibly gotten any more fortunate than to get Curtis Armstrong to play him.

Curtis Armstrong: We were shooting it outdoors in some neighborhood in Los Angeles until two in the morning, as usual. I seem to remember the key grip was on the verge of tears, if he heard me sing it one more time. It drove them crazy. They hated it so deeply, because it was one of

Herbert (badly) serenades Ms. Dipesto, who looks on from her window.

those things, you have to do a bunch of takes, different angles, and all that. They—honest to God—wanted to die. It was "Kill me before I hear this again."

Jeff Reno: When you have a romantic comedy where the two leads are never in a scene together, you have a shaky season. Nobody wanted to see Curtis, because they wanted to see David and Maddie. I think that's why so much hate started. It became a different series. It was a broader comedy. Curtis and Allyce were not leading men and women. They're just fun. Audiences wanted to get back to David and Maddie, and that was the downfall of a show.

Glenn Gordon Caron: Viewers show up to see Bruce and Cybill. They get angry when they're not there.

Allyce Beasley: I try to be a healthy human being. I felt really badly about my experience on the show for a very long time—not like it messed up my life. I didn't start shooting heroin or anything. [Laughs.] It was just really hard on me. It was really sad.

Sheryl Main: That was very difficult. We got through it the best that we could. When you're dealing with creative types, and networks and deliverables, there's a certain amount of tension and stress. It's a heightened kind of atmosphere. I can't say those were the fondest memories, but I have to give everybody credit for just getting through it, because it wasn't easy. There were a lot of challenges on many different levels, and everybody stepped up as much as they could. There was a lot of discussion about how they hate each other and how miserable everybody is, but if you weren't there you can't possibly know what it was like to have so many things happen and *still* have to deliver a show.

Roger Director: That was such a challenging time, with some headwinds against us. We did a pretty damn good job under the circumstances. The actors, Allan Arkush, and everyone did a damn good job building some really quality stuff. I'm aware that most people do consider this season a drop-off, and I suppose it probably was. I was sort of the guy on deck there because Glenn was away. So we had to be making decisions about going forward with things. He knew what the episodes were about. I'm sure Jay kept him informed. I think some of the episodes that we did that season were actually mighty fine.

Jay Daniel: I was very concerned that Bruce and Cybill weren't in scenes together, but what were we gonna do? Emotionally, for me, this was the hardest season, not from a shooting standpoint—Season 3 was much harder—but on pure emotion, this was hard. Roger and Chic did an excellent job, but the magic was just not there because the magic is the two of them together.

Roger Director: I suppose I still have a little bit of a chip on my shoulder about some of that. Glenn was in Philadelphia at that point, shooting *Clean and Sober*. I spoke to him on the phone a few times when we had different situations to deal with.

Glenn Gordon Caron: Roger didn't have the experience of having gone through this with Bruce. He kind of didn't have any capital with which to talk to Bruce. He was the guy who was going to run the show, but he wasn't as big a presence on the show prior to that.

Roger Director: Bruce was confined on a plane set for a day or two of shooting with Robert Webber in "Father Knows Last." He was not happy about it. Bruce wanted the sequence to be rewritten. He did not want to be confined inside an airplane because he felt that was constraining as an actor, and as an artist. He wanted to have more free range to voice what this character was thinking and feeling at that point. He voiced his concerns to me, and I tried to explain that given certain constraints of the story, as we had previously been locked into shooting, that it would be difficult to rewrite that part of the script. Bruce called Glenn.

Glenn Gordon Caron: I have the vaguest of recollections about that. I remember getting a phone call from Bruce. I can't remember about the specifics of the scene. I remember talking to Jay and saying, "Jay, what's going on?"

PHOTO COURTESY OF DEBRA FRANK

There's a shift in the balance of power on Season 4, as Glenn departs, Cybill takes a break, and Bruce remains.

Jay Daniel: Roger didn't step to the forefront on stage. He wasn't a presence that Bruce would think was next in command. He was just one of the writers to Bruce. Plus, he was missing Glenn. Bruce and Glenn always had a great one-on-one. Bruce trusted Glenn. He didn't know if he could trust Roger because he didn't know Roger. It was a minor battle.

Allan Arkush: Roger Director was in charge. Whatever Roger was doing, Bruce and Cybill would take turns beating up on Roger. That was my impression. There was a lot of second-guessing. It becomes more like a regular show, in the sense of actors having opinions and going to talk to the writer about it.

Roger Director: I understood Bruce's frustration. I understood as an actor that he felt that he was being denied access to some of the tools that he likes to use as an actor. And I really respected that. I regretted that he felt constrained like that. And I regretted that I hadn't been able to provide him satisfaction. It was a challenging time, and with a couple of road bumps in it. People don't offer a whole lot of kudos for some of the work that year, but given the challenges, I think we did rather well. But there were also certain regrets, and we were forced into some situations where Bruce felt a little bit shackled. His words to me at the time were that he felt like he was being robbed of his gifts.

Allan Arkush: When it was Glenn in charge, he maintained control by being late. That's why the network couldn't give notes. That's how it worked. That's why he did it. Because he controlled it. You couldn't stop it. I mean, when you're handing in a finished episode at 9:00 a.m. on the night it's supposed to air at 9:00 p.m.—that's the ultimate control. And so with Roger, there was a lot of second-guessing everything. There were a lot of big rewrites for the actors, which never happened before Glenn left the show. Glenn would listen to them and make adjustments, but he wouldn't rewrite a scene.

Roger Director: You can talk about the story and the script all you want, but your job as a writer is to put the actor in the best possible position to give you the best possible performance in the best possible minute on film. That's your job. There are sometimes difficult discussions that have to be had. I don't think Bruce was happy about that episode, but I understand why.

Glenn Gordon Caron: The dynamic on the show was shifting. I wasn't there. Bruce and I were very tight. We'd gone through this extraordinary experience together. But I wasn't there. I sort of counted on Jay to be that person that Bruce could talk to because Jay had been there from the beginning. But Jay did a very curious thing, which I'm sure made great sense to him. He decided to become Cybill's protector.

Jay Daniel: Years later, ABC asked me to do *Roseanne* because they knew I could talk to Roseanne. I was able to communicate with her for five seasons. I learned how to do that from working with Cybill. It was pretty much the same thing. You had to make Cybill feel like she was being listened to. I utilized what I learned in dealing with Cybill with Roseanne. Bruce's professionalism was being taken advantage of.

Glenn Gordon Caron: I think Jay realized, from a production point of view, that the biggest detriment to getting things done was Cybill, and that by sort of befriending her and protecting her he could make sure that production moved, but in doing that I think he alienated Bruce, in the sense of Bruce would come in and say, "Hey, is there any way I can get off Friday?" and Jay would say, "No, you've got to shoot these things." But Bruce saw him make accommodations for Cybill.

Jay Daniel: That was probably the hardest season I had ever been through in the past or even till today. There were just so many things thrown at us that hampered our ability to do the show. The show was never an easy show to do. In the beginning the difficulty was set high in terms of getting the scripts into a form that Glenn was willing to shoot. His system of writing and all of that made it difficult. But it was well worth the wait because the pages always worked. Then Bruce realized he was becoming a star. He was still there and willing to work, but even so, those episodes were difficult. When I look back on all that was thrown at us, I am proud of what we accomplished. But at the same time, I wondered,

"Am I gonna die?" [Laughs.] The normal stuff we could handle, but at the same time it got more difficult, for so many different reasons. It was one of the most difficult things I ever had to do.

Roger Director: You've got to hear the actors; they make the script work. The writers don't make it work. Writers make it work on the level of the storytelling and the dialogue, but it's the actors who put the performance on film. Every time you type in a character name in a script, you give yourself the opportunity to write something as good as Hamlet's soliloquy. But if your actor cannot perform that soliloquy or they are better at getting the "thought" of Hamlet's soliloquy by saying, "What the fuck is going on here?" then you tear up Hamlet's soliloquy and write, "What the fuck is going on here?"

Allan Arkush: I was looking to leave during these episodes. There was just too much anxiety.

Roger Director: Then Cybill finally came back, and all hell broke loose. I'm not sure whose idea it was to have Maddie get married. You wanna talk about strike three?

CHAPTER 12

Citizen Caron

"I don't know how to run a newspaper, Mr. Thatcher.
I just try everything I can think of."[1]

—Charles Foster Kane, *Citizen Kane*.

If you changed "newspaper" to "television series" and changed the three-named man to Glenn Gordon Caron, you'd have a good description of *Moonlighting's* game plan. It was created as anarchy personified in a detective series. Four years in, it had hit the heights of creativity and popularity, then started its downward slide. Glenn admitted that his main goal with the series was to open the door to directing movies. He got that chance and took it. Ironically, while he was on sabbatical from the series to achieve that dream, Cybill was off tending to her family. Their relationship was like a waning moon at this point. But whether the series was at a low point or not, Cybill was returning, and so was Glenn. The twosome would reunite with Bruce Willis, but was the threesome ready for it? In the meantime, viewers had been handed a steady dose of Addison only. In the beginning of the series, Maddie-and-David arguments were served with a scoop of Maddie and a scoop of David. For the first half of the season, the viewer was fed only one flavor, and the

---

1   *Citizen Kane*. Written by Welles, Mankiewicz. Directed by Welles. RKO Radio Pictures. 1941.

show suffered because of it.

Maddie left David *before* she knew she was pregnant. She left David with a broken heart and a business to run. It's hard to take her side on that one. Viewers watched David pine away for her for eight episodes. Meanwhile, Maddie wasn't pining for David; she was hiding. David went to JAIL, for goodness sakes, and she still couldn't get on the phone with him. It's understandable from a production standpoint that the creative team couldn't change what had already been filmed, but as a result all the empathy viewers had felt for Maddie had been sucked out. Now she was returning. Could that empathy be restored? For the series to survive, it was crucial that the two characters were equals, not just in the battle of the sexes but also in the empathy department. With all that had occurred between Glenn and Cybill, would personal feelings seep into the scripts? Glenn came up with the storyline that would bring Maddie back into the fold. He had her take a train back to LA and marry a stranger (Walter Bishop, played by Dennis Dugan) whom she meets on the train. She also informs David that he was not the father, even though in previous episodes we had watched him prepare to be a father. Feel any empathy for her now? Maybe the Urban Dictionary should define the *Moonlighting* Curse as what happens when writers start to make viewers care for only one side of a couple.

Jay Daniel: I don't think it was intentional. Maddie is a very opinionated character, and so was the actress playing her. Dave was a character that you just had to like. He could turn it from being funny and then show his heart in a moment. It was a different thing. But I don't think it was ever a problem in writing the characters. It was a problem to everyone working on the show, but I don't think it was in the writing.

Jeff Reno: I hope the level of empathy wasn't an issue in the writing of the two characters during that time. Cybill's pregnancy created a production challenge. We had to separate the two people in the show, a huge problem in a romantic comedy centering on their two characters. I'm convinced that was the central reason for the show's decline. Getting them together is usually pointed to as the undoing of the show, but the much bigger problem was doing a rom-com that was all about these two people going at it and suddenly not being able to put them in the same room. I think we knew the audience would side with Bruce a little, since Cybill was the one who left town, but I remember doing our best to make what she was doing as understandable and palatable as possible. I truly don't think any feelings about the cast entered into anything we talked about in story meetings or wrote into the scripts. But I can only really speak for myself.

Roger Director: There's a part of me that thinks it was when Maddie got married—if you want to talk about a nail in the coffin, that might be it. Not that there hadn't been some hammer blows before that.

Karen Hall: I had empathy for Maddie because I kind of felt like I understood Cybill, being surrounded by guys and trying to work, because I had the same thing. That was the thing about being a woman writing a woman: I could completely understand her circumstances. I always liked writing men. But there was a difference when I was writing women, because I am not guessing at how they think.

Ron Osborn: In terms of Maddie, life was dictating art at this point. Because of Cybill's pregnancy—giving her all due respect to that fact— we had to scramble. This is a show that on a good day was scrambling; this was kind of scrambling squared. I think decisions were made that were just not in the best interests of the series.

Cybill Shepherd: That pregnancy went on for like ten months on the series.

Glenn Gordon Caron: I thought, "I've got to come up with something really wonderful and inventive." I really thought I had, but clearly I hadn't. We all suspected the show was going to suffer, because people tuned in to see Abbott AND Costello. They don't want to see just Abbott. I tried to be as clever as I could, but I couldn't solve that problem. At that point, Cybill's acrimony toward me was really high.

Jeff Reno: Glenn had just come back to the show and came in with the

idea that Walter Bishop, played by Dennis Dugan, comes on the show and marries Cybill. I *really* hated it. Glenn and I kind of fought about it, which was unusual and no fun. But I just didn't think it was gonna work. And I don't think it did. I don't think people liked it so much.

Ron Osborn: I remember going to his office and discussing our problems with this. His response was "Come up with something better if you don't like it." Which I think is a valid response. I am sure we had ideas, but I don't remember what they were. But I would have bought a more solid and interesting, worldly guy. I would have bought David's equal. Part of Glenn's idea was to surprise.

Chic Eglee: I think it made perfect sense. I think marrying Walter is exactly the opposite of marrying David. Maddie thinks, "I'm gonna just marry somebody that represents a real common-sense decision." I think it was an impulse in Maddie. I kind of dug the idea that she would marry a nice, sensible guy.

Roger Director: By that point we had reached a point where there was no clear, easy answer to the situation. Walter Bishop was one flash of a radically different, surprising turn of events. It had that appeal.

Glenn Gordon Caron: Necessity is the mother of invention. Dennis Dugan had done a wonderful audition to play David Addison. I always remembered how he wrote me this heartbreaking letter. He had heard through his agent that the audition was fantastic, but I just didn't see him as somebody I would put next to Cybill Shepherd. He wasn't a leading man in that sense. He wrote me this fantastic letter where he said, "When I wake up in the morning and I look at myself, I'm a leading man. I can do this." I needed her to marry someone. I thought, "Hey, we'll get Dennis Dugan."

Dennis Dugan (Walter Bishop): I got a call on New Year's Eve. They said, "Cybill is pregnant in the show, and they need someone to marry her. They want you to come in Sunday for wardrobe and come in Monday to film the episode and get married. You'll do this season and all of next season."

Ron Osborn: The staff wasn't crazy about that idea.

Melissa Gelineau: I love Dennis Dugan, but it wasn't the show. I think Dennis is unbelievably appealing and he was fun. Everybody liked him, but he's not David Addison. It just became a different show.

Sheryl Main: Clearly Maddie was attracted to men who are the opposite of her. I didn't see it totally out of her realm. But meeting Dennis Dugan was key. Aside from the fact that I still work with him, he is one of my dearest friends.

Ron Osborn: I don't ever remember a discussion about "What does a Maddie/Walter relationship feel like, look like, taste like? What stories are we going to build around that?" I just remember "This is the decision, and we're going to do it."

Roger Director: We had spent so much time and effort chewing over a whole range of possibilities. When Glenn wanted this to happen, we rendered it the best we could.

Ron Osborn: Had she come back with Ralph Bellamy [*His Girl Friday*], we would have got it. I could see Maddie doing that. We didn't understand the casting. It was basically given to us. That was Glenn's idea. There was a lot of Sturm und Drang sitting there discussing that. That was staff written, because I remember writing the scene where David sees Maddie for the first time and she tells him she's married.

Jeff Reno: I have huge respect for Glenn and so many of the decisions he made on the show, but he and I disagreed about that one and actually had a pretty big argument about it. I lost, but I remember doing my best to make the situation work.

Debra Frank: I would never have made that choice in a hundred years. I have a story credit on that episode, and I get a check for a penny every couple years. I should give it back to them! I never worked on the story. I don't know what happened.

Ron Osborn: I told Glenn, "I don't know how to write this." At least he listened to that. He responded to that as a writer. We had a discussion where I got to a place where obviously I did write it. I registered a pseudonym while we were writing the script in case I ever had to put my name on it, and it was Les Worth.

Debra Frank: I have a great pseudonym: Kay Sara.

Glenn Gordon Caron: It was a colossally bad idea. The audience just hated the whole concept of it.

Cybill Shepherd: Dennis Dugan was a very good actor but his character was rather wimpy. I remember Glenn saying he got so much hate mail. I mean like tons of letters in giant sacks. Glenn and I had already had some kind of falling out by this point.

Dennis Dugan played the unpopular Walter Bishop.

Sheryl Main: It was probably a positive thing that we didn't have the Internet. Viewers had to actually write a physical letter or call the network to complain. I think it confused some of the viewers, particularly the female viewers.

Roger Director: The time slot for the show was 9:00 p.m. At 10:00 p.m. Eastern time, the phone started ringing in our office. I was there and received a few angry phone calls. I realized when the phone started ringing and we were getting an intense negative reaction to it that there was trouble.

Glenn Gordon Caron: I remember writing the line for Dennis when we took him off the show. He literally turned to the camera and said, "There. Are you happy now?"

Dennis Dugan: I didn't care. It wasn't me; it was Walter. It never bothered me for a second.

Glenn Gordon Caron: He came to me and said, "I really want to direct, and I do get along with Cybill rather well. It might be a great thing." So it was the beginning of a great directing career. He's gone on to direct a lot of really successful films, like *Happy Gilmore*.

Sheryl Main: People think about him being Walter Bishop, and they don't understand the contribution he made to *Moonlighting* as a director.

Chic Eglee: That kind of launched Dennis's directing career as a go-to comedy guy. And he obviously has proven that with the great success that he's enjoyed as a director since *Moonlighting*. He got along really well with Cybill, which by that point in the show was a very big box to check. He's super funny. He got along with everybody.

Sheryl Main: Dennis Dugan totally understood the humor. He's a wonderful, collaborative director. He listens. He's an actor's director. You have to remember it's Cybill and Bruce's show. They pretty much embraced all of the directors. I don't want to say 100 percent, but I never felt there was a big problem between them and the directors. They did embrace Dennis, because he was one of them. He was an actor and he knew the show, which definitely helps.

Dennis Dugan: It was all so much chaotic fun. I love Bruce. We got along great. I was actually happy because I really wanted to start my directing career, and working on *Moonlighting* was a gift. It was better that I directed it, instead of act on it for another season and a half.

THE PLAN BECAME to get Walter Bishop out and the romance back in. At this time, the series did the annual Dipesto episode but with a new twist: Herbert Viola would be the centerpiece. The assignment fell to Jeff Reno and Ron Osborn, who had written the Shakespeare episode the previous year. They decided to tackle a different classic, *Casablanca*. Directed by Artie Mandelberg, the episode features Herbert playing Bogie and Ms. Dipesto playing Bergman. The episode is as creative and funny as anything the series had done before. It's such a spot-on spoof of *Casablanca* that I strongly suggest everyone watch them back-to-back. While the episode was a writing success, it was not a ratings one.

Curtis Armstrong: Actually, as I recall, it was the lowest-rated episode of *Moonlighting* in its history. Usually Dipesto episodes would start with David and Maddie, and then it would turn into a Dipesto episode. "Here's Living with You, Kid" is the one time that didn't happen. It's the only episode where Bruce and Cybill never appear. And that was the lowest-rated episode of the season, of any year. I'm not surprised people don't remember it.

Neil Mandelberg: I wish they'd done more with Curtis's character. I loved his character. I loved Allyce's character. But the few times we did those episodes, the audience just didn't respond the way we hoped they would.

Sheryl Main: I liked the episodes that Bruce and Cybill weren't in. I know people didn't care for them. But Curtis and Allyce were so sweet. It's just an example of how creative our team was to keep the show going.

A rare color photo of Curtis Armstrong as Humphrey Bogart in *Casablanca*.

Roger Director: The production schedule for Cybill and Bruce was exhausting. They were in nearly every scene. Glenn wanted to shoot episodes featuring Agnes. It was only natural that Glenn added Herbert and gave him flight clearance. He paired up with everyone, worked great with the rest of the actors.

Curtis Armstrong: In high school, I used to do Bogart imitations all the time. I was obsessed with him. It was like, "Well, now you're going to play Bogart." I said, "Hold my beer." My whole life has been toward this moment, and then being on that set and everything down to the camera angle when I signed "Bert," which is right out of *Casablanca*. It was just an amazing experience.

Allyce Beasley: I watched the movie a bunch. Curtis was a great Bogey. It was easy to imagine we were those characters. Jack Blessing [MacGillicuddy] did a great job, too. It was so fun. I tried to channel Ingrid Bergman.

Curtis Armstrong: I had seen *Casablanca* nine hundred times. It's one of

The late Jack Blessing and Allyce Beasley in the *Casablanca* spoof.

my top-five movies. For me, this was a dream come true. When they have Rick's Café set up and using set pieces from the film—our set dresser got the original table lanterns from *Casablanca*. They were in storage still. In some ways, it was like a gift that made up for all the other stuff. It was remarkable.

Ron Osborn: *Casablanca* is maybe my all-time favorite film. It was actually a lot of fun to write. Allyce and Curtis were so great.

Curtis Armstrong: The way they set up the airport-tarmac scene—which was done on a soundstage at Fox—with the forced perspective so that the plane looks like it's far off and regular size. And that car that we drove up in was actually one of George Raft's cars. It was from his collection of antique cars. So there was a double thing, of George Raft and Bogart. Jack Blessing was hysterical as Paul Henreid.

Ron Osborn: Curtis is just one of the good people. So is Allyce. They really just had the misfortune of working under the people and conditions that they did. Allyce and Curtis probably weren't treasured enough while they were there. Those episodes were totally to give Cybill and Bruce time off.

Allyce Beasley: I had fallen asleep in my trailer completely dressed while wearing my Ingrid Bergman wig. I was still nursing my son. I was so happy to do an episode but was exhausted. They just woke me up, brought me on set, and stood me on my mark, but didn't tell me what scene we were filming or where we were. I said, "I don't know what the hell we are shooting! Where the fuck am I?" I didn't even know what the setup for the shot was. That was the only time I ever cracked. It was a bridge too far for me. I don't want to look bad and not do my work. They all got mad at me. They chewed me out. I didn't even have a second to understand what I was going through. I was just destroyed by it. You just had to survive. No one was going to help me. Curtis was a friend, and we respected each other's work, but I wasn't gonna lean on him because it wouldn't have been fair. He had his own stuff to deal with. When you are the good kid in a family—when you are calm and loving—the day that kid steps out of line, the parents destroy that kid because you have a role to play in the family. That was exactly what happened that day. That was the only day my heart broke. I just didn't know where I was. They took me off set and chewed me out, and then we shot the scene.

Curtis Armstrong: I know it's primarily Bruce and Cybill, but Allyce was a really important part of the dynamic that made that show work. I think an underregarded part of the magic of that show—when it was magic—was Allyce. I can't imagine how difficult it would be to have been part of something that significant, as part of the trio, and then wind up having it go awry. That was a situation which I didn't have anything to do with, because I came in as a day player and then was extended. I never had a feeling like I was a part of it. I was *sort of* a part of it. I didn't come into it with any preconceptions about how I would be treated or the kind of roles that I would play or episodes that would be written for me or anything like that.

Glenn Gordon Caron: Allyce and Curtis were really an important part of what held the show together. And I loved what they did. I felt badly that they would show up and people would be so consumed with the fact that it wasn't Bruce and Cybill that they couldn't appreciate what they were doing. I did feel badly about that. But my sense was that Curtis was hip to it, and never let it get him down.

Sheryl Main: They got overlooked because people got too hung up on Dave and Maddie instead of watching the show and going, "Wow, that was cool." Allyce and Curtis carried some heavy water there.

Jeff Reno: There was a Dipesto episode each year. Ron and I just loved the idea of doing a Bogart takeoff. We thought that Curtis would do it well. He's such an underrated guy. He's just really, really good. And by then we totally knew we could give him all kinds of stuff. He just had such great enthusiasm about getting a chance like that, which was so nice.

Ron Osborn: We both had a lot of fun on "Here's Living with You, Kid."

Allyce Beasley: Jeff and Ron were just wonderful writers.

Neil Mandelberg: I edited "Here's Living with You, Kid" entirely with my brother Artie, who directed the episode, because he wanted me to do it with him. We enjoyed working on it together because it was creative. It was hard for him, because it was pressure packed. He was a producer also, but he stepped up. Artie let pressure affect him more than I think the rest of us did, because he was a new director and you're much more public as a director than an editor. So it can certainly have an impact on who you are and how you see things. But he did a wonderful job with a good episode. We stepped outside the norm.

Roger Director: I remember the way we re-created the final shot in *Casablanca*. Jay moved a small plane into a darkened soundstage. I am amazed at how great Curtis was as Herbert Viola and Allyce was as Agnes Dipesto. They were made for each other.

Jay Daniel: We put the plane way across the stage so, in perspective, it looked like a larger plane. It matched very closely to the plane used in the movie.

Chic Eglee: Allyce and Curtis were just so great. I mean, Roger created the Herbert Viola character. It was just a perfect Roger creation. I love that character because he took himself so seriously. I used to try to write the longest gobbledygook stuff to put in his mouth because Curtis was so literate. He could just say anything. Then it became sort of a challenge to write dialogue for him that was nearly impossible to say, which I'm sure was hilarious for me, and just made his life miserable.

Curtis Armstrong: It's an old truism that anybody who works in TV or film will tell you: if the writing is good, it's not hard to learn it. They were really good at what they did. They figured out who I was, and they were able to write for me. It just was a real gift is all I can say.

Allyce Beasley: I loved the "Play it again, Sam" part when he doesn't play "As Time Goes By." He plays "Chopsticks." How brilliant is that writing?

Roger Director: Bert's opening surveillance sequence in the episode "Here's Living with You, Kid" is a sweet sample of vintage Viola, as is that entire episode about Bert and Agnes, including its dream sequences. A writer can't ask for more than the chance to watch Curtis Armstrong work his magic on your Bert Viola pages.

Jeff Reno: We really loved "Here's Living with You, Kid." It was a fun show to do, with the different styles and everything. We had a great time doing it, but it just wasn't quite *Moonlighting* anymore. That's how I feel. We left at the end of Season 4. We started doing movies.

Jay Daniel: It got a twenty-seven share overnight. So the ratings were not so hot. It was a well-done episode, and Curtis and Allyce were good, but this was a time where keeping up and doing what we had to do was really hard. To work on a Viola show where Curtis would hit his mark and do his job was a nice break.

Ron Osborn: We left the show right after that episode to write *Radioland Murders*.

Jeff Reno: George Lucas hired us because of our work on *Moonlighting*, and Ron Howard was originally set to direct. The script we wrote was one of our all-time favorites, very much in that same screwball vein, but it was unfortunately gutted a few weeks before production started.

AFTER THE *CASABLANCA* episode, *Moonlighting*, along with all of television, was hit by a writers' strike. They were in the middle of filming "And the Flesh Was Made Word" when the strike started. They couldn't finish the episode because, of course, they weren't ahead on scripts, not even the one they were filming. There was nothing they could do to finish the hour but sing and dance.

Jay Daniel: The writers' strike started in March, and it didn't end until August 7, 1988. It was a twenty-two-week strike.

Margie Arnett (Maddie's Stand-in/Photo Double): They were going to do a 3D episode filmed at Magic Mountain. They used the stand-ins, David Willis (Bruce's brother) and myself as Maddie. I think I remember a script, but they didn't get that far.

Jay Daniel: We were talking about doing a 3D episode. I was looking into it. There was a technique that someone had come up with that would allow you to shoot 3D. I wanted to research it and see if it was feasible. I went with a small crew and directed a chase scene to see how it would work. It was interesting, but there were limitations to it. It only worked when something was moving. We couldn't really do a full episode. We spent a day out there. It was fun, but wasted time.

Margie Arnett: The writers went on strike, and shooting ceased. The stars never shot the script, but I had a great time running around the park.

Melissa Gelineau: I was an assistant, not a guild member, but I remember thinking, "Really, you guys aren't going to finish this episode? You get paid a lot and you can't finish it?"

Roger Director: It was extremely frustrating, from the point of view that we were about to finish the episode and couldn't, although I was definitely down with the strike and complied with everything that the Writers Guild wanted. I understood it completely. And as frustrating as it was, it hurts. It hit people in the pocketbook. In talking about it with Jay, we cleared it with the Writers Guild that we would not be able to write. So we sat at some desks on the soundstage.

Melissa Gelineau: At the end of "And the Flesh Was Made Word," we literally turned the camera on the crew because we didn't have enough pages. I remember that because they had all of us sit there. I don't like having a camera on me, and I was in the front. I couldn't look up because I didn't know what to do. I remember my parents being super annoyed. "You never looked up. You looked down the entire time." I didn't want to be on camera.

Chic Eglee: I remember being on camera for the writers' strike bit. It's funny being on the other side of the camera for a change.

Roger Director: It was not fun looking at myself, I'll tell you that.

Ron Osborn: I've got frames of that scene with us on screen hanging up in my office at home. There was no script; there was nothing written down. We were all told, "You're going to assemble on the set." I choreographed the hand move in the beginning. Then Curtis just lip-synched to "Wooly Bully" and we listened.

Roger Director: In Curtis's hands, Bert was asked to do almost anything—not least, hold his own with Bruce Willis—and Curtis was always up for it. He took the bits and pieces of Viola the writers gave him and made the character his own. There's a cave painting of him somewhere in the Pyrenees, and a carving of his head some believe to be the work of human hands on the moon.

Jay Daniel: You could sing a song, but you couldn't write a script.

Ron Osborn: Bruce came up with some lines. I don't remember there being a piece of paper anywhere around. Now, there might have been something that I didn't know about, but we didn't write it.

Jeff Reno: Who doesn't wanna see a group of writers in a chorus line? Curtis singing the song was just a fun idea, and as far as I know the guild didn't have a problem at all because we actually did stop writing when the strike began.

Jay Daniel: There was some talk about Glenn getting in trouble for breaking the rules, but it didn't amount to much. You just didn't know when it was gonna end. It really was a killer for all series—more for us because of the way things happened on our show.

Roger Director: It was the typical *Moonlighting* response to things. We were breaking the fourth wall, trying to connect with our audience, and to know that they were real writers here but that we couldn't write anything. It was a little sort of trippy and surreal, but not altogether different than anything else that show had done.

Jay Daniel: I directed that scene. We shot it on March 17. It was fun to do. Because we were out of scripts and ratings were down, I was concerned. I wrote in my journal: "Could this be the last thing we ever shoot of *Moonlighting*?"

THE CONCERNS WERE justified. The writers' strike meant that after waiting a year for Maddie and Dave to return to the screen together, viewers were rewarded with just three and a half episodes of them together. Problem was that in those three and a half episodes, Maddie was married to someone else. Production problems started to resurface. It was taking even longer to finish an episode. If the show returned for Season 5, Glenn would be finished with his work on *Clean and Sober* and return as showrunner. ABC was concerned about how that would play out with Cybill Shepherd, but it wanted to renew the series.. Ratings had slipped in Season 4, but the series was still cracking the top twenty. When *Moonlighting* was bringing in huge ratings, ABC didn't mind the bills. Now things had changed. ABC was looking to get *Moonlighting* under control.

Glenn Gordon Caron: Brandon Stoddard was running the network. The writers' strike was happening. Cybill, more and more often, would be sick. When a lead actor on a television show is sick, the way it normally works is the studio sends a doctor because they have to file an insurance claim. They have to verify that the person is ill. But when Cybill would get ill, ABC wouldn't send a doctor because they were terrified that they would discover that she wasn't ill, which they strongly suspected.

Jay Daniel: The way this whole season was working out was that either Cybill was sick or she would go to her trailer for a while to tend to the twins. Episodes were taking a really long time to make. We had one episode in this period where I was cutting the episode at noon and it aired that night. With Bruce having *Die Hard* coming out the upcoming summer and knowing he was going to be a movie star, his attitude changed a bit. His attitude about waiting was starting to get to him. When he saw a movie career ahead of him, he got more impatient with waiting for Cybill. It hurt the show in a number of ways.

Glenn Gordon Caron: I was constantly saying, "You've got to send a doctor. We have to put a stop to this. How do we countenance this?" Brandon Stoddard said, "We've got a writers' strike. We're down for a few months. We're going to deal with this. You need to have a meeting with her and her representatives. You need to tell them ABC is prepared to pick up the show for another season. But we're only prepared to pick her up on an episode-by-episode basis, and if she misbehaves, then she's gone." So I dutifully call this meeting.

Melissa Gelineau: I remember the circumstances that led up to that. We were not at our *Moonlighting* offices. We were at Glenn's Warner Bros. offices because we were in post for *Clean and Sober*. ABC came to Glenn and said, "You need three elements for *Moonlighting* to work: Bruce Willis, Cybill Shepherd, and Glenn Caron. You need all three." At the time, they felt that we had a lot of issues, primarily because of Cybill, in terms of the amount of work she did and the delays.

Jay Daniel: April 15 it was decided, due to the writers' strike, we wouldn't film any more this season. On April 19, we set the meeting with Cybill, her agent, and her lawyer.

Glenn Gordon Caron: My representatives were there, her representatives were there, and we had the insurance company there. Literally, I think it was the Fireman's Fund that put a guy on the stage for the entire season who would clock when she was called to the set and when she would arrive. Sometimes we would call, "We are ready for Cybill now," and an hour or two hours later she'd show up. She would do one take. She walked out. And everybody would be like, "What do we do now?" It was really, really, really difficult. They had clocked it and said, "Here's what she's cost in production time—in waiting time."

Cybill Shepherd: I remember that somebody was going to time Bruce and I's bathroom breaks. So if you were gonna go to your trailer, you were going to have to be back in five minutes. My lawyer Walter Teller said, "That's ridiculous. You can't time somebody's bathroom break." Everyone realized that was stupid.

Melissa Gelineau: I partly remember this because Jay had me compile all these stats of the amount of pages we did when she was there, amount of pages we did when she wasn't there, just all these various stats. It took me like two days because I had to go through every single call sheet and production report. ABC said, "You have to do this, because of the budget."

Glenn Gordon Caron: We had all these figures and facts and we presented it all, and then I presented ABC's thing that they were prepared to pick up the show but they would only pick her up on an episode-by-episode basis. I always remember, she looked at me and went, "Fuck you." I said, "Cybill, it's not fuck me. I mean, it's fuck you." She stood up, and then her representatives stood up. It was like in those cartoons where they go, "Beep, boop, boop," and then they get traction, and they're out the door.

Melissa Gelineau: The door was closed, and then all of a sudden we heard raised voices. Then she storms out and slams the door. We all looked at each other and just figured, "I guess it's over. *Moonlighting*'s done."

Jay Daniel: The network was all over the show for not being able to get shows on the air.

Melissa Gelineau: I think all of the delays are what sort of led to the big come-to-Jesus moment that they pushed Glenn to do with Cybill, which then backfired. It was a culmination of all of that in terms of not having episodes.

Glenn Gordon Caron: I called Brandon Stoddard. He said, "How'd it go?" I said, "It didn't go well. She didn't seem at all concerned with the ultimatum." He said, "Well, we have months now, and I'm going to get involved and I will bring her to heel." A couple of weeks later, I called and asked, "Did you connect with Cybill?" He confessed that she didn't take his call. We were getting to where he had to pick up the show. It was getting closer and closer. No word.

Melissa Gelineau: I can't remember specifically if it was that Cybill called Brandon Stoddard from ABC or he reached out to her. Next thing you know, ABC calls Glenn, and I think that ABC thought they would be able to smooth it over and Glenn couldn't. They had him confront her and lay all this stuff and say, "You've got to shape up." Then they didn't support it; they chickened out. They really left him no alternative, but I truly, truly believe that they figured that he would come back.

Glenn Gordon Caron: She basically said to the network that "you've got to pick one of us." And as a famous producer said to me shortly after I left, "Glenn, what did you think was gonna happen?" Honestly, it hadn't occurred to me that it would go that way. It didn't. My naivete was huge. I think she thought I made it much harder than it needed to be, and in some aspects she was probably right about that. But in others, I'd like to think I gave as good as I got.

Chic Eglee: Cybill sort of ran Glenn off his own show.

Allyce Beasley: It was terribly sad. I was crazy about Glenn. Whatever everyone else felt about him, he was always wonderful to me. Cybill was pushing him off the show. I don't like that kind of stuff. I don't think anyone has the right to do that. It made me feel so bad. I have worked for Glenn since. I was supportive of him. It was all so awkward and sad. I just hate when people like that get their way. I hate that Hollywood gives in to that. Other shows didn't.

Melissa Gelineau: So Glenn couldn't return. I know that Bruce was really upset that Glenn didn't come back. I really understood that he had to, but I was really sad, because this was Glenn's baby and it was very much his vision. And no disrespect to any of the amazing writers we had on staff, but this was Glenn's voice.

Chic Eglee: I know how much pain there was for Glenn. I didn't at the time, but I've been separated from my own shows. It's really frickin' traumatic, especially something as much of a white-hot hit as that was. It had to be just awful for Glenn.

Jay Daniel: The network decided that either Cybill or Glenn had to go. In their infinite wisdom, they chose the face on the screen instead of the writer/creator behind the scenes. I think they thought the audience believed actors make up their own lines anyway. So they broke Glenn's heart. Well, they broke all our hearts.

Sheryl Main: As for losing Glenn, it was really difficult. I had a tremendous amount of respect for Jay and Artie and all those guys. It wasn't that they couldn't do it. It was that Glenn truly was the creative force. There's some David in Glenn, and losing him had a big impact on me, personally. Because he was our leader; he was the guy. He took me under his wing.

Melissa Gelineau: I don't want to be disingenuous and say, "He left because he was done with it." Because that wasn't it. It was a matter of pride. Glenn upheld his side of the bargain; ABC did not. They did not deserve him to come back, even though the show certainly suffered without him.

Jay Daniel: It was a huge loss to not have Glenn. I don't know what their thinking was.

Allyce Beasley: Glenn was really young. He loved Bruce. He didn't know how to deal with Cybill. She was always envious of Bruce, from day one, and she had no reason to be, in terms of how much Glenn wanted her for the role of Maddie. I used to say, "Either you belonged to her or you belonged to Glenn." Once she decided that Bruce was a star too and Glenn liked him, she wasn't having any of it. Glenn did his best to placate her. Bruce was supposed to be invisible, an afterthought. Once she saw that Bruce wasn't, there was nothing Glenn could do right. So when she was able to drive him off the show that way, it just broke my heart.

Glenn Gordon Caron: Brandon Stoddard confessed that he did speak to Cybill. He said, "I picked up the show, and I picked up her." I said, "Oh, how's that gonna work? I gave her an ultimatum, and we can't countenance this behavior. And you basically have said that doesn't matter." He said, "Maybe you can't run the show. Maybe you can't tell her what to do, but you can still write." And apparently, *she* had given *him* some kind of an ultimatum. I was never privy to the exact wording, but I was gone. There were operational problems with the show that I was asked to fix. To do that, I needed to confront Cybill about some stuff. And frankly, when the smoke cleared, Cybill was still there and I wasn't. I honestly believe that if I would have been able to stay, there was a fascinating story to be told about two people who clearly, on some level, yearned for each other but who, in the business of living day to day, weren't meant to be together in that way. But I never quite got to tell that story, because the two actors were not available at the same time and then, at a precipitous moment, I simply was no longer there. I was the one who felt the story in his bones. I couldn't write it. I really couldn't share it with anybody. It was heartbreaking. It was just heartbreaking. I don't know what story you've heard, but that's the . . .

. . . [SILENCE] . . .

"Rosebud."

Chapter 13
Viewer Come Back

How are you doing? Are you hanging in there? This was a comedy show, right? Remember the rhyming secretary? Remember the pie fights? That was fun, wasn't it? Seems like a long time ago. Now imagine, after all that had just transpired, having to write something that makes people laugh and also brings Dave and Maddie back to where they were. That was the task for those in charge of the Season 5 premiere. The other redefining change that happened during the twenty-two-week writers' strike was something that had been brewing for more than a year.

Jay Daniel: *Die Hard* came out on July 23, and I wrote in my notebook: "Shit, he's gonna be a movie star." [Laughs.]

Ron Osborn: I teach screenwriting at a couple of colleges. I point to the first *Die Hard* as the thinking-person's action movie. It's fourteen minutes in until you cut to a truck, and then it's sixteen minutes until they come into the building to shoot it up. You cannot do that now. Times have changed.

IT'S IMPORTANT TO put into context just how influential *Die Hard* was in the summer of 1988. Movies today come and go. In the eighties, popular movies stayed. *Die Hard* stayed, and changed how movies were written. Yes, studios today try to convince ticket buyers that the latest superhero movie is a must-see, and they may even convince droves of people to go see it on opening weekend, but then everyone forgets it immediately. Movies don't have legs anymore. They are consumed and then the waiting begins for the next, exact-same sequel. *Die Hard* truly changed movies—and not just action movies, but movies altogether. Just like David Addison in television, John McClane changed the male lead in movies. Now everyone was making snide comments and had a laissez-faire attitude about their circumstances. Paul Newman and Robert Redford never said, "Come out to the coast, we'll get together, have a few laughs" in the middle of an action sequence at the pinnacle of the film. They CARED. The movie also viewed reporters and the media as the bad guys. They weren't helping John McClane stop the terrorists; they were assisting them. The same went for the police. All the American institutions were the bad guys. Only one rogue man could save the day. Every movie after that became *Die Hard* on a bus, *Die Hard* in a rodeo, *Die Hard* in a *Die Hard* movie. Bruce Willis became the biggest star on the planet. His reward? A diaper.

Neil Mandelberg: When I saw Bruce as the baby, I burst out laughing, because I had not read the script before I saw the dailies.

Jay Daniel: Bruce was a sport about playing the baby. The concept was very interesting. It's sort of a sweet, touching episode. I was very grateful that it was the first thing we did for Season 5 because I could prep. I didn't have pages, but we could at least create the womb and how they would talk through it.

IF YOU DON'T remember the episode, "A Womb with a View," you must be mighty confused by that last statement. There was, in addition to all the behind-the-scenes drama, a drama taking place on screen: the writers had to address Maddie's pregnancy, and her claim that David was not the father. They decided that Bruce Willis would play the baby inside Maddie's womb. The baby is visited by an angel/guide played by Joseph Maher (*Heaven Can Wait, Seinfeld*). Seeing David as the baby lets viewers know the child was not Sam's, but David's. The following hour takes viewers through a recap of Dave and Maddie's relationship, teaches the child about good and evil, and, in the end, teaches all of us about death. As Maddie goes into what appears to be labor, it becomes clear that something is wrong. The angel receives a call telling him this baby was just not meant to be. The storyline that had caused so much trouble was now gone. The scene is handled the way *Moonlighting* handles things: the child, instead of being born to Dave and Maddie and growing up on that TV series, will be sent to another TV series, either *Growing Pains* or *The Cosby Show*. Well, let's hope he ended up with Alan Thicke and Joanna Kerns. The child and the angel dance their way up a set of stairs and sing "On the Sunny Side of the Street." If this sounds to you like a creative idea and seems like it needed that Glenn Gordon Caron touch that was no longer available to the show, you wouldn't be the only one who thought so.

Chic Eglee: Ron and Jeff had left, Glenn was gone, and I hung in there. I didn't want to take a higher credit at that point because of the people who had been doing extraordinary work, like Artie Mandelberg. I just didn't want to bump up over anybody's credit. So I just kept my same producer credit all the way through. As Steven Bochco was fond of saying, "It doesn't matter what they call you or what title you have or how much they pay you; at the end of the day, we're all story editors." And that's one of the truest things I've ever heard about showrunning for television.

Jay Daniel: Jeff, Ron, and Roger left. Chic took over as head writer. I tried my best to convince Roger to come back, but he just couldn't.

Chic Eglee: Roger Director left because it was a rough show to do. Even now, when I've been doing this for a while, I look back on *Moonlighting* and it's kind of good that I didn't really know what I was getting into, because now that I know how intricate and hard these shows are to do, the idea that I was the showrunner was kind of crazy.

Jay Daniel: Chic had done a first draft on "A Womb with a View."

Chic Eglee: I remember having written a long, different opening, about

God. And it was sort of God being on a TV set looking in on people's lives and cracking wise.

Jay Daniel: It was actually Bruce that called Glenn and said, "They came up with an interesting script here, and you should put it through your typewriter." I don't remember how much it changed.

Glenn Gordon Caron: Chic had the original idea, and Bruce called me and said, "Will you write the season opener?" I confess I have a very difficult time saying no to Bruce. I was also sort of bitter and mad. But remember, I get a real kick out of doing something so provocative. There's a part of me that does like that.

Chic Eglee: I remember Glenn hating what I'd written. He thought, "We've seen this a hundred times before, and it's not fresh." I remember hearing that Glenn called Jay because he wanted to know if I was OK, because Glenn is such a sensitive, sweet man, and after saying that he

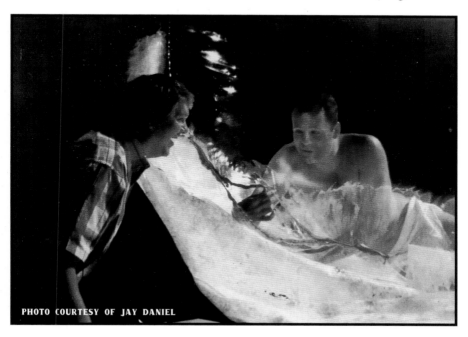

PHOTO COURTESY OF JAY DANIEL

Bruce Willis gets direction from Jay Daniel while he is inside the womb set on "A Womb with a View."

hated this segment, he was worried that I had taken it badly, which I hadn't. I do remember there was some chaos attached to that episode, as there was to a lot of those shows.

Glenn Gordon Caron: I had sort of gotten us into this jam. I had these two people get together. "Let's go for it. Let's make them pregnant." Some of that was because Cybill was pregnant. It was the easiest way to deal with that. Now I had to pay it off in some way. I thought, "Maybe this baby was never meant to be." But then how do you articulate that? Bruce called me, because I was officially off the show at that point.

Jay Daniel: Cybill didn't care if he wrote "A Womb with a View." She just didn't want him around. I don't think she really knew how very important his involvement to the show was. He was not coming to the stage. So in her mind, she won.

Glenn Gordon Caron: It was weird going back to a place you knew you were very welcome, people were very nice to me, but at the same time, you'd been evicted by the landlord.

Chic Eglee: Glenn would go behind closed doors and write. I just remember at one point walking by Glenn's office and the door opening and hearing, "I'm going to need like an eight-foot piece of broccoli."

Jay Daniel (Director of "A Womb with a View"): I knew that if Glenn was writing it, it was going to be good. The technology that we had back then is night and day in terms of what we could do. It wasn't edited on a computer. You had to plan for any special effects before you got on stage to shoot it. A lot of my focus was on storyboarding.

Glenn Gordon Caron: It's very personal, because I was at that age where I was having children. I am not very religious. But the basic fundamental idea of faith is something that I think about quite a bit. I'm fascinated by it, by the need for it, and how we process it.

Chic Eglee: I loved Glenn's conception of the idea of the baby dying.

It was his idea to do the baby dying as a song and to have it be kind of bittersweet. It wasn't about abortion. It was about losing a child from the baby's point of view. It was so sweet and beautiful. I remember that episode being particularly trippy.

Glenn Gordon Caron: I love the idea that maybe people contemplated for a moment the business of faith, and "What is this gift of life? How does that work?"

Neil Mandelberg: And that's really about Glenn understanding the rhythms of his series. That's why we had so much trouble once he left. Not because the other writers and directors weren't talented or smart, but because Glenn understood *Moonlighting*.

Glenn Gordon Caron: The public seemed to be obsessed with "Whose baby was it? Is it Bruce Willis's or Mark Harmon's baby?" What better way to say the answer to that question than actually see the baby? So there were a bunch of different ideas and influences at work.

Cybill Shepherd: You knew I was pregnant but you didn't know who's baby it was. By doing that, Glenn was setting up the show to go longer. We build in the suspense of "Whose baby is it?"

Jay Daniel: James Agazzi designed the set for the womb. He was a very talented guy and won an Emmy for that episode. That kind of simplicity worked really well. We didn't try to create the rest of her body. Bruce was sealed in. The womb was a plastic bubble that was inflated by pushing air in. So when the inflator was off, Bruce would crawl through the hole to get in and out. It did affect the sound, but we were able to muffle the inflator sound. We covered the device with soundproof material. Bruce's voice is affected by the bubble.

Glenn Gordon Caron: I remember Bruce quite liking that episode. He thought it was kind of a hoot. He gets to sing and dance in a diaper. Particularly for an action hero, if you can put him in that kind of circumstance, he's going to owe you for the rest of his life. [Laughs.]

Sheryl Main: I thought it was beautifully done. Glenn is a thinker. He wouldn't have broached that subject in that way if he didn't feel very strongly about it. It was an odd episode, with the baby dancing off to heaven, but there was something so basic and fundamental about it. That's what touched me. People want to put their own thing into it; sometimes they don't want to see things for what they are.

Melissa Gelineau: We got calls. People were so appalled. "How could you make a mockery of miscarriage?" It was really distressing. But we didn't mean to. We're just trying, in a thoughtful way, to show what happened. People were just appalled that we would kill a baby, which we didn't.

Glenn Gordon Caron: I'm not completely surprised that it isn't well loved, because it was 1988 and it ends with the death of a child. That wasn't a dialogue you could have in this country, even though it wasn't like she went in and got an abortion. But I don't think people were prepared for that. I mean there's Bruce Willis in a diaper. It may be that the high was too high and the low is too low at that moment in our culture.

Jay Daniel: People took issue with the ending of the baby dying. The reaction was a little more than we thought it would be. The first thing that was agreed upon was that it wasn't going to be a great idea to have a baby on the show. It was decided that the show wouldn't work with Maddie being a mother. This was the solution to it. A lot of thought was given to it. Controversial as it was, it had a huge heart. For me, that shone brightly.

Melissa Gelineau: I remember thinking it was really creative. I don't know if it was one of my favorite episodes. I think I knew that it was something we had to do because we knew we could not have a baby as part of this series. It just complicates an already very complicated show and situation. I remember thinking, "That's sort of a unique, creative way of dealing with this."

Cybill Shepherd: I see Glenn shooting himself in the foot. Would the show have gone on longer if we had it be David's baby from the start? It's a good question. Glenn has admitted it was a mistake to do that. It was like everyone in the world was waiting for this. They could have ended the show with David and Maddie having a child. It would have been lovely.

Jay Daniel: Some critics didn't like it. They felt it trivialized the death of an infant. That baby isn't gone into darkness. He is going up the stairway to heaven and is gonna go to another TV set of parents. The baby dances up the stairs to go to *Growing Pains* or *The Cosby Show*. Maybe that is a reference we should get rid of.

Glenn Gordon Caron: I remember it being very bittersweet and that the episode was rather remarkable. Even though it ends in the miscarriage of the baby, there was something very sentimental about it at the same time. I will always be really excited and keen to mix up different feelings.

MOONLIGHTING **CAME BACK** in December of 1988 for Season 5. Since a few episodes were already in the can, reruns weren't going to be an issue. Bruce Willis was a movie star, so star power wasn't a problem. The following episodes all had cases, chase scenes, and lots of great comic lines. So that wasn't the problem. The problem was no one watched. The moment of Dave and Maddie had passed. The season had great guest stars, like Virginia Madsen, Demi Moore, Colleen Dewhurst, Jennifer Tilly, Rita Wilson, and Ray Wise. It wasn't enough.

Ray Wise (Guest Star): I had a scene where I ran after Cybill in a parking garage. I injured my left achilles tendon, and it snapped in two. It was operated on the next day. Two weeks later they constructed this cart in which I could sit, and they would shoot me from the waist up. I would pretend that I was running and they would pull the cart, and I finished up my run after Cybill.

Jay Daniel: I directed that sequence with Ray when his tendon gave way. Ray Wise was in some real pain. But he is a total pro. He had a great attitude through the entire episode. He never lost his sense of humor.

Dennis Dugan: Rita Wilson was in an episode. I had cast her in an episode of *Hunter*. We shared a back fence. When this came along, I offered it to her and she said yeah. She's really great. Colleen Dewhurst was wonderful because she's a real New York Broadway actress and was just completely classy.

EVEN THE TENSION on the set slipped away, according to Margie Arnett, who stood in for Cybill on over-the-shoulder shots and for lighting setups.

Margie Arnett (Maddie's Stand-in/Photo Double): I'm sure you've heard there was tension on the set. I was there daily, and it wasn't as bad as it was played up in the entertainment magazines. I remember waiting for Bruce or Cybill to leave their motor homes to come back to the set after it was lit. They called the lighting process "Hurry up and wait." I started when Cybill returned from maternity leave, still breastfeeding those adorable twin babies. Looking back, I think she had a great work ethic.

Melissa Gelineau: The last season is sort of a blur, I think because it was just totally different, because everyone knew Glenn was gone. They moved us from Tuesday night to Sunday, which killed us. The irony is they gave our time slot to *Roseanne*. Cut to a year later, Jay and I are working on *Roseanne*. Sunday put the nail in the coffin. Look, it was a really expensive show. Originally they needed it and they just paid all the overages, but then it started getting harder.

Jay Daniel: ABC came to me and asked if I would take over as the executive producer of *Roseanne*. It seemed she had fired the head writer, so I jumped from frying pan to frying pan.

Neil Mandelberg: We thought it should have ended better than it started, which was hard to do. But with all the changes, the last year was difficult for everybody. It was getting to the point where almost everybody was tired of the show because of the problems we had.

THERE WAS NOT much that could save the show. The ratings dropped, and ABC canceled the series. Whether it was the loss of Glenn, the season that kept the stars apart, the plot decisions, or (as everyone in the world will say even with all that is in this book) that Dave and Maddie did it, it doesn't matter. The show came to an end. Before we get to the final episode, we have to spend a moment on the Anselmo case. Starting in Season 3, whenever Dave, Maddie, or Herbert worked a case off-screen, it was the Anselmo case. Viewers were never told what this case entailed. Herbert spent more time working this case than he did shaving in the morning. It ran all the way through the series. The final episode, "Lunar Eclipse," was directed by Dennis Dugan, and despite the screen credit to Ron Clark, it was actually written by Chic Eglee.

Chic Eglee: I wrote the last episode. But I had in my mind that it's Glenn's show, and it just didn't feel right to slather my name all over somebody else's show. But I absolutely did put the Anselmo case in *Moonlighting*. It's not quite as ubiquitous as Tommy Westphall [a reference to the famous snow globe ending of *St. Elsewhere*], but it's up there.

Curtis Armstrong: The Anselmo case is from [comedy troupe] Firesign Theatre. It's a private-eye thing that Firesign did referring to the Anselmo case. So it was just an inside joke about that.

Chic Eglee: Fireside Theatre was this series of super smart people from Yale, Peter Bergman and Philip Proctor. They did a skit that was a send-up of Dashiell Hammett called "Nick Danger's Third Eye." It was sort of a forties gumshoe thing that was written by guys on acid, and in passing they make reference to the Anselmo pederasty case. I just threw it in a script. I might have used it in *St. Elsewhere*. But I definitely used it in *Moonlighting*, *The Shield*, *Civil Wars,* and *Murder One*. Herbert Viola was always up to his ass on the Anselmo case.

Curtis Armstrong: Obviously there wasn't an Anselmo case. But I've always loved the fact that the last screen on the show ever was "The Anselmo Case was never solved . . . and remains a mystery today."

Chic Eglee: I did write that the Anselmo case was never solved as the last line for the show. I remember very specifically writing the final episode. I wanted the screwball comedy to end with a wedding, just not Dave and Maddie's wedding. It ends with Viola and Dipesto's wedding. It was such a complete mess by the end, with people just not wanting to be there. The show was so expensive, and they were looking for a way to cancel it. It was just time to let that show go. I don't want to comment on the interpersonal dynamics there because people are still alive. I wanted to tell the story of what went wrong. It was this idea that in forty-two minutes, we're going to cease to exist as TV characters. It's a show about death.

Curtis Armstrong: MacGillicuddy died in that episode. I had this scene where I was over his dead body, and Mr. Addison was there. I'm crying and talking about MacGillicuddy. Bruce had done his close-up and had left. So I wound up having to do a silly, but emotional, scene with one guy who's dead and another guy who isn't there—again, exhausted and sad. As I was doing it, Bruce walked through the soundstage on his way to his car. He heard that I was doing that scene and he wasn't there. He stopped and came over and said, "Wait a second. Let me do it with you." So he stayed and did my off-camera for the first time in about two years. I mean, it had been a long time since he'd been doing my off-camera. I should say it was gratifying, but at the same time, really, a professional person does that without it being a big deal. But it was a big deal. Partially because it was so emotional.

Allyce Beasley: I didn't want it to be over. I loved *Moonlighting*. It was always threatening to self-combust. It never made sense to me. You have the opportunity of a lifetime with these characters, and how could you not want to do it? It should have gone on longer than it did.

Curtis Armstrong: I did at least two other shows after *Moonlighting* where the stars hated each other. We're not talking about stars on the level of Bruce and Cybill necessarily, but in both cases they sort of bragged to me that it would be familiar to me because they were, in a weird way, shooting for the same level of hostility that legendarily Bruce and Cybill had. So I would say that I came out of it, at the time, with an increased facility at learning lines on the fly and a better knowledge of dealing with difficult actors—namely by just being professional and not trying to fight back in situations like that, because it's not my place. That was the thing: because I never felt it was my place.

Allyce Beasley: When we all fell in the pool at Agnes and Bert's wedding on the very last episode, Curtis and I were really heartbroken. We didn't want to see the show destroyed. It was very hard. It was a great thing. You don't want to see it destroyed. And you don't want to see it destroyed by two people that are out to destroy it because it's their whim. It's not a good thing to be around if you are not that kind of person. I was upset for a very long time. I never thought that I could be in the same room with either of them again, and actually, I haven't been.

Glenn Gordon Caron: I think Allyce had a bunch of anger about how short-lived *Moonlighting* was. There was a sense that "Hey, this is one of those experiences that doesn't happen very often in an actor's life. Why are we throwing this away?" I've always felt badly about that.

Sheryl Main: I was there at the pool scene. It was Chic, Allyce in her wedding gown, and Melissa and everybody jumping in the pool. We were all there. It was so much fun. Timothy Leary performed their wedding service.

The final episode features a wedding, but it's Viola and Dipesto who marry, not David and Maddie.

Curtis Armstrong: It was really sad more than anything, except for having Timothy Leary perform the ceremony, which I'm sure was Chic's idea. I don't think they make any reference to the fact that it's Timothy Leary. If you knew it was Timothy Leary, then it was a nice inside joke, sort of out of nowhere, but he was just this guy showing up unexplained, which was one of those *Moonlighting* things, which I loved. This was the guy who'd been on John Lennon's "Give Peace a Chance."

Chic Eglee: We got ahold of Timothy Leary. I could have seen him around, and I wrote that wedding service for him. He said to me about his lines, "Can you believe we actually used to believe this stuff?" He was just in such a different place. But he was perfectly delightful. Glenn got Orson Welles and Ray Charles; I got Timothy Leary.

Dennis Dugan: That was on the last day of shooting. There were two units. I didn't direct Timothy Leary; I think maybe Chic directed that. They were doing the Timothy Leary thing over near Hugh Hefner's house. The church scene was the last scene that was filmed.

Chic Eglee: So the idea was that Dave and Maddie, in a desperate bid to save themselves, are gonna get married, and they race to the church. But first they go to the screening room to meet Cy.

Dennis Dugan: We had a guy who was gonna play Cy, and he got sick in the middle of the day, when we were setting up. They called me to his dressing room and said he was really sick and they called the ambulance. I called up to Jay and said, "I got bad news and good news. The bad news is that the actor who's playing Cy is getting wheeled into an ambulance." And we were literally almost ready to shoot. He said, "Well, what's the good news?" I said, "We've got this really, really good actor that is going down to wardrobe as he talks to you." So I played Cy as Walter Bishop.

Chic Eglee: I based Cy on Sam Arkoff from American International Pictures. He was an old-time Hollywood guy, heavyset, bald, big cigars, a movie mogul. Cy says, "You kids had it all, but you lost it. You just forgot to care about each other." Because that's very much what happened.

Separate and apart from the story twists and setbacks, it was a high-wire act with some pretty volatile personalities, people who were becoming movie stars. And because there was so much attention on it, people began to get out of scale with the show.

Dennis Dugan: Everybody at the end was just goofing around. We were all going to have fake names in the credits. My directing credit was going to be Sharon Dugan's husband, but the DGA wouldn't let me. It was all going to be goofy credits. I think the "Walter Bishop as Cy" credit may have just slipped through.

Chic Eglee: Then Dave and Maddie go to the church. That'll fix everything. They're so desperate to get married, clearly for reasons having to do with something way different than the sanctity of marriage, and the priest won't marry them. The idea was that they were supposed to go out and sit on the steps and essentially, without knowingly doing it, reflect on the years together. It's the moment when they really do tell each other how they feel about each other. And it was supposed to be kind of sweet. What happened was there was a performer, I won't say who, that simply didn't want to say those words. They said, "We can stay here all night, and I am not going to say those words." So they pulled the plug on it, we had to build that moment in flashback, which was really sad.

Dennis Dugan: There were dialogue changes all the time. An actor would want some changes; Chic would do it. There's nothing special about a day in which dialogue changed.

Melissa Gelineau: I don't think anyone, in a million years, thought the show would go down like it did. You never think that.

Sheryl Main: The problem was not about Dave and Maddie getting together. People had their feelings about that based on how that was going to affect their on-camera relationship. But that was not the demise of the show. Nothing lasts forever, but *Moonlighting* probably should have had a longer shelf life. But when you look at the body of work, what we delivered for every episode, the stuff we did, you go, "How did they do that? If it was so crazy?" We probably couldn't. That's what I keep telling people: you can't deliver quality when it's total chaos. People stepped up; they knew they had a job to do. They did the best they could do. That show wasn't perfect. And that was part of the beauty of it.

Chic Eglee: The intention never was to have Dave and Maddie marry, because it would fundamentally violate the pact with the audience, and in a way the pact had already broken.

Neil Mandelberg: Once the babies were born, Cybill would be on set from seven to ten, then be gone till two and leave at six. How do you write her into a lot of the show with that? And she was needed. Bruce's attitude changed that last season. He had just done his first *Die Hard*. We didn't have Glenn. So when you put all those things together, without being disrespectful, it was like cutting a lot of the other failed television shows that I worked on. It just didn't give the audience what they wanted. It was sad that *Moonlighting* turned into that, because it didn't have to.

Suzanne Gangursky: Bruce and Cybill changed over the course of the series. I think their commitment and how much they were invested in the series changed. It could have even bordered on resentment. When we started off, it was like a new romance, with the charm of "Everyone loves us; we are a hit." Everybody was happy. But then things happened. Bruce started becoming a movie star in *Die Hard*. For Cybill, her aspirations were having a family. She had done this before.

Cybill Shepherd: I had the opportunity to take $50,000 worth of wardrobe when the series was over, but I was so overwhelmed with raising the twins that I didn't take any of it.

Jay Daniel: It was the best of times, it was the worst of times, and I wouldn't trade the best part of that experience for anything in the world.

Melissa Gelineau: I think that as sad as everyone was—especially the crew, who had been there for a good portion of it—the show had lost its steam. It was sort of painful. The people that we worked with—it was an amazing crew, but it wasn't always the easiest set to be on. The numbers were so bad, and you hate to see that. I remember it not being a surprise it was canceled. But I think it's just hard to keep up the quality when you have so many factors fighting against you— the whole Maddie and David together, and then her getting married and all that. It just wasn't the same show.

Sheryl Main: It becomes bittersweet, because we're having a blast, we know it's ending. But how can you be sad that it is over when you are having the experience of your life, or your career? I mean, what is there to be sad about? I am a kid from Pennsylvania! It was surreal.

Neil Mandelberg: I can't picture a single frame from that episode. I'm so upset now. Holy shit! I have to go watch that episode again to find out how we ended.

Chapter 14
The Moonlighting Story

They were "moonlighting strangers who just met 'long the way." It wasn't destiny. It wasn't meant to be. It was just a lark. But that lark helped inspire a revolution in formula television whose effects can still be seen today. They most certainly gave cable channels looking to break the mold with scripted programming something to aspire to. When *Moonlighting* was at its best, it was doing the unexpected. It's easy to see the influence of the series on shows like *Community*, *Atlanta*, and *Fargo*. Shows that don't follow a formula. Shows that offer surprises week in and week out. If this book serves any purpose, my hope would be that it reveals the factors involved behind the scenes that caused the demise of *Moonlighting*. It most certainly wasn't because the couple had sex. What a pedestrian way to look at something. Just imagine how disappointing it would have been if they had *not* gotten together at that exact moment in time. Glenn made the decision, but he didn't know that Cybill was going to leave the show for a year and that Bruce was going to make *Die Hard*. Just think if those four episodes in Season 3 were just typical episodes, with cases. Then Maddie left for a year, and then, when the couple reunited, the show was canceled. How sad would it have been if we didn't have that four-part arc? It didn't cause the end; it cemented its legacy. There would never have been another moment when the country and the characters were more in sync than spring of 1987. Season 3 is the high point of the series. Those episodes are the *Sgt. Pepper* of the series. Sure, the band may end up breaking up because of what they went through making it, but what a piece of art they left behind.

As for the "bad behavior," it can't be laid at the feet of one person. Everyone I talked to mentioned how tired everyone was. How crazy their job was. It's hard to stay on your best behavior when you are pushed to the brink. Glenn was writing as fast as he could. He was writing dialogue that was nowhere else to be found at that moment. He was also learning the business. If he had already had the experience he needed to know that he should follow a schedule, he would have never attempted to do all those classic episodes, and then we would have lost out on so much. I am forever inspired by the fact that if something wasn't good, he wouldn't film it. I want to live in a world where all TV is done that way. So let's forgive and forget the late scripts and inflated budgets. I am pretty sure ABC is still in business.

Cybill Shepherd created one of the strongest, most well-rounded female characters of that decade, and probably the next. She was also caught in the middle of a boys'-club TV show in the middle of a boys'-club industry, stacked inside a boys'-club country. There was no #MeToo then. It was all #Him and #HimToo. Being a parent of twins myself, I can concur that caring for twins is tremendous work. Her work on the show is amazing, inspiring. Who knows how many young businesswomen she inspired? How many of those young girls are now grown women running their own business and fighting to break the glass ceiling? A ceiling that was made of brick when Cybill started fighting to be treated equally. Let's forgive and forget her latenesses and power plays. I am pretty sure time has proven the business wasn't fair to actresses.

Bruce Willis changed the concept of the leading man as we knew it. Here we are over thirty years later and I can't think of another actor who has come along to change it again. He is in the same category as Cary Grant, John Wayne, and Clint Eastwood as influencers in how men were portrayed by Hollywood in their time. Every casting agent spent the rest of their career looking for the next iteration of him. He carried the show by himself when Glenn and Cybill left. He didn't leave the show. His heart may not have been in the last season, but neither were viewers'. Everyone will take away what they want, but when I look at what the three of them went through during this incredibly pressure-packed time, I can't help but conclude that any bad behavior is at least understandable.

Allyce Beasley and Curtis Armstrong should win lifetime Emmys for being the best supporting actors ever. They had to stand to the side patiently when they were told and then be ready to jump into a spotlight that was designed for others, whenever they were told. They created characters whom viewers never forgot, and more importantly, every coworker had only the kindest words to say about them.

When you think about what Jay Daniel did, balancing all these egos and still making all those deadlines, it confounds me at how he managed it. How could one man run to all sides and keep it all going? He may have let everyone lean toward that bad behavior, but in doing so he helped facilitate artists who produced some of the most creative moments in television. The show wouldn't have made it to air without him.

Moonlighting was as innovative in front of the camera as it was behind the scenes. All the crew and writers gave their time and overtime to create a comedy show for five seasons. As of the printing of this book, the DVDs are out of print, the show doesn't stream, and it's not in syndication. It runs the risk of slipping away into obscurity. Fans of the series, myself included, hope that doesn't happen. It was a moment in television that really can't ever be re-created. There is no way any show is going to get a forty-nine share in our time. But once there was such a show.

The mistakes of *Moonlighting* are as much a part of its history as its successes. But that shouldn't be the show's legacy. What I see in talking with everyone and delving into the history of the series is that the show slipped through a crack in the wall that accountants and money-obsessed network executives erected between creative, ambitious artists and the constraints of commercial television. TV shows exist not to entertain, not to educate, not to surprise, and not to allow a self-proclaimed provocateur to create anarchy. No, television exists to make money for people who already have money. But in that brief moment, a large corporation was trying out an idea that would make its pockets even deeper. Some executive thought, "What if we owned the shows that we ran? Couldn't we then buy the show from ourselves and make money off the ads as well?" So they let *Moonlighting* be born out of that. They picked Glenn Gordon Caron to run this experiment. They knew nothing of Glenn's revolutionary idea of making TV programming not because seven days had passed since the last program had been made, but rather writing and producing a TV show when an idea presented itself that was worthy of being made. The bills piled up, but because Glenn was doing something new, ratings piled up too. How fortunate for the people of my generation that it was Glenn who was tapped for this experiment. Someone who wanted to try something daring and inventive. Once the accountants knew these companies inside of companies would work, another executive said, "Well, couldn't we make more money if we made average TV as well? Kept on a budget. And had a couple that isn't as magic as Cybill and Bruce, but are less trouble and cheaper?" The answer was, well, you can turn on TV right now and see the answer for yourself. You'll see *The Voice. Survivor. How to Win a Stupid Thing You Don't Need.* And *N.C.I.Law-Chicago-Fire-Police Edition.*

Moonlighting was an inspired moment in television history. I was there watching it as a teenager. It made me desire something unexpected from television. It's why I watched *thirtysomething, Twin Peaks,* and *China Beach.* And then, years later, *The X-Files, Ally McBeal, The Sopranos,* and *The Wire.* Quality TV survived the tightening of the screws from the suits, but it never quite had the bombastic ego of a *Moonlighting* again. I will be forever grateful to all the ego, blood, sweat, tears, and anger that created this piece of art. Learning more about it just gives us a better understanding of what it takes to do something groundbreaking.

The lyric that haunted me throughout working on this project was the one that started the book. I will use it to end it. "Isn't it nice to know a lot? And a little bit not."—Stephen Sondheim.

I leave you with final thoughts from the people who were so kind to share their stories. Also, here are a few longer stories that I couldn't quite find a place for earlier. And speaking of stories of forgiveness coming from another time, this one from Chic Eglee is a humdinger.

Chic Eglee: It used to be a whole lot more fun, before the lawyers took over this business. On *Moonlighting*, it was the eighties and it was just a whole other time in a different sensibility. We were shooting; it was the end of the week. We had shot some episode that everybody was feeling good about. It was kind of at the end of the run of the series. I believe it was a Dipesto/Viola-heavy episode. Those were always fun to shoot because everybody got along, and people weren't walking on eggshells. We'd wrapped at around nine o'clock, and everybody sort of retired to the trailers that were around Stage 20. They were partying and playing Motown music, and out came the beer. And it being the eighties, the blow came out. I'm sitting in, I want to say, Curtis Armstrong's trailer, and I hear this bump, a rumble, and a jolt. All of a sudden, the trailer we're sitting in starts moving.

The Teamsters, who were part of our party, because that crew was all very close and everybody loved each other on that show, had hooked Curtis's trailer up to another trailer that had people in it, which was hooked up to another trailer. They put this train together and then hooked it up to a tow vehicle and started pulling this train of four or five trailers—full of *Moonlighting* actors and crew—driving around the lot. People were jumping out of the trailers and saying, "Somebody has sangria in the fifth trailer." People jump out to get that. All of a sudden this train is going out the entrance from the Fox lot, and we pull out onto Pico Boulevard. Now we're on the city streets! It makes a left turn onto Avenue of the Stars. It ends up going through the back gate of the Fox lot, which is where the *Die Hard* building is. I didn't particularly think of it as anything weird at the time—it was just a party—but the idea that we would do that now? I probably would get jail time for just general recklessness.

Cybill Shepherd: When I was doing *Moonlighting* there was a lot of cocaine going around. I am not naming any names. I did caviar. If you get the best caviar in the world, it costs about the same as cocaine, but it tastes better and it's a lot safer.

Neil Mandelberg: We had edited and locked two reels of film. We called the driver to pick them up and take it to the lab. We get a phone call twenty minutes later. They say, "We only have one reel. Why didn't you send the other?" We say, "We gave the driver both reels." Holy shit, it was not in his car. We're talking about a full cut! Ten minutes of cut footage, and it's not backed up. We're going crazy. We don't know what happened. Forty-five minutes later, a homeless-looking man comes walking up the driveway at Fox. We get a phone call from the front gate. He found a reel of film and thought it probably belonged to the studio. The driver had left one of the reels on top of his car. When he made a left turn out of the Fox lot, the reel slid off the top of his car and landed on the curb. This man saw it and brought it in. I said, "Keep him there." I ran to Glenn's office and said, "Glenn, give me a hundred dollars." He said, "What do you mean?" I told him what happened. We gave the guy a hundred and said, "Thank you so much." We almost lost a cut reel of film on a Saturday when it was airing on that Tuesday. We saved ourselves, because we would have had to recut everything and we might not have made it. I can't remember which episode it was, but I can certainly remember what the gate looked like with the twelve of us screaming, "What happened?"

Allan Arkush: It was about the third or fourth day shooting on my first episode. I show up and Jay pulls me aside and says, "I gotta take you to wardrobe. Glenn wrote a part for you. He needed someone in the porn shop and decided that you were going to play it." So I get in the costume and I'm directing. I've only been directing on the show less than a week. So I'm not totally in the groove there. Every time I look at Bruce I laugh, because I'm like this close to him. I put on sunglasses so I could squint a little bit and not look at him so much, because he was cracking me up. We were filming in a real porn store. It was on Western Avenue. We were surrounded all day long by the world of hardcore pornography on paper, which I don't think exists anymore. This was not like *Playboy* magazine. There was a section, not just one magazine, but a section of every kind of kink and perversion—not making a judgment. Cybill was outspoken about how offensive it was. At a certain point she said, "Okay, let's have a contest. Let's give an award to the kink we never expected to see." I believe the winner was *Jugs in Tubs*.

Melissa Gelineau: I worked in the office, and we would get calls from people who would need help on a case and needed Maddie and David. There were a couple of times when people called with massive problems. You'd be really nice and say. "I'm sorry, but this is a TV show. They're not really detectives." This was something that went on throughout. They thought that these were real people.

Debra Frank: *Moonlighting* didn't use union-approved extras. Well, my parents were extras in the business, and one day I am driving through the gates at 20th Century Fox and there were all these people picketing the show. I see my parents on the picket line. My mom is yelling, "Hi, honey. Meet you for lunch later today?"

Curtis Armstrong: With *Moonlighting* you had to learn very fast. It was hardest of all of course on Bruce and Cybill. It was hard for them because they obviously had the lion's share. They suffered from it much more than anyone did. It was all a matter of whether you had the facility to just get things at the last minute. It's not like sending the changes online. It was on different-colored pages that would be driven across town in the middle of the night. I would get up at four thirty in the morning and go out and look to see if there were pages. I would go over whatever they sent me. I had never done television before. I just assumed that's the way everyone did it. It was frustrating and hard, but I thought, "OK, well, this is TV." It would never have occurred to me that this was a unique situation.

Roger Director: The work was so intense and so enervating after a while for Bruce and Cybill. They were in every freaking scene of one-hundred-page scripts. This was an overwhelming amount of work, week in and week out. It was draining. Now you can get paid any amount of money and receive any amount of fame, but it's going to take a physical toll on you after a while. One of the great reasons for the explosion of ensemble dramas is that the actors aren't in every scene. You've got five to nine actors, some of them are working twice a week, and if someone's sick or gotten on the wrong side of something, then they're just not in an episode. But you've got these two main characters in an hour-long drama; the energy that was required of them was enormous. I can remember a moment sitting outside the soundstage in a trailer with the two of them, the three of us sitting there, almost too exhausted to talk. We were spent. And that may be a thought to throw in here somewhere. We were spent. They were spent at some points. And just being spent might be what caused all the trouble. Some marriages last for forty years, some last for twenty years. It doesn't mean because it lasted only twenty years, not forty years, it was a bad marriage.

Dennis Dugan: It was like going to film school and getting paid to do it. When you've done a year of *Moonlighting*, like I did, there's nothing you can throw at me that I won't go, "OK, I can solve that. Yeah, good, fine."

Glenn Gordon Caron: I don't regret any of the sort of bodacious ideas that I had or the things I tried to do. Everyone I worked for is still in business. I didn't bankrupt anybody. In fact, I made a lot of money with my recklessness. Everybody that was associated with the show went on and did rather well. So it's hard to look back on it with many regrets.

Karen Hall: The best writers out there are writing for television right now, whatever you want to call TV. We can't call this TV writing anymore because that's going to be meaningless in five years. Everybody's going to be watching it on some screen. Call it screenwriting, because it will be writing for screens, but there really is no TV right now.

PHOTO COURTESY OF DEBRA FRANK

Roger Director, Glenn Gordon Caron, Debra Frank, Ron Osborn, and Jeff Reno reunited a few years ago to relive old times.

Glenn Gordon Caron: I certainly was in television jail for a while, but I didn't care. I thought, "If you make a show that's genuinely entertaining, if you're willing to spend the money to do that and work on it long enough to do that, you will have a show that's more repeatable than most." This was in an age when there were repeats. So I would shoot a show until I thought it was worthy of being broadcast. I wasn't much concerned whether that was seven days or twelve days. Because my other feeling was "If I do this and do this well, I won't do TV anymore. I'll do movies." I couldn't have anticipated the world in which we live today, when some of the best material is on television. So if I burn the town down to get things done, so what?

Jeff Reno: First, you look at the sophistication of the material, and then you look at the fact that a woman was absolutely as smart and as strong and as able to deliver the dialogue as the male character. She became a really strong character with sophisticated stuff. Somewhere in there is the success of the show—a few of those elements combined. I would probably throw in there that Bruce had a unique charisma that helped the show take off.

Roger Director: Maddie and Dave were as right as two people can ever be right. Which is to say that there's always a lot of wrong in the right.

Peter Werner: Here's what made the chemistry with both of them. They were really good actors and really good stars. And then, of course, they had that really good writing. So it was a great match of two tennis players at the top of their game.

Melissa Gelineau: I think it was one of those magical things that probably can never be repeated given the time and the circumstances and what we did. I think that's why people responded.

Ron Osborn: It was a whole different kind of storytelling, which was all credit to Glenn. It was a placebo detective show. It smelled and tasted like one, but in fact, it was a romantic comedy. When you were coming up with the stories, it really wasn't about solving the mystery. It was always to illuminate some aspect of David and Maddie's relationship.

Sheryl Main: We were in the middle of these characters being created. So our perspective, those of us who were there to the end, is so very different. It's almost like you don't see the forest for the trees. There was so much going on. [Laughs.]

Neil Mandelberg: *Moonlighting* gave me an opportunity to have a career, so I am forever grateful to everybody involved. I met Will Mackenzie, who hired me whenever he could. I met Allan Arkush, and we worked for years together.

Allan Arkush: *Moonlighting* made me a much better director. I learned how to work so fast. Every day the call sheet for tomorrow was the same: "Blue Moon agency, eight pages, to be announced." I learned how to really think on my feet and how to make things stylish. From Jerry Finnerman I learned so much about cameras. He was very forthcoming. That's when I met Neil, and he is a fabulous editor.

Debra Frank: For all of the craziness that went on, no one was ever belittled. No one was ever put down. There was never any kind of verbal abuse. That happens so often in these situations. So for me, that's just the best.

Chic Eglee: *Moonlighting* was a place where you could throw all kinds of weird ideas out there. There were no wrong ideas. Sometimes you write a bad idea to get to a good idea. I learned a lot of that working on that show. That was pure Glenn. He insulated the writers on the show from consequence in terms of money and network intervention. It's not like there was an army of executives crawling all over everybody the way they do now, where everything has to be vetted by network executives.

Karen Hall: I have a lot of just unbelievably great mentors. I had Steven Bochco. I had all the *M*A*S*H* writers. Glenn was a great mentor. I had David Chase, later. So I've had the best education you can get. I learned a lot from Glenn. His scripts were just alive. And I don't know what that means. I don't know if it was the pace of them, but they just purred when you read them. And I tried to emulate that. I think I learned a lot about writing dialogue from him.

Jeff Reno: We really learned a lot from Glenn. He is probably the one guy I can point to that made me a better writer along the way. After writing half-hour comedy, he instilled in me about following the truth of the character from one scene to the next.

Chic Eglee: What I'm especially grateful to Glenn for is the idea that you can kind of be intellectually, emotionally, and spiritually free to write what you want to write. As Jim Cameron said to me some years later, "Sometimes you just write shit that you want to see." And Glenn absolutely embodies that sensibility and really just helped me grow as a writer.

Roger Director: At one point, Glenn used an adjective to describe me and my sensibility, and the word was "bent." And I get that, and I have to say how lucky and fortunate I was, because there were not a lot of TV shows where I felt I could wholly, adequately, successfully deliver that cockeyed or bent part of me and have it be met approvingly. Whereas with Glenn, he saw that and he liked that. He didn't want me to stifle that.

Debra Frank: Apparently there were lots of battles that went on with the network. Glenn was very savvy. One of the things that I learned, which is very tricky, was that if Glenn wanted to sneak something into a show, and he knew he was going to have problems with the network, he would put something else in the show that they would find offensive. He took the onus off of what he didn't want them to take out, and all of a sudden everyone's focused on this new bit, which he had no intention of putting into the show. And then finally he said, "We'll take that out." And then the network thought they won that battle.

Allan Arkush: Here's the only time the network ever censored the show: Bruce takes Curtis out to show him how to date women. Bruce explains to Curtis about "don't put all your eggs in one basket." And while they're talking to these two women across the bar, Curtis leans over and says, "Mr. Addison, whose basket do you want to put your eggs in?" Because the network couldn't do anything about it because they got the print in the morning to air that night, they literally cut it off when it aired on TV. It is not in the show.

Neil Mandelberg: My favorite line in the entire five years was in a scene where they come sliding down a fireplace. David lands at the bottom of the fireplace and the line is, "That's the last time I get in a hole that tight with my clothes on."

Glenn Gordon Caron: It was really the product of youth and enthusiasm and ignorance to some extent, in a good way. You forge friendships going through all of that. I had great compatriots. Bruce and I come from very similar backgrounds. Both of us were amazed that we were being allowed to do what we were doing. And neither one of us felt like we better play it safe. Our attitude was that we better give it absolutely everything we have because you only get one bite at this apple.

Melissa Gelineau: We had a parade around the 20th lot. It was the "Curtis Armstrong Day" parade. We all dressed up in weird outfits and did this wild thing.

Curtis Armstrong: I think it was something that came up in the production office. People were running on fumes at that point, and they were looking for something to distract everybody. So they started to make jokes about it being "Curtis Armstrong Day." I didn't know anything about it. I think it was a private joke, and then Bruce caught wind of it. Or it was Bruce's idea from the beginning. Once he got hold of it, it went totally out of control. We started off on a parade around the 20th Century lot. John Ritter was shooting *Hooperman* at the lot across from ours. John was standing outside applauding and cheering all by himself.

Sheryl Main: We created "Curtis Armstrong Day" on the lot at Fox. I think Cybill was in a convertible, and we had people who worked on the show dressed as cheerleaders. We did it for some reason that I don't recall. We also had a one-man band. It was hilarious.

Allyce Beasley: Curtis and I were such good friends, and we went through such a bonding experience. It took three or four years for me to not have that weight on my heart. But you have to move forward, and you can't carry that with you. Being on *Moonlighting* was not commonplace. It was very vivid.

Dennis Dugan: Curtis and Allyce were funny as they could be. They were a great squad. They were really wonderful actors who just literally went with the flow no matter what happened.

Allan Arkush: I worked with Cybill again, on *The Client List*. We were great together, and it was really nice. We still talked movies. She was so well-read, so informed, and so much in sync with my politics. With Bruce, his energy would always be there. He would yell stuff like, "It's the fourth quarter. Let's go!" Very guy things.

Sheryl Main: That was my TV experience. I got to work with amazing people like Glenn and Bruce and Cybill. I have to say Cybill was very, very kind to me. Bruce was very kind to me, Curtis, Allyce, Jack Blessing, our cast. They were really wonderful people. And we did have a pretty spectacular crew.

Cybill Shepherd: When I got the call for *Moonlighting*, it was the biggest break of my entire career. Everything I did after was because I did *Moonlighting*. I will be forever grateful to Glenn.

Debra Frank: *Moonlighting* has to be at the very top of my career. I learned so much there. I'm forever grateful to Glenn for saying, "The only time you fail is when you don't try." It just was so freeing, and wonderful. And the fact that you could just come up with just any idea about anything and it would not be made fun of.

Bob Butler: I'd put *Moonlighting* up near the top and not at the top of my career. *Hill Street Blues* was much more familiar to me because it was not so comedic. I put *Moonlighting* around the fourth or fifth to a bunch of really good shows. I must say on my good days, during teaching, when it holds up for me, it looks just delightful. It looks light, fast, fun, and dangerous.

Melissa Gelineau: It was something special, and for a first real job, someone coming out to LA who literally had nobody in the business, I loved every minute of it, good and bad.

Allan Arkush: I've done two shows that were in the zeitgeist of men and women in society, *Moonlighting* in the eighties and *Ally McBeal* in the nineties. I think they both served different waves of feminism and different waves of the male-female relationships.

Sheryl Main: It changed my life. I'd be surprised if everybody who worked on the show didn't have the same feeling that I do, that we were so fortunate to be a part of something so crazy, wonderful, new, exciting, tough, weird, and wacky. That's a pretty high bar.

Chic Eglee: I learned that writing could actually be really fun and really enjoyable. I learned a lot from Glenn. It was a really good time for me creatively, growthwise. It's really sort of my transition into becoming a grown-up writer. I was fortunate enough to get paid while learning.

Ron Osborn: It's a bit like being in a foxhole with people where you could die. Suddenly you remember all the camaraderie and the good times you had in the foxhole.

Roger Director: We shot out of a cannon, and it did great. It had its own natural life. Could things have turned out differently given this or that decision among a million other decisions? I suppose it could have.

Debra Frank: When you're under such pressure and you're sharing that pressure with everybody, you all understand what you're going through. And because of that, I think there is a deep affection.

Jay Daniel: I am glad I made all these scribbles when we were doing it or I wouldn't remember any of it.

Neil Mandelberg: Jay would bring this calmness to any problem and solve it. We'd have like six hours to delivery and we're still mixing. He's got his legs crossed, leaning back, and just calm.

Will Mackenzie: Jay is one of the nicest people I ever worked with. What a doll. He was so much help to me. I learned a lot, especially about photography and staging. He just was one of the great unsung heroes, because Glenn, rightfully so, gets the glory. But Jay was the one that put it all together. He did take over Roseanne's show after *Moonlighting* and wanted me to come on as a director, and I said, "No way!"

Debra Frank: Jay is brilliant. Also, he is the guy who works with difficult people, and when everybody else was having a nervous breakdown, he calms the situation. He is amazing.

Karen Hall: I love Jay. He is wonderful. He always had really good notes—not from a line producer's standpoint, but from a good overall view. You know, he was a huge part of what the show was, but he doesn't tend to get much credit.

Alicia Witt (Worked with Jay on *Cybill*): I just remember Jay's smile more than anything. My memory of Jay is this great, big, gregarious energy. He always had a big hug for me and everyone else on set. I had nothing but a great experience with him. I'm grateful to have gotten the chance to have a steady job from the ages of nineteen to twenty-three.

Dennis Dugan: Jay Daniel's great. He's the most detailed guy. I just loved the way he looked at the monitor and looked and looked. He saw stuff that God wouldn't see.

Peter Werner: Jay is such a wonderful man. He really knew how to delegate. He was the rock. It was obviously a wild ride, and somebody needed to make sure that they were on the ground holding the string.

Glenn Gordon Caron: Jay Daniel is one of the best people in the world and a fantastic line producer and exactly who I needed at that moment, because I had no idea. We formed this company called Picturemaker Productions. We weren't aligned with the studio. So there was no one standing around saying, "You can't do that. You shouldn't do this. We're not going to let you do that." The closest thing we had to that was Jay, but Jay very quickly became a facilitator.

Allyce Beasley: A bunch of people in their thirties saw me when I was in LA recently, and they went batshit crazy. They were so excited to see me. They had just binged *Moonlighting*. They loved it, and it was nice to see another generation embracing it. It seemed to disappear off the face of the Earth for a while. So it's nice to see people discovering it. I was glad to have a positive impact on people.

Dennis Dugan: Who didn't like that show? It was great. They just broke every rule in the book.

Allyce Beasley:. I am glad you are writing a book from the creative viewpoint. That was the amazing thing about it. The show deserves to be thought of in positive ways. I don't think anyone was ready to talk about it before.

Curtis Armstrong: There was a point when the show was still on where somebody was writing a book about *Moonlighting*, but it never got anywhere. I think because it was too raw and nobody wanted to revisit it. But now seems like it's as good a time as any.

Chic Eglee: It seemed like we were doing the biggest thing in the history of the universe at the time, because it was on the cover of *Newsweek*. There was all this heady talk about "There will be books written about this show." Twelve years later, I was lecturing at Yale and I made reference to *Moonlighting*. I look out at this sea of blank faces. Nobody knew what *Moonlighting* was. It's funny how something that just seems so colossal and noteworthy just ends up being very much of its time.

Cybill Shepherd: You have to have that little extra magic that takes off, and *Moonlighting* had that. I can't think of any comedy, movies or television, that did anything like that or even attempted to do anything like that. And I went to the Peter Bogdanovich school of film. Just when you think that you can't top it, something would top it, and it kept coming back to Maddie and David and Ms. Dipesto—the touchstones. I have never seen anything like it. I was blown away by rewatching it.

Karen Hall: I was unpopular in high school. When I worked on *Moonlighting*, I just thought, "I'm finally in the coolest place on Earth. There's no place cooler than this." So it did wonders for my self-esteem. I have felt that way at a Bruce Springsteen concert. When I was at *Moonlighting*, I knew there was nowhere I could be that would be cooler than that.

Glenn Gordon Caron: None of what anyone said was true. I just want to close with that.

Chic Eglee: The Anselmo case has never been solved.

Special Thanks

An oral history only happens if participants are willing to share their truth with a complete stranger. I am so grateful to the names listed below, that they trusted me and spent hours on the phone with me reliving a crazy time in their lives. When I was a teenager, all of these people helped shape me as a writer, comic, and human.

Glenn Gordon Caron agreed to do a *Red Room Podcast* interview with me in 2015 for *Moonlighting*'s thirtieth anniversary. I have been asking him ever since we finished that interview if we could do a book about *Moonlighting*. In June of 2019, he finally acquiesced. He was so open and willing to help with anything and everything. He knew that not everything would come out sunshine and roses, but that never stopped him. I sent Glenn the first three chapters. Two days later, he called me and said, "You've got me hooked. This is great." If you can have one of your writing influences compliment your work, I suggest you do that. It can keep you going, even in the midst of a global quarantine. He then said, "I just got off the phone with Bruce Willis, and Bruce is willing to be in the book." In the end, we couldn't work it out with Bruce, but it was exciting for a moment. Glenn's writing and propensity for surprise truly inspired me. The first script I ever wrote, at the age of eighteen, was an episode of *Moonlighting*. I played David (of course) and my girlfriend played Maddie. I've been using that template for my writing ever since. I am not showing anyone that movie (called *Spooflighting*), but his impact on me as a writer can't be overstated. So in other words, if you hated this book, blame him.

The saddest part of this book being over is that I won't be on the phone for hours with **Jay Daniel**. Nothing was more fun than looking down at my phone to see Jay Daniel is calling. He was so helpful with research. I would send him an email and say, "Can you confirm that you filmed the

Honeymooners scene in April 1987?" A day later, he would call me and tell me the exact day and a million other details. This book is a monument to his work and dedication to *Moonlighting*. I wish my next book could be about *Roseanne* or *Cybill* just so I can keep working with him. But I think maybe my next book should be about a show that millennials have at least heard of. I mean, I'd like to eat at some point. Thank you, Jay, for doing this book with me. I knew I couldn't do it without you because of your importance to the series, but now I know I couldn't do it without you because of your friendship and support.

Roger Director is a name that I have thought about for as long as I can remember. Why was he a producer and writer only? Roger and I had two really great calls. He didn't know that I loved "Cool Hand Dave" more than anyone in America, and I didn't know that he needed to be reminded of how wonderful an episode it was. I could tell that Roger still carried the weight of Season 4 with him. I hope our talk and this book lighten his load. It's a really fascinating piece of art that needs to be studied more. Roger took on a herculean task and nailed it. No one could have done it better. I am so happy this book will finally put what he did in perspective. He is a profound thinker and wonderful writer, and I feel the need to tell him that he is *capo di tutti capi*, even if Chic wrote the line.

Allan Arkush directed episodes of *Ally McBeal*, which is one of my favorite shows. It was really hard not to beg him for stories from that show, because he is the BEST storyteller I have ever interviewed. He told such details. They were incredible. (Go back and read the details in his Ray Charles story.) Allan, more than anyone, shaped this book and really sent it on its path. We FaceTimed twice in the same day for two interview sessions. The first call, he was upbeat, excited, smiling, and full of laughter. We ended the first session when Dave and Maddie had sex. We picked up three hours later to discuss the latter half of the series. His mood was sour, his stories darker, his smile was replaced with a furrowed brow as he struggled with the flood of tough memories that came back. It was that night that this book changed from an episode guide to a story about the series. That interview was the book. I could see so clearly that the moment that David and Maddie "did it" just happened to coincide with the beginning of the trauma that the crew went through. (And make no mistake, it was trauma. Most of the interviewees went through some PTSD while reliving their experiences.) He also helped me with the chapter titles. He is a classic-movie savant.

Bob Butler freaking directed the original *Star Trek*, and I got to talk to him. He was so classy. It felt like talking to TV itself. The amount of quality television he is responsible for is mind-blowing. The best part of my job is getting to talk to extraordinary people who have a skill. Skill can never be discounted. I thank Jay for making this interview happen.

I tried really hard to get **Curtis Armstrong** to say *capo di tutti capi* during our interview. I mean, I did everything but beg him. It didn't work. Which I understand. But he did something even better. When he was talking about a scene with Bruce Willis, he called him Mr. Addison. He sounded just like Herbert Viola. That was the coolest two seconds of doing the entire book. Curtis's memoir is a great companion piece to this book. Check it out.

Allyce Beasley talks faster than a speeding bullet. Transcribing a New Yorker should be illegal. Allyce is so sweet and kind. She made all kinds of jokes that were really funny and totally appropriate but just wouldn't have worked in print. I am fearful that her quotes will come off darker than she is. Make no mistake, she is pissed. But she is lovely, sweet, and hilarious and invited me for coffee next time I am in New York. (And this was before COVID, so when she asked, it might have actually happened.) I sure hope I get that coffee someday.

Suzanne Gangursky and I talked politics for just about the same amount of time that we talked about *Moonlighting*. I remember some big political thing occurred that day, but since I am an American, I already forget what it was. I am so thankful that she saved the first script with Glenn's note on it. I think that was a great insight to how different the series was.

Ron Osborn kept offering his help. He paved the way for my interview with Curtis Armstrong, which led me to Allyce. He was so helpful and such a great guy. I want to take his class where he talks about *Die Hard*. That might be a class that I could pass. I feel bad I ended up cutting his comment about how his wife helped with the solving of one of the cases. Guess you'll have to get your bonus points elsewhere.

Reuben Cannon is a name I have known forever, but I wouldn't think I would get to speak with him. He didn't need any prep from me. You could tell he had told the casting-Bruce Willis story a time or two. I am glad it was captured here.

Jeff Reno came up with "Atomic Shakespeare," and then he talked with me for the book. That was incredible for me. I have seen that episode so many times, I didn't even have to watch it once during the writing of this book. It's implanted in my brain like the lyrics to "We Didn't Start the Fire." When my wife found out he wrote *Meet Joe Black*, I think she might have finally been impressed with me.

Debra Frank and I talked a few times, and she is such a sweetheart. I liked her immediately. I sent her the black-and-white chapter to make sure it was accurate. Her first comment about it was not on everyone's interviews but on my writing. To be complimented by the person who wrote one of the most famous hours of TV will keep me going for a long time. Thanks so much for sharing your photos with the world. I have been trying to convince her to write a book for FMP. I wonder if by the time this book is published I will have convinced her or not.

Melissa Gelineau gave such an honest and open interview. She was sitting right there when just about everything happened. The main actors of TV shows usually only know what happened when they were on set. The staff knows it all. She also mentioned having some *Moonlighting* swag. I am really hoping some of that shows up on my doorstep some day.

Chic Eglee doesn't know this, but I have had two songs that he wrote in my phone for years: "Another, Opening" from "Womb" and "Call Collect Chicago" from "Cool Hand Dave." I can sing every word to them. Finding out that he was the one who wrote those songs and that he added the Anselmo case made the two years I worked on this book all worth it. Chic cares so much about *Moonlighting* that we rescheduled our interview over ten times. That isn't me being snarky. He was in the writers' room for a new show, planning out a season. He was just really busy. I talked to his assistant so many times I think I should send him a Christmas card. But Chic wanted to be in the book so badly he kept trying to find the time. Thank goodness he did, because he had all the info and so many great stories. He is responsible for some great lines in the show and in this book.

When **Peter Werner** and I finished our interview, he asked if I would send him the audio. I started to get nervous. I thought, "Uh-oh. This guy is gonna sue me or he wants to double-check me and he doesn't trust me." Nope. He said he wanted it for his son so his son would know what his father had done. Peter and I also pitched a series about a popular show where the leads don't like each other and you follow the behind-the-scenes drama. Anyone want to option that idea?

I had contacted **Sheryl Main** to get an interview with Dennis Dugan. Then in doing research I saw she also worked on *Moonlighting*. I felt so bad that she didn't tell me in any of our correspondence. When I finally asked if she wanted to be interviewed, she said she had to think about it. I am so glad she decided to talk. She had a great perspective on postproduction. All the pieces matter.

Karen Hall was a rough interview. She didn't want to give me much. I think she was so protective that our first forty minutes were a lot of one-word answers. I think that once we started to break down "Mulberry Street," she began to get that I was not out to trick anyone. She wrote such an incredible hour of television. She had so much good writing advice to give. I was lucky to receive it.

Neil Mandelberg started telling me about *Moonlighting* before I could really even ask my first question. He, like the majority of the interviewees, seemed like he had been waiting for someone to call and ask him about the series for the last thirty years. I am not sure he realized I had also been waiting that long to hear his stories.

Will Mackenzie is about as pleasant a guy as you can ask for. He also bravely turned off Wimbledon to talk to me. I understood what a sacrifice that was. He also hung up with me and called Cybill Shepherd to tell her about the book and how she should talk to the nice young man he had just spoken with. That is an act of kindness I will remember every time I think about him.

Dennis Dugan is a comedy legend. The movies he has directed have been a part of my viewing experiences for years. But it was his acting in a different movie that I had to bring up, at the end of our interview. I had to tell him that whenever one of my bosses told me to work a bit harder to get that promotion or raise, I always thought of him telling Steve Martin to "dazzle" him in *Parenthood*.

My good friend Brad Dukes wrote a *China Beach* book, and that led me to **Chris Leitch**. We had a fun time talking about Hitchcock and directing on two amazing ABC series. He may have done only one *Moonlighting*, but it sure is a classic.

Mel Harris has now been in two of my books. I was talking to her about the *thirtysomething* reboot that ABC axed. I mentioned to her that my next book was about *Moonlighting*, and she told me the story about her being cut from the black-and-white episode. I think that tidbit is my favorite thing in the book, because I believe I am the only human who could have uncovered that. I am the link between *Moonlighting* and *thirtysomething*. (Side note: It annoys me that the cold open where David mentions Mel on *thirtysomething* was not put on the DVDs. Let's put it on a complete Blu-ray release.)

Dana Delany is also in two of my books. I interviewed her for *The Red Room Podcast* and talked to her about her career and have been using those moments for years. I think I am out of shows that she was in that I would write about. But I am not out of my infatuation with McMurphy. That lasts for life.

Whenever I interview an actor who was in *Moonlighting*, I always ask them about it. So when I spoke to **David Patrick Kelly** about *Twin Peaks* for *The Blue Rose* magazine Issue #8, I had to talk about *Moonlighting*. He is such a cool cat. Check out his daughter and him singing a Beatles song on the online *Twin Peaks* event I did for *The Blue Rose*. You won't be sorry.

My phone rang late on a Saturday night weeks after I had interviewed **Sandahl Bergman**. I looked down and my phone said "Sandahl." I answered, wondering what she could possibly want. She said, "Hey, kiddo. Sorry, I butt-dialed you. I am inviting people to my mom's birthday party. Want to come?" I have never wished I lived on the West Coast more than in that moment. I would have totally gone. (By the way, I could listen to her call me "Kiddo" for another couple of years.) I am a huge Broadway baby, so we talked a lot of Fosse. Finding her and getting her for this book were a delight. Call me anytime, Sandahl.

I was on vacation in Florida looking for swim stuff in a Walmart, and an unknown number called me. It was **Bill Landrum** calling from a beach in Mexico. Sandahl had given him my number (unclear if she was just calling him to invite him to her mom's party or if she butt-dialed him). I loved putting the pieces together of how they developed "Big Man on Mulberry Street." That is my favorite Billy Joel song, and has always been my favorite. Bill gave me some dish on some Hollywood actors he has worked with. But that goes to my grave.

Margie Arnett was so kind and helpful with information and was always kind on social media. Thanks so much.

Ray Wise can't stop showing up in my books. *Twin Peaks*, *The Massillon Tigers*, and now here. He is the only man whom I gladly watched kiss my wife and took a picture of it. He is truly one of my favorite actors around. I am proud to call him my friend.

Alicia Witt is another Twin Peaks alum whom I interviewed for *The Blue Rose* (Issue #14). We had to talk about Jay, since he was a mutual friend. I didn't list her in the list of participates in the book, but she can never go unmentioned. I love her and her music.

Bruce Willis agreed to be in the book, but his schedule just didn't work out. I know that he wanted to do it and that is pretty cool by itself. I got to send him my Letterman book and thank him for making my family's favorite holiday film: *Die Hard*.

The first time I talked to **Cybill Shepherd** on the phone it was her twins' birthday. The ones who were born during *Moonlighting*'s run. That is the kind of kismet that I like. Cybill was a delight every time we talked. She taught me about the song "This Funny World" by Tony Bennett and it became the soundtrack to me transcribing our talks. Cybill sang these words to me: "This funny world can laugh at the dreams you're alive for." But getting to meet her, and having her in my phone and me in hers (she put me in as "Moon Scott," which I loved), is a dream come true. "This Funny World" is working out just right. Thanks so much Cybill Shepherd for everything. Can't wait till our next catch-up call.

To *my friends*: Janet Jarnagin (Look! You are first, just like you like), Josh Minton, Mindy Fortune, David Lee Morgan, Jr., Matt Marrone, Brad Dukes, Lisa Mercado-Fernandez, Rachel Minton, Bryon Kozaczka, Marybeth Mayhew Whalen, HoBro, Mya McBriar, Ben Durant, Tony Stanic, Anita Dunning-Rehn, Mary Hütter, Richard Green, Rose Thorne, Ben Louche, Roger Dicker, Wimberly Hill Brackett, Charlotte Stewart, Diana Maiocco, Tiffany Cunnningham, Charlotte Stewart, Matt Zoller Seitz, Jami Keller, Huppie, Alyssa Fye, Michael Ryan, Amanda Beatty, Melanie Mullen, Amy Shiels, Diana Stavroulakis, and my children.

To *Don Giller* for the Letterman appearance photo.

To *James Sheridan* for his knowledge of classic TV in general, and Betty White in particular, and *Jay Fialkov* for the advice.

To *Shameeka*, you said I had potential way before Fiona ever said it. Thanks for all you have done for me. My postal BFF is the best.

To *Courtenay Stallings*, you have taught me so much—most of it I didn't wanna learn. You have been important to every project I work on and a real inspiration to me.

To *David Bushman*, you are a great business partner and the person who has made me a better writer over the last four years. Your support means the world to me. I would go over a cliff for you, and with the cost of doing this book in color, I think we just might. Thanks for editing the book and for all the support. Thanks for the use of your interview with Glenn about the "Dream Sequence" episode.

Erin O'Neil dropped into my life, and it has made things so much better. Every writer needs that writer friend to bounce ideas off of, commiserate with, and share all the stories that other people don't want to hear. You have been such a great friend. I am proud of all you have done. If a reader needs a good book, check out her *Gui Ren*. Pronounced: bhjadklfhdsaulfj.

Lisa-Lou Hession, I love you for being my friend, my family, and my heart for all these years. You have always been the Mona Lisa to my Mad Hatter. I thank the Lord there's people out there like you. Thank you for teaching me what love is. Agatha Picklepants has nothing on you.

Alex Ryan is a constant enjoyment in my life. He has been a big help to FMP, running reports and showing his old man what spreadsheets can do. I am proud to call him my son and my friend. I leave you my *Moonlighting* DVDs, which are probably the thing I own that are worth any money.

To *Jason Jarnagin*, thank you so much for your insight and suggestions. They truly made this book what it is. I would never have thought of interviewing Cybill and Bruce for a *Moonlighting* book if it wasn't for you. How do you come up with such groundbreaking ideas and be a mentor to me as well? It's astounding. You are a hero to all of us.

Mom, thanks for making me watch *Moonlighting* and for supporting me in all my projects. I wouldn't be an artist today if you weren't always working on a project when I was growing up. I learned how to be a good worker and be disciplined with deadlines because I watched you do it. I am forever grateful that you encouraged me to create even when the path was bumpy. I love you and am thankful for you.

Jen Ryan is the best thing that ever happened to me. Not sure what I would do without you but luckily I won't have to find out because, like a fool, you signed up with me for life. I have had all success since we met, unfortunately for you, not monetarily, but artistically. I love running my ideas past you first and will be forever thankful for all that you do so that my dreams of being a writer can come true. "Loving you is not a choice, it's who I am."—Sondheim.

Before you go, I want to pitch you my religion. It's called kindness. Our country has gone through too much the last few years. We will never be able to beat power and greed if we don't start being kind to each other. Be kind not to get kindness back. Be kind knowing you won't get it back. That is the true act of kindness. Once we all do that, kindness will win. Might I suggest you only comment on social media if it's kind. Glenn's and Jay's kindness to a stranger allowed this book to exist. Cybill was so kind to talk and sing to me over multiple phone calls. Kindness works. Try it.

If you have kind words about the book, send me an email at Superted455@gmail.com and follow me on Twitter @Scottluckstory

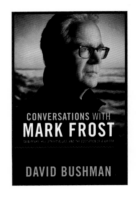

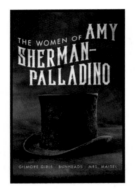

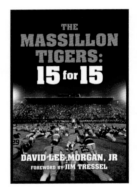

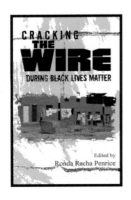

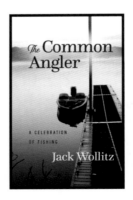

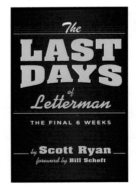